The Lost World
of Music Hall

The Lost World of Music Hall

a celebration of ten greats

Derek Sculthorpe

BearManor Media
2021

The Lost World of Music Hall: A celebration of ten greats

© 2021 by Derek Sculthorpe

All rights reserved.

No portion of this publication may be reproduced, stored, and/or copied electronically (except for academic use as a source), nor transmitted in any form or by any means without the prior written permission of the publisher and/or author.

Published in the United States of America by:

BearManor Media
1317 Edgewater Dr #110
Orlando FL 32804

bearmanormedia.com

Printed in the United States.

Typesetting and layout by John Teehan

ISBN—978-1-62933-802-6

Table of Contents

Acknowledgements ix

Introduction 1

The Rise and Fall of the Halls: A Brief Resume 3

Nellie Wallace: The Essence of Eccentricity 5
    (I)   Child Star 5
    (II)   A Unique Comedienne 10
    (III)   The Immortal Nellie 16

Lily Morris "Why am I always the Bridesmaid?" 27
    (I)   Teenage Prodigy 27
    (II)   'Our Lil' 31
    (III)   Lily in Bloom 36
    (IV)   American Sensation 45
    (V)   A Great Artiste 51

Billy Bennett: Almost a Gentleman 59
    (I)   Soldier Boy 59
    (II)   The Making of a Gentleman 64
    (III)   A Versatile Artist 72
    (IV)   The Royal Command Comedian 78
    (V)   The Art of Comedy 83
    (VI)   Echo of Laughter 88

Charlie Higgins: 'It's good, isn't it?' 95
   (I)   Double-Act 95
   (II)   Solo Turn and Revue Artist 100

Alfred Lester 'Always merry and bright' 111

Tom Foy: The Fool of the Family 127

Vivian Foster: The Vicar of Mirth 'Yes, I think so!'' 133

The Art of the Female Impersonator 143

Bert Errol, The Lady (?) with the Tetrazzini Voice 147

The Entertainer at the Piano 161

Margaret Cooper: The Diva of the Humorous Song 167
   (I)   Meddlesome Matty 167
   (II)   Nights at the Palace: From Concert Hall
          to Music Hall 172
   (III) Mrs. Humble-Crofts on Tour 179
   (IV) Her Glory Days 187

Norman Long: A Smile, a Song and Piano 193
   (I)   Concert Party 193
   (II)   All for Ten Shillings a Year 197
   (III) We Can't Let You Broadcast That! 203
   (IV) Keep Smiling 210

Epilogue 217

Appendix	221
Bibliography	269
Notes	281
Index	305

Acknowledgements

WITH GRATEFUL THANKS especially to Tony Barker for all his work over so many years in the field of Music Hall. Thank you to John Lovell for his invaluable input and fascinating discussions on Nellie Wallace. With acknowledgements also to Peter Charlton and David Read of the British Music Hall Society. With thanks as ever to my family for their patience, support and encouragement.

Introduction

"The music hall is dying, and with it, a significant part of England. Some of the heart of England has gone; something that once belonged to everyone, for this was truly a folk art."

– John Osborne, author's note
for *The Entertainer* (1957)

MUSIC HALL WAS THE ENTERTAINMENT of the ordinary folk between the middle of the nineteenth century until the early-mid-twentieth. In essence it was generous-spirited, open-hearted, robust and lively. It was patriotic, sentimental, sociable, vigorous, honest, vulgar and revelled in debunking pomposity. It could also be subtle and was a place of genuine artistry. It reflected the values of the wider community and was imbued with warmth and a sense of belonging. At its best it encapsulated the British spirit of eccentricity in full flower, and although long gone its influence lingers.

There have been numerous works on the history of the genre. My book is not intended as a general history of music hall, or Variety, which have already been well-covered, particularly by Richard Anthony Baker's *British Music Hall*, which is widely available. Nor is it about the biggest stars—Dan Leno, Marie Lloyd, George Robey—they too have been discussed extensively by others and most of these have more than one biography about them. Listed in the bibliography are those books I consulted and recommend. *Little Tich—Giant of the Music Hall* is one of the finest biographies I have read. It was written with heart and did full justice to its subject and his place in the pantheon. I hope my reference book can be supplemental to the existing literature on the subject and add to that of a crucial period in history. The era I discuss is, generally speaking, from the 1890s until the advent of the Second World War but concentrating particularly on the period of the changeover from Music Hall to Variety. The years both before and after the First World War are crucial in understanding the great changes wrought in society and how they were reflected in entertainment of the time. The Edwardian era marked the glory years not just of the Music-Hall, but was witness to a great blossoming of British individuality and eccentricity. My intention is to focus on a handful of less well known but nonetheless significant entertainers who are not well represented elsewhere. All of them had that joyous sense of the ridiculous that was so essential to British humour. Through the prism of their lives I hope to illuminate the whole.

I consider their songs and patter in the context of social history. Included is a discography and a full list of credits for each artist. I endeavoured to provide a list of songs, monologues and recitations known to have been rendered by them, including, where possible, the publisher of the sheet music. While these lists are in no way exhaustive, they are in more detail than any I have hitherto found anywhere else for these artists. I have tried to write for an audience that is at least partially familiar with the subject but also in a way that is accessible and entertaining to the casual observer.

I chose these artists for various reasons, some of them personal, but I could easily have chosen a dozen others—or two dozen. It is perhaps an idiosyncratic selection but reflects those I felt had been overlooked and not previously given their due. This was especially true in the case of Malcolm Scott, who I first came across on a compilation LP, *On the Halls*. I was surprised at the paucity of material there was available about him, much of it inaccurate. The fruits of my researches appear as the companion volume *The Woman Who Knows*. The same was true of Norman Long and Tom Foy, both of whom I first encountered through my grandfather's records. In a way those records were a personal link to my grandfather who I had never known because he died long before I was born. Many of the others I became aware of through the beguiling medium of radio, which was a profound influence on me. As a devotee of John Peel's show, alongside tracks by Sonic Youth and The Fall I recall him playing some by Lily Morris and Billy Bennett among others; and it was thanks to Frank Wappat on Radio Newcastle that I was introduced to Charlie Higgins. I recall a design of silhouettes of bygone stars at the City Varieties in Leeds which pictured Nellie Wallace alongside Charlie Chaplin. That always intrigued me, because so few people could be recognized by their silhouette alone. From these beginnings grew the kernel of the idea for this book, which is my tribute to Music Hall and the world it represented.

Most of those I discuss spent the greater portion of their life on stage. Some appeared in films, and most made at least a few records. Nonetheless it is harder to bring to life long-dead stars of the stage than any others in the entire entertainment field. If they made lots of films, they live for all time—or at least for as long as film stock survives. If they were singers, their voices were recorded. However, even the great stage stars of a hundred years ago are little more than shadowy figures now. If they seldom or never stepped before a camera or a microphone, they are, to all intents and purposes, dead to us. We are reliant on what was said about them while they lived to form any kind of impression. This impression will be imperfect at best and requires a little imagination. Like Ezekiel and the dry bones in the desert, I have tried to make these ten stars live again in the hope of rekindling interest in a neglected corner of our entertainment past.

THE RISE AND FALL OF THE HALLS: A BRIEF RESUME

"Come on boys and girls, let's enjoy ourselves!"

MUSIC HALLS DEVELOPED from the Song and Supper Rooms and the Free and Easies of mid-nineteenth century London. The first 'halls' proper were attached to pubs, and indeed, food, drink and entertainment went hand-in-hand from the beginning. Customers bought the package and got a whole night's dining and entertainment for a reasonable price. The Song and Supper Rooms were essentially dining clubs where the patrons were encouraged to get up and perform. These grew out of the earlier Free and Easies, where amateurs, professionals and different classes of society mingled. These had a poor reputation by and large, principally because of drunkenness and profligacy. Among the most famous of the Supper Rooms were The Coal Hole in the Strand and Evans' in Covent Garden, both of which eventually lost their licences. Some of the earliest purpose-built halls were established in the 1840s and 1850s. Charles Morton is often credited as "the Father of the Halls" with the Canterbury on Westminster Bridge Road. The success of this model led to many others. The later halls were better organised and more respectable, thus they attracted families.

The first popular entertainers were singers and Lion Comiques. These latter were larger-than-life personalities who sent up the upper-class 'masher' or 'swell'. Such names as Alfred Vance and especially George Leybourne with his anthem "Champagne Charlie." The strength of their personalities alone attracted patrons to different halls. Each hall had a chairman, who introduced up to ten acts a night, all different kinds of artists including ventriloquists, conjurers and novelty acts. The halls competed with one another to attract the biggest stars. By the 1880s the set-up had altered and the chairmen all but disappeared, although the figure was retained in television's affectionate tribute to the halls, *The Good Old Days*. A number of theatre syndicates formed and before long there were music halls in every town and city in all parts of the British Isles including Ireland. This was the great age of theatre-building when the many Palaces and Empires popped up all over the place like mushrooms and ushered in entertainment for the masses. Some of the finest were designed by Frank Matcham. By the end of the nineteenth century the music-halls reached the height of their popularity, when the great names of Marie Lloyd, Dan Leno et al were in their pomp. After Queen Victoria died in 1901, the reign of Edward VII saw a certain relaxation in society and consequently the full blossoming of the halls in national life.

Nellie Wallace
(1870–1948)
The Essence of Eccentricity

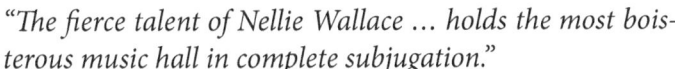

"*The fierce talent of Nellie Wallace ... holds the most boisterous music hall in complete subjugation.*"

– T. S. Eliot[1]

(I) CHILD STAR

NELLIE WALLACE WAS A COMEDIENNE of unique appearance whose career spanned seven decades. Small, buck-toothed, hook-nosed, she was ribald and salty, her songs and patter strewn with innuendo and *double-entendre*. In her act she portrayed the character of a continually thwarted but defiant spinster desperate to find a man. A true grotesque on stage, she entertained generations and became part of the national consciousness.

Eleanor Jane Wallis Tayler was born on 18 March 1870 in Hutchesonton, Glasgow, the daughter of Francis George Tayler and Eleanor Ann (nee Fromow). Her father started out as a schoolmaster; his own father, also Francis Tayler, was a clergyman. One of his ancestors had been a vocalist. Nellie's mother Eleanor was born in Norfolk, the daughter of Stephen Fromow, a cattle salesman. Francis and Eleanor married at St. George's, Colgate, Norfolk, on 27 September, 1855, and by the following year, Francis had already abandoned his teaching career and was de-

The inimitable Nellie Wallace as she appeared in her famous act, c1906

scribed as an agent.² The family moved to Glasgow, where Francis ran the Scotia Music Hall. Nellie was one of five children, two brothers and three sisters, but both brothers died in infancy. By the time of her birth, Francis Tayler was established as a musician and vocalist, and Eleanor was also a professional singer, although neither achieved any measure of fame on their own account.

As the youngest daughter, Nellie was ushered on stage from the age of at least six. She is reputed to have made her debut as a clog dancer at the Steam-Clock Music-Hall, Birmingham, billed as "The Little Ray of Sunshine."[3] She was then cast in a pantomime and appeared as a Roc's egg in *Sinbad the Sailor* in which she "made such a lively egg" that she was "one of the heroines of the show."[4] During the 1870s and 1880s, she toured the country with her sisters Emma and Fanny in a clog dancing act as "The Three Sisters Wallace." From early on she was also billed singly as "La Petite Nellie." Her natural comedic ability was already apparent; by the age of eleven she had won four medals for her performances and was listed as a vocal comedienne. The sisters joined the London company of Harry Monkhouse and, in a provincial tour of the farce *Larks* drew some attention from one critic, who remarked; "The three sisters ... are graceful and accomplished dancers, and their efforts were warmly applauded."[5]

Little is known about her off-stage life, which she seldom if ever spoke about. Considering that her father was once a schoolmaster and that her mother had been a governess, one would assume the daughters were educated, presumably at home. However, little stood in the way of their stage careers. Being such a young age adrift in the louche life of the stage, they were presumably chaperoned. But whether or not the parents were watchful enough, Nellie fell pregnant at the age of fourteen and in 1885 gave birth to a daughter, Daisy Wallis. Nothing is known about the father. Her parents saw to it that the child was adopted by a childless couple, James and Agnes Timmins, who took great care of her, and she had a loving home.[6]

Nellie joined the Milton-Rays troupe (1890-91) and had her first experience in panto as Chee-Kee in *Aladdin*. In her early years she was a soubrette, and her clever delivery of a lyric was appreciated. With her sisters she appeared in a *Faust* burlesque at the Standard (July 1891) which starred three of the famous Lupino family; George, Arthur and Harry. A reviewer declared; "The three sisters Wallace (Nellie, Emma and Fanny) are smart dancers; and one of them is especially brisk and vigorous, every step being done by her with dashing rapidity and intense spirit."[7] She joined various stock companies and spent many months on the road. From the first she excelled in eccentric supporting roles, playing a gallery of chambermaids and comic characters despite her youth. With Harry Bruce's company she appeared in such plays as *Two Hussars* and *The New Barmaid* in the North East. At Hartlepool she made an impression as Gypsy Nell, "irrepressible inmate of a prison."[8] She displayed her skill as a dancer in the Cockney comedy *Glorie Aston* with Charles Williams' company. At Croydon she was again singled out for praise; "The life and soul of the piece is undoubtedly Shrove Tuesday, played with wonderful abandon and vivacity by Miss Nellie Wallace."[9] The Irish actor and comedian William Henry Liddy was a member of the company and came from County Limerick. They married on 18 November 1895 at St. Philip's, Salford while the company were on tour in Lancashire. Their daughter Nora was born the following year. William became her manager, for which she paid him a set wage. She was always keen to secure herself financially, and keener still to ensure that no-one else got their hands on her money. This grasping nature where money was concerned implies that she had been done out of what she felt was rightfully hers at some stage early on in her career, possibly by her own family, or at least by those shepherding her.

Her years touring the provinces and play-

Nellie played all kinds of roles during her career as an actress touring the provinces before she found her niche in the music hall.

ing skivvies coupled with her training in dancing and singing gave her an excellent grounding both in the practical difficulties of touring and helped to shape the nature of her future act. She was able to assume a character easily, although it was one that was far removed from her real self.

An early breakthrough came in the panto *Jack and Jill* at the Comedy, Manchester (1894-95), when she was understudying the principal girl, Ada Reeve. When Reeve fell pregnant and it became impossible to hide the fact, Wallace stepped in. Reeve recalled in her memoir her impressions of the 25-year-old Nellie: "She had not developed her own distinctive style at that time, but was still trying to compete with prettier girls in ordinary show business."[10] Her career in the legitimate theatre was not such a success, not only because of her lack of looks, but because she tended to get laughs at all the wrong times, for instance at a great dramatic or tragic moment. By the early 1900s she turned her attention instead to the music hall and began to form the act for which she was so fondly remembered. She toured the provincial halls and in 1903 made her London debut. One of her biggest song hits in her early career was "Down by the Ri-hivvah Side" at the Tivoli, where she proved so popular that her stay was extended to three months. She even appeared in a short for the film pioneer James Williamson. In *A Lady's First Lesson on a Bicycle* (1902) she played the lady of the title.

She had such a singular and striking appearance and worked with so much vigour, that many in the audience were extremely unkind to her and believed she was in reality a man. Once at the Artillery Theatre, Woolwich, some of the men even had a wager about it, and were only convinced of the truth when she appeared on stage at the end of the show with her husband and daughter.[11] She was one of the few women to play the dame successfully in pantomime, and followed Malcolm Scott as Widow Twankey in *Aladdin* at the Prince's Theatre, Manchester. She was so successful in those roles that she was besieged by offers to play solely dame roles, but she declined them.

She obviously had none of the sex appeal of most female singers of the time. Instead of making herself as attractive as possible, she took the opposite route to appear as peculiar as she could. Hence, she broke new ground as a comedienne and billed herself variously as a "comicess" and "The Only Female Comedian." She was by no means the first comedienne, and others with whom she was comparable included Jenny Hill, known as the "Queen of the Halls" and Louise Freear. As some academics have indicated, there were perhaps more female laughter-makers even in the

Victorian era than most people imagine. However, Wallace was, like the others, swimming against the prevailing tide in a male-dominated world, and her male counterparts gave no credence to the notion that a female comic even existed. The celebrated Swiss clown Grock declared bluntly; "...women are never funny. They want to look attractive before the public. Besides, people don't like to watch a woman play the fool. The nearest approach to a woman comedian was Nellie Wallace, but she was more of a fun-maker than a clown."[12] People also seemed to think they could say what they wanted to her, but never spared her feelings, whether telling her bluntly that she looked seventy even though she was in her forties at the time, or constantly reminding her how ugly she was. The public imagined that so-called public figures were their property, that they had no feelings or a life away from the glare of the spotlight.

She was a prominent supporter of the Music Hall strike of 1906-07. This dispute arose because of poor pay and working conditions for artists and stagehands, prompted by a rise in working hours. The big stars of the halls, chief among them Marie Lloyd, essentially took a stand for the small-time turns who were earning between 30s. and £3 a week for twice nightly and matinees too. The strike began at the Holborn Empire and was centred on the London theatres. It was keenly advocated by leading figures in the Trade Union movement including Ben Tillett and Keir Hardie. After two weeks the strikers' demands were essentially met, with a minimum wage and maximum hours agreed.

(II) A Unique Comedienne

> *"Miss Wallace can remain here as long as she likes, as her effervescent good humour and evident intent to please will win her many warm admirers."*
>
> *– The New York Dramatic Mirror*

IN THE YEARS BEFORE THE GREAT WAR, Wallace continued to develop her act and made several successful tours of America. That period when she was establishing herself was in many ways the golden age of Music Hall of which she was an indispensable part.

In 1906-07 she embarked on the first of four tours of the United States. Initially, audiences did not quite know what to make of her, having seen nothing like her previously. New England was hardly prepared for the shock, and Bostonians in the better houses found her act "too strong" for their taste. Elsewhere she was appreciated for her uniquely grotesque appearance and her boundless energy. Lovers of Vaudeville in New York immediately took to her; *The New York Dramatic Mirror* declared; "She is extremely lively on her feet and does some eccentric dance steps that are alone worth the price of admission. She has plenty of self-assurance and some magnetism, and has no trouble keeping her audience amused and interested."[1] The following year she was engaged to tour South Africa, but according to one source ill-health forced her to abandon those plans.[2] However, she did tour the country because a South African writer recalled seeing her on stage in 1909 when she sang "Daisy."[3] She returned to America for at least two further tours up until 1910. Away from the East coast she proved to be something of an acquired taste. Some critics declared her humour too broad or too coarse, and others believed that she over-emphasised or went on too long. In her show at the Temple theatre, Detroit, for instance, where she was the headline act, her conception of comedy was at variance with that of the audience.[4] She fared better in Philadelphia where critic George Young declared; "Her eccentricities reach about the extreme of her sex, and while it was a bit hard for the staid Quakers to grasp her at first, she quickly won them over and had them well in hand at the finish."[5] It was difficult for a visiting artist to make a big impression in America, and others famously failed there for various reasons, or had limited success, Marie Lloyd being a case in point. It took time and effort for foreign artists to build up a following, and although some, such as Vesta Victoria and Harry Lauder did well, many discovered they just could not make the transition. When Nellie toured there, she was often compared to a fellow English artiste, Katie Barry, who had toured the country a few years earlier. In 1908-09, Nellie ventured further afield in the United States, but with mixed results. She proved a hit in Newark, they laughed in Cincinnati, but she had a lukewarm reception in Indianapolis, and in Chicago they hardly understood a word. Even so, she won many audiences over and was making distinct progress. After finishing her fourth successive tour in 1910, she announced that she would return the following season, this time for Percy Williams, and not William Morris, but in the event, she abandoned those plans and although she visited the country a number of times in the en-

The American Music Hall in Chicago, one of the theatres Nellie played during her successful tour in 1913. She visited the United States several times between 1906 and 1914.

suing years, she never toured again. Her U. S. tours had been successful on balance and were financially rewarding. It is surprising that she discontinued them. She concentrated on her core audience who knew and loved her but did make further visits to South Africa and Australia.

The secret of her success as a comedienne was in finding her own unique style of act; something highly individual that set her apart from the others. She developed a vivid stage persona that emphasised her unusual appearance and was essentially a caricature that made a visual impact. Combined with her songs and the patter, the character of the grotesque and deluded spinster was complete.

All comedians become associated with particular costumes, and especially, headgear. Whether it was Chaplin the tramp with his bowler, baggy trousers and cane, or Laurel and Hardy with their different-sized bowler hats, every comic had their own style, a kind of visual shorthand which identified them immediately. Nellie's wardrobe was inimitable, with her moth-eaten coats, her "bit o' vermin" stole, and grotesque hats with feathers. It was integral to her act, exaggerating all her physical imperfections. In his memoirs, Alec Guinness related how he was mesmerised by her as a child when he first saw her at the Coliseum. He described her appearance, with special attention to her clothes:

> "She wore a loud tweed jacket and skirt, an Alpine hat with an enormous, bent pheasant's feather, and dark woollen stockings, which ended in neat, absurd, twinkling button boots. Her voice was hoarse and scratchy, her walk swift and aggressive; she appeared to be always bent forward from the waist, as if looking for someone to punch. She was very small."[6]

She assembled her costume carefully and everything was totally in keeping with her stage character. Some of the items were bought at second-hand shops, and many were given to her by those in the profession who knew of her interest. A great source was a little stall in Brixton market that sold what were charmingly referred to as Post Office Findings—once-desired things that had been lost or were no longer desired by their former owners. There was something curiously melancholy and yet inspiringly comic about her habiliments. An air of faded finery pervaded. Everything had seen better days, like its wearer. She always managed to latch on to the most piquant and apposite garments, with an especial knack of finding remarkable hats. They were often adorned with feathers which was a touch of pure genius; these emphasised her small stature and made her nose seem even more like a parrot's beak. Some of her hats had been made by the finest milliners in France and one had even been seen at a long-ago Paris Exhibition. That creation, described, even by Nellie, as "weird-looking" was presented to her by a couple of ladies after they saw her act one night.[7]

Publicity photo of Nellie in typically outlandish habiliments, c1928.

The other key element of her act was her songs. In her early career she used to buy between 100 and 150 songs a year, but out of them she only found a handful that suited her. She bought the titles from their composers, which cost her between 30s. and two guineas. After she hit the big time the costs increased of course. Two of her most popular numbers were "My Mother's Piecrust" and "Under the Bed" both of which she recorded. The latter stands as an abiding anthem for the thwarted spinster, with its refrain

> "My mother said, 'Always look under the bed,
> Before you blow the candle out
> See if there's a man about;'
> I always do, you can make a bet
> But it's never been my luck to find a man there yet!"

She glorified in the joyful absurdity of "Queenie the Carnival Queen"

> "I dance at the ball of the Carnival,
> And add to the masculine woes,
> Young men of degree
> Fight madly for me,
> They lay out the wounded in rows.
> With thirst the poor fellows lie dying,
> The waiters stand useless about,
> Enthralled by my gaze,
> They drop all their trays,
> And that's why they ordered me out.
> I'm Queenie, the Carnival Queen,
> The fairest in all the procession.
> Each time I appear on the scene,
> That's when the p'lice take possession.
> I asked the M.C. would he please be so kind
> To settle the dispute—my partner to find;
> He shouted out, 'Wanted! Some blighter that's blind,
> For Queenie, the Carnival Queen.'"

The songs she favoured exploited her appearance to the full and employed sardonic humour and cheerful self-mockery to hide a deeper sense of despair. One such was the doleful ditty "I Was Born on a Friday"

> "I went to see the monkeys once, it's true without a doubt
> They kept me there for eighteen months before they let me out
> I saw a dog in Brighton swim, the owner looked at me
> He thought I was a walking stick and threw me in the sea.
> *I was born on a Friday*
> *I was born on a Friday*
> *Never be born on a Friday*
> *It's a most unlucky day*
> *My Father was out*
> *Across the raging foam*
> *And I was born on a Friday*
> *When my Mother wasn't home."*

In real life she insisted that Friday was her luckiest day, because she was married and her daughter Norah was born on that day. Another in a similar vein was "Isn't It A Cruel World?"

> "Once, when in doubt, I found that I was doubting
> So I went out, but only for an outing.
> I got a shock—the shock was really shocking
> There on a rock—I saw a man was rocking
> I thought to nab the nearest man worth nabbing
> I made a grab, to find that I was grabbing
> I seized his hair, just where he'd let his hair grow
> Oh! Girls, the scare—'twas nothing but a scarecrow.
> *It's a cruel world! A wicked world!*
> *Oh, goodness gracious me*
> *Oh, men why do you miss me?*
> *Will no-one come and kiss me?*
> *Isn't it a cruel world?"*

Her ironic paeans to love were a curious combination of ludicrousness and genuine pathos:

> "Ah, woe is me, a broken heart
> My true love left, the tear drops start
> He's gone afar to Africee,

> *That's farther than he went with me*
> *To make his fortune off he flit*
> *They must have caught him making it*
> *The years have fled, but he no doubt*
> *Will come back when they let him out.*
> *But he kissed me when he left me*
> *And he told me to be true*
> *When he wooed me by the wood yard*
> *Where we used to woo to woo*
> *And he gave me a geranium*
> *And I placed it in me ferns*
> *And I wore his geranium*
> *Till my true love returns."*

As time passed, she found it increasingly difficult to find songs that suited her particular style. This led her away from the variety stage and persuaded her to pursue a career in revue instead.

(III) The Immortal Nellie

> *"During a pantomime, I went to have my photograph taken. I done in five or six different characters, and at the finish the young lady operator said: 'I think I will take a funny one of you now.' The saucy minx! I did not know which way to take her remark."*
>
> – Nellie Wallace "Should a Woman Tell Her Age?" 1921.

After the Great War, Nellie moved away from the variety stage and into revue. Although she said she preferred revue, it only occasionally gave her opportunities to be seen at her best as a unique act. She continued to appear on the halls and in panto and recorded a dozen of her best songs. Her film career was also reignited, although she was disappointed that many of her big screen ambitions, especially in the United States, did not come to fruition. Her popularity spread thanks to her BBC broadcasts, although the corporation's "blue pencil" hovered nervously over some of her utterances. She became the darling of the *cognoscenti* when she was noticed by leading poets and even photographed by the society photographer of the age, Cecil Beaton.

At the same time as her career was on the up-and-up, she suffered personal loss when her husband Frank Liddy died on 5 March 1921 aged 63. He had accompanied her on her tours to the United States, although they had spent periods apart by necessity through her heavy work schedule. Nellie continued to mourn him, and on the anniversary of his death each year put a memorial notice in *The Stage*. In the early 1920s it was reported that she had a serious breakdown, but no details ever came to light.

The offstage Nellie preferred a more refined sartorial style. Photo repro by S Georges.

On stage, she was once again a big hit as Widow Twankey in *Aladdin* at the London Hippodrome (1920-21) and on tour. She was also seen to effect at the Palladium in *Dick Whittington* (1923-4). She made another film, *The Golden Pippin Girl* (1920) otherwise known as *Why Men Leave Home*. This would-be satire of the film business drew scorn from *Variety* as an "alleged comedy" and was further derided as "pitifully crude stuff of the "stuffed stick" and eccentric order, and what little humour there is in it is obtained from the "star's" makeup and weird attire."[1] She hoped to make films in America, following in the footsteps of her favourite star, Marie Dressler. Unfortunately for various reasons it did not happen.

Musical comedy revues were the order of the day in the inter-war years, and her first, *The Whirl of the World* (March 1924), also at the Palladium, was probably her best. *The Whirl of the World* gave her ample opportunity to show her acting and singing ability, and the real stroke of genius was to team her with the great Billy Merson as the most unlikely romantic couple of the age. The highlight was a burlesque of Rudolph Valentino the great lover, with the short-statured Merson as Valentino and Nellie as his desert queen. Although normally a solo act, several reviewers commented on how well she worked with her fellow performers, a skill that she had learnt as a young actress playing in stock. The show was an artistic and commercial triumph, and lasted for 54 weeks, a Palladium record that stood for twenty years. She next appeared in *Sky High*, starring George Robey (March to September 1925), which to begin with was mostly composed of dazzling set piece scenes and ballet dancing interludes. After some criticism it was revamped, and more comedy was introduced. Nellie's highlight was her song "Finesse." She said she much preferred revues to being a singular Music Hall turn. For one thing it was less stressful, and she found it "much brighter and jollier working with a company."[2]

In 1926-27, she toured the Tivoli circuit in Australia for E. J. Tait. Despite her long stage experience, she was nervous for her first shows in Sydney, but was given much encouragement by the audience, especially when she admitted her nervousness in a closing speech at the curtain.[3] It took some time for her to catch on with audiences down under, who seemed to consider her act too crude and old hat. Critics implied she needed to modernise her material. She was deemed acceptable in Sydney but not so much in staid Melbourne where there was some predictable criticism of her blueness. The general feeling was that away from London and her old stomping ground of the Holborn Empire she was a fish out of water, and that antipodean audiences would have preferred to have seen her as a pantomime dame.[4] On her return, it was reported that she had received offers of film work in Hollywood, but had turned them down because she had already signed up for the Maurice Cowan revue *Love and Money* in which she toured in 1927-28.[5] This consisted of twelve scenes, with Nellie as a woman who stands to inherit £50,000, provided she can find a man to marry her within six months.

In 1928 she came close to marriage with Selwyn Smithers, an engineer originally from Derby. They had first met five years earlier when she was appearing in panto in Cardiff. Smithers had once lived at Hugglescote in Leicestershire, and their engagement was announced from the stage of the Leicester Palace. Rumours spread that they had married in London, but she soon scotched the myth. The following year she said that their engagement had been broken off by mutual consent, but when asked about

Nellie achieved good notices as the nurse in *The Golden Toy* starring Peggy Ashcroft at the Coliseum, 1931, with dances choreographed by Ninette de Valois.

it a couple of years later denied it, saying they were still engaged. They never married because he wanted her to quit the stage and that was something she would never do.[6]

She continued touring in revue and spent two years in *All Fit* (1928-30) which featured the famous Tiller Girls. As the star of the show, Nellie was practically on stage for the duration. Some of the dialogue was considered weak, especially in a Girl Guide scene, but she occasionally came into her own, for instance in "Neighbours" in which she played an eccentric character far closer to that of her familiar act. Any faults in the script were largely overlooked, and the audience were so pleased to see her they laughed anyway. Her remarkable energy prompted one reviewer to marvel at her "vivacious and incredible" personality.[7] In 1932 she appeared in *The Queen of Clubs* which was later retitled *The Revue Superb*. At the Coliseum she played Nana the nurse in *The Golden Toy* (February, 1934), a spectacular show with a large cast including Peggy Ashcroft and Ernest Thesiger. Loosely based on an old Indian play with music by Robert Schu-

Nellie in character, possibly from a pantomime.

mann, the production boasted an elephant and the biggest revolving stage ever seen. *The Play Pictorial* declared; "Nellie Wallace proves she is not only a wonderful comedienne, but also a very fine actress."[8] During 1934-35 she toured variety theatres in the show *Laughter Zone*.

From 1930 onwards she became a popular broadcaster, and was regularly heard on such programmes as *Vaudeville, Variety, Music-Hall* and *Palace of Varieties*. Despite her popularity, the BBC were watchful that any of her notorious *double-entendres* did not stray over the borders of taste. It was sometimes a running battle between Nellie and her employers. She was touchy about any slight, deliberate or otherwise, and once demanded an apology when she was faded out because the news bulletin was running late. After her death, the corporation celebrated her regularly on various shows of reminiscences including *The Ladies of the Halls* (1958), *Gert and Daisy Remember* (1978), *Trinder's Hall of Fame* (1979) and *Top of the Bill* (1980).

In 1935 at the Vaudeville, Nellie appeared as Carabosse the witch in an unusual take on the panto *Sleeping Beauty* or *What a Witch!* This innovative adaptation, *sans* traditional elements such as principal boy, dame and leading comics, was perhaps one of the most *avant garde* versions of the tale to be seen in London. The modernization by Andre Charlot, doyen of revues, was welcomed by many for injecting new life into a venerable institution, but unfortunately it turned out to be his sole excursion into pantomime. The show made a welcome return in December 1936. In 1938, Nellie was asked to take over from George Robey as the dame in *Jack and the Beanstalk* at Brighton, in which she was again a great success.

After a lull, her film career re-ignited in the 1930s and she made several features. A so-called Quota quickie *The Wishbone* (1933) was filmed at the newly fitted out Sound City studios at Shepperton. Nellie played an old woman who inherits £50 and goes on a spree. She was one of the highlights of *Radio Parade of 1935* (1934) in a duet with Lily Morris as a couple of charwomen singing "I'm Not What I Used Ter Be." The two were reunited in *Variety* (1935), and although there were plans to team them in a film series, that never came about. It was just as well because they could not abide one another. Nellie had a prominent role in *Boys Will Be Girls* (1937), a so-so farce about a group of relatives who gather for the reading of their eccentric great aunt's will. She even got to sing "Lo, Hear the Gentle Lark" as only she could. The film was originally known as *Big-Hearted Bill* and was the first of three she was due to make for American producer Joe Rock. However, Rock did not exercise his option on the other films, which were never made. More pertinently to her, she was not paid. Consequently, she sued Rock and won £3,500 plus costs.⁹

Her act was seemingly improvised but carefully worked out; she was not a natural ad-libber and understandably did not take kindly to anything unexpected or to any spontaneous intrusions. One time she followed the performing seals in a bill, and one of the seals came back on the stage during her turn. As she started singing the seal began barking; when she stopped, the seal stopped, and when she started again, so did the seal. "This happened several times and meanwhile the audience were in roars," she recalled, "while I was overcome with confusion, but at last a man rushed on to help me deal with the recalcitrant seal, and together we hauled the noisy brute off the stage. But it was some time before I recovered my composure, and my performance was quite spoilt by the incident."¹⁰

Lily Morris (left) with Nellie, Gallaher cigarette card 1935. Despite their mutual antipathy, the two great comediennes of the age appeared together to great effect as washerwomen in The Radio Parade of 1935 (1934).

She made surprisingly few recordings, most of which have appeared on several classic comedy compilations over the years. Her dozen sides were gathered on CD on the Cylidisc label (with G. H. Elliott) and later by Windyridge, (with Maidie Scott). One of her best and most catchy ditties was Noel Gay's "Let's Have a Tiddley at the Milk Bar" which caught on to the curious vogue for milk bars as an anodyne replacement for the real thing:

"So, let's have a tiddley at the milk bar,
Let's make a night of it tonight!
Let's have a tiddley at the milk bar,
Let's paint the town a lovely white!

You buy half a pint,
I'll buy half a pint,
We'll try to drink a pint somehow.
So let's have a tiddley at the milk bar,
And drink to the dear old cow!"

Some of her appearances on stage and radio have also been issued, and of special interest is *Through the Looking Glass* (1945) in which she was perfectly cast as the Red Queen with fellow comedienne Jeanne de Casalis as the White Queen. This was a charity record in aid of the Great Ormond Street Hospital for Sick Children. It was a follow-up to the successful version of *Alice in Wonderland* (1941) with Ann Stephens in the title role. A short Pathe film, *Alice Makes a Record* (1945) shows excerpts of the principals recording the production.

Her final touring revue was *That'll Be the Day* with Sonny Hale in the summer of 1945, a joyful time after the end of the war in Europe. Nellie also continued to appear in pantomime, but variety was in flux and once again the war ushered in a change in the nature of entertainment. However, there was a revival of interest in music-hall, just as it was in the process of fast disappearing and becoming a thing of history. This led to *Thanks for the Memory*, an unashamedly nostalgic show full of old-timers, organised by Don Ross. The other performers included Randolph Sutton, Ella Shields, G. H. Elliott and Gertie Gitana. Well into her seventies, Nellie was still as agile and full of pep as ever. She was also just as testy, and bickered constantly backstage with Shields, with whom she had a long-standing feud. The public had no inkling of this, and audiences flocked to see the stars of yore on their valedictory tour of the variety theatres of Britain. It gave the old-stagers a new lease of life when it seemed they were all but forgotten. Just as things appeared to be going well for Nellie, her beloved daughter Nora was diagnosed with cancer and she took time out from the show to look after her. Sadly, Nora died in March 1948 aged 51. Nellie was devastated by the loss, but nonetheless returned to work, probably as a way to cope. The company tried to cheer her the best they could, but she had lost heart. Her final appearance on stage was with the *Thanks for the*

Nellie in evening attire, signed photo dated 1938.

Memory players at the Royal Command Performance on 1st November 1948. Ted Ray and the American star Danny Kaye were the big draws in that year's show which marked the debut of a 13-year-old Julie Andrews. Oddly enough, it was Nellie's first appearance, too, a late reward to crown her amazing career. Her act went down well and she finished with "A Boy's Best Friend is His Mother." After leaving the stage she was taken ill in the wings and was whisked away to a nursing home.[11] She took a turn for the worse in the middle of the month and died on the 23rd November at the age of 78. A friend was quoted as saying "She had been deeply grieved since her daughter died last Easter. It left her broken-hearted."[12] She left all her money to charity. Her estate worth £8,439 was divided equally between cancer charities and the R. S. P. C. A.[13]

Wallace presented an act so unique and an image so bizarre that she became part of the national consciousness of her time and beyond. A cultural icon, she was a cartoonist's dream and was frequently caricatured. Even renowned artists such as the surrealist Edward Burra immortalised her on canvas. She was an early inspiration for a seven-year-old Alec Guinness and admired by leading poets of the century T. S. Eliot and Dame Edith Sitwell. This "re-discovery" of so-called "low" culture by the literati, was part of a wider resurgence of interest in music hall as a phenomenon worthy of study, almost in the same way that Ben Nicholson elevated the work of Cornish self-taught artist Alfred Wallis as folk art. Hitherto it had been dismissed as mere amateurism, and given no credence by the art establishment in artistic terms. The same was to an extent true of Music Hall which, as it was in the process of disintegrating suddenly became of lasting cultural value. Rather surprisingly, Eliot was a frequenter of the halls, and wrote about some of the leading lights and their effect on an audience. Sitwell saw Wallace whenever she could and told of her sheer joy when she was once mistaken for her outside the Finsbury Park Empire. Sitwell rated her highly, although she spoke in a rather condescending tone about her, and the variety stage in general:

> "In her own way she is an extremely fine artist—one of the only fine artists on the English stage. She is an extraordinary mime, has great personality, and has the most significant appearance I have seen in an English actress. Everything acts: her cheeks (which she flaps as though they were being blown by the wind, when she cries), her hands, her feet, her body. She is very tragic, although she is a low comedy actress: the epitome of starvation."[14]

Edith's brother Sacheverell even persuaded Cecil Beaton to take photographs of Nellie, in 1931. Beaton found her a patient subject and wrote that she embodied "the ageless spirit, half sprite, quarter cockatoo, quarter human, of harlequinade."[15]

Nellie Wallace was not blessed with looks, or a shining personality. She had a singular appearance which she embellished on stage in an act which brought her great popularity, but off-stage she was not widely liked and had a reputation as a difficult, touchy woman. For all her failings she was compensated by the priceless ability to make people laugh. Perhaps she would rather have been pretty in her heart of hearts, but then she would not have been the comic she was. She worked hard for over seventy years to please the shifting tastes of a hard-to-satisfy public. As she once reflected; "Keep coming up with something new for the folks who put you where you are … or else the buggers will forget… they're a fickle bunch, they are."[16] A unique comedienne, she was truly one of the immortals of British entertainment and a pioneer for female comics everywhere.

See discography and list of credits on page 221.

Lily Morris
(1882–1952)
Why am I always the Bridesmaid?

"Miss Morris is now and ever shall be one of Variety's mainstays. Her art lies in and dear to, the heart of London."

– "The Passing Shows" *The Tatler*, 1931

(I) TEENAGE PRODIGY

Some commentators contend that there are no funny women, but Lily Morris for one disproved this maxim. There were admittedly few comediennes at that time and for many years Nellie Wallace held sway as the most famous. Like Wallace, Morris was on stage from childhood and was something of a teenage phenomenon. She was a doyen of pantomime and enjoyed her greatest popularity on the variety stage in the immediate post-war era. In her prime she presented a blousy figure and had a great way with a song, in the tradition of Marie Lloyd, with whom she was often compared. Usually, Morris in character was one over the eight, and delivered her songs in a disarming way but they were true gems of social comment, and she did full justice to them.

Lilles Mary Crosby was born in Holborn on 30 September 1882, the daughter of Maurice and Mary Anne Crosby (nee Davies). Her father was a tobacconist who at one time manufactured his own brand of cigars. He had been born in Ireland, the son of a bricklayer from County Kerry. The

Morris was a perennial principal boy since her teenage years. Seen here as Colin in *Mother Goose* at the Prince's Theatre, Bristol, 1905-06.

family settled in the Hoxton area which contained one of the earliest and most vibrant music halls. She had several siblings, some of whom were employed in the family cigar business.

As a child Lily often sang at family parties and when she was eight or nine, she started to appear in charity concerts wearing a little white frock singing songs written by her father, an amateur songwriter. The manager of the Empire, Bow, happened to see her one night and asked her mother if she would agree to letting her daughter appear on stage. Although her parents thought she was too young they nonetheless allowed her to sing at the theatre for which she was paid three gold sovereigns and ten shillings for the two-week engagement. Her parents were not well off, and she always vowed that if she did find success on the stage, she would buy her mother a house, which she did. For her first outing she sang a song called "When I'm A Little Older" composed by her father, a number which became a mainstay in her repertoire in those years. "That first appearance really decided my career," she said, "for a man who saw me on that occasion took me round to Drury Lane to interview the great Sir Augustus Harris." The result of the interview was the role of a fairy in a prestigious pantomime *Dick Whittington and His Cat* alongside Dan Leno, Herbert Campbell and Ada Blanche.[1]

She appeared at several London music-halls and immediately stood out as a child performer of natural talent with a strong appeal. She was receiving some glowing notices, such as that from *The Referee* for an appearance in south London as early as June, 1894:

"Miss Lily [Morris] is only ten years old, but she plays with all the confidence and considerably more than the usual ability of a full-grown artist, and withal there is in her no trace of self-consciousness. The infant phenomenon is usually my pet aversion, but Lily Morris is different goods. She is a perfect little artist, charming all the time."[2]

At that early stage she was far from being the finished article, and she was criticised for her failings. Various commentators faulted her pronunciation of certain words and her slowness of delivery. Others felt that she over-emphasised at times and questioned her choice of song. However,

Lily started singing from childhood and had one of her biggest early hits with Joseph Tabrar's "Lardy-Doodi-Day"

she had the temperament to succeed because she took all the criticisms on board and learnt quickly. It was a case of practice makes perfect, and she improved both her singing and the projection of her songs. She gained much experience playing theatres up and down the land, getting used to the widely different audiences, finding what pleased them and what did not work. Even though she was little more than a child she was judged to be better than some of her material, and her natural talent was obvious to spectators from the first. She already had the knack for making more out of a song than appeared to be there. In this she often outshone her seniors.

Lily later said that her parents were "horrified by the stage" to begin with, and that it was in fact an uncle who took an interest in her and shepherded her early career. Whatever the truth of the matter, once she was whisked into pantomime at Drury Lane at Christmas, she was already in demand elsewhere, having been sought out for the Grand, Islington. Dressed in a little white baby frock and bonnet she sang many sentimental favourites of the day including "Two Little Girls in Blue" and "My Soldier Boy" as well as comedy nonsense songs, of which Joseph Tabrar's "Lardy-Doodi-Day" was one of the most popular. By August Bank Holiday of 1895 she was declared to be "decidedly the cleverest little girl on the variety stage today" by one reviewer of an evening at The Middlesex, who further commented; "There is a spontaneity about her whole performance, a perfect appropriateness in her gestures and a skill in facial expression remarkable in an artist of so tender years."[3] At the Canterbury around the same time she was further praised for her intelligence and "lively sense of comedy."[4] She began to appear outside the capitol and had some of her earliest triumphs at the Empire, Brighton. Shortly after she made her first appearance in Scotland at the Empire Palace, Edinburgh. Sir Augustus Harris thought highly of her and sought her out for more engagements. However, instead she signed with Messrs. Moss and Thornton for a tour of their extensive regional circuit and returned to them for several years in succession.

In his memoirs, the pianist/accompanist Joe Batten recalled visiting Lily in her early days: "Her father kept a tobacconist shop in Stoke Newington High Street," he recalled, "I was taken there to play over a new song. The year was 1897. I, twelve, she thirteen, and regarded as a prodigy."[5] At the time of Batten's visit, she was a teenage sensation, and earning almost £100 a week, when the average 13-year-old-girl was unlikely to see more than a few shillings and a 25-year-old male bank clerk might be glad to get £1. Her star was on the rise to such an extent that she had offers from all over, including some for tours to America and

Africa, but because she was underage at that time, she was not able to accept them. She worked hard and was always supported by her family; her sister Katie made many of her dresses, which drew glowing approval from fashion critics. By the Christmas panto of 1896 she was effectively the principal girl as the Fairy Queen in *Dick Whittington* at the Theatre Royal and was considered "intelligent and vivacious" in the role.[6] The following year she was elevated to the leading role in *Cinderella* for Arthur Roberts at Nottingham (1897-98). Critics hailed her singing and dancing and one noted that "the dainty and graceful Cinderella of Lily Morris captured the hearts as well as the applause of the house."[7]

As a sign of her great advance in September, 1899 Lily was even called upon to replace an indisposed Marie Lloyd, the "Queen of the Halls" one night at the Oxford, which she did most successfully.[8] One of the secrets of her success, apart from her work ethic, was a knack of finding catchy songs. Ever since her early days with "Lardy-Doodi-Day" she found numbers which took with her audiences so that by the end of the second verse they were joining in the chorus. She was ever on the lookout for new material and often used the songs of Joseph Tabrar at the beginning of her career. Among her most popular numbers then were such songs as "I Wasn't Born with a Silver Spoon in My Mouth" and "A Poor Soldier's Daughter in England" which appealed strongly to working class Cockney audiences. She fought her corner for the rights of independent women everywhere in her own way and struck a blow for the dignity of female labour in "She's No Lady Some Might Say." There was also the time-honoured theme of how money changes people for the worse in such songs as "Since I Have Had a Row of Houses." She had many admirers and received lots of presents and keepsakes, especially jewellery. She was fond of jewellery and even had a necklace that had once belonged to the actress Sarah Siddons.

(II) 'OUR LIL'

> "Lilly Morris is an artiste to her fingertips and her exuberant spirits are positively infectious."[1]

Lily appeared in pantomime practically every year since she was ten, and by the 1900s was a veteran. She played the Principal Boy or Girl many times in some fondly recalled productions and was especially loved in

Scotland. It was not just because she married a Scotsman and was based in Glasgow for several years, but because she was such a wholehearted performer with an infectious good humour that she had a wide appeal and was known affectionately as 'Our Lil.'

Most of her pantomimes were produced by the great Robert Arthurs. A sixteen-year-old Lily won over the hearts of Kennington in the title role of *Cinderella* (1898-99), and was lauded as "a graceful dancer, a sweet singer, and a vivacious actress."[2] Two years later her winsomeness captivated the same theatre when she played Polly Pansy in *Robinson Crusoe* (1900-01). That season she scored a big hit with Joseph Tabrar's

Lily as Jack in Jack and Jill at Bristol, 1907-08.

"I'll Buy a Mangle, Polly." She was just as popular at the Shakespeare, Liverpool as a dainty and winning fairy queen in *Dick Whittington*. In *Puss in Boots* at the Grand, Woolwich (1901-02) against the background of the Boer War she sang "Dolly Gray" to great effect.

From 1903 she lived some of the year in Scotland and was associated with the Princess Theatre, Glasgow. She first appeared there in *Mother Hubbard* (1903-04) which starred local favourite Neil Kenyon. She was often recalled for several songs and two of her biggest hits that year were "I'm Coming Home to You Love" and "The Good Old Summer Time." The follow up season she was a bright Principal Boy in *Goosy Gander* (1904-05) which incorporated a much-admired facsimile of Ayr racecourse. In between panto seasons she toured variety theatres across Britain on the Tivoli circuit singing her songs. She was back to panto duty as Colin in *Mother Goose* at the Prince's Theatre, Bristol, 1905-06, with the great Wilkie Bard as the Goose. She showed plenty of spirit as *Aladdin* at the Theatre Royal, Newcastle, 1906-07. It was during the run that she married Archibald McDougall, a whiskey distiller, on 18 February 1907 in Newcastle. She was 25 and he was 38. They had no children but were a totally devoted couple and early on he became her manager.[3]

For Arthur Roberts she played a "rogueish and vivacious" Jack in *Jack and Jill* at Bristol (1907-08) in which she gave a rousing version of "Put Me Amongst the Girls." Another hit of that show was "She's a Lassie from Lancashire" complete with clog-dancing chorus. While in the city she took time out to give a concert for the unfortunate inmates of the nearby Eastville Workhouse.[4] The ensuing season she made a "handsome and dashing Humpty" in *Humpty Dumpty* at the Royal Court, Liverpool (1908-09). That production was recalled long afterwards because of an accident that occurred when a trap door gave way unexpectedly and two chorus girls fell a long way and were badly injured.[5]

One of her most successful productions of the decade was *Mother Goose* (1909-10) at the Grand, Glasgow. It was there she introduced "Ship Ahoy" the chorus of which was eagerly taken up by the audience, who demanded and got numerous encores. The people of the city responded to her warmth and adopted her as one of their own. As a reviewer wrote, "On her first entrance she received the enthusiastic welcome reserved for special favourites and carried the audience by storm right to the end. No one can deliver lines with more point or infuse such spirit into her songs."[6] In her next, *Dick Whittington*, (1910-11) there was so much cheering on her first appearance that it stopped the show for several

Morris in the title role of *Humpty Dumpty* at the Royal Court, Liverpool in 1908-09.

minutes. She was feted on the first night with flowers and gifts galore and enough chocolates to stock a small shop. Her popular songs of that Fred Karno production were "Fall in and Follow Me" and "The Chocolate Major." One of Karno's biographers maintained that she also appeared in his panto *The House That Jack Built* in the city.[7] Lily was truly loved at Glasgow, where she was affectionately known as 'Our Lil.' As a sign of that affection she was once again presented with seven baskets of flowers on the opening night. A keen football supporter, she was only too pleased to hand out the medals at the Scottish Junior cup final. She was happier still that her favourite side Ashfield were the winners on that occasion. She often entertained at football club concerts and regularly kicked off at matches.

The next season she was back to playing the Principal Boy in *Jack and Jill* at the Theatre Royal, Birmingham (1911-12) and although it was her first visit to the city in pantomime, she soon had the house on her side singing along. In 1912-13 she was at the Shakespeare, Liverpool as Principal Girl opposite Maidie Scott in *Jack Horner*. She preferred playing boy's parts for a number of reasons—chiefly because they were better-paid, although she did not like wearing tights on account of the difficulty of sitting down. "I first played a boy in Glasgow, and I do enjoy being Dick Whittington or Aladdin," she revealed. "The latter for preference, as the cave scene gives a chance for the dramatic element."[8]

Music Hall was patriotic by nature and came to the forefront of national life during the Great War. Lily was a terrific morale-booster in wartime and sang many of the defining songs of the era, either in pantomime or in her Variety turn. All were rendered with her inimitable gusto. At Christmas, 1914 she introduced "Tipperary" in *Cinderella* at the Theatre Royal, Edinburgh. In *Jack and the Beanstalk* at the King's in the same city, her most popular numbers included "My Soldier Laddie" and "We Must All Fall In." At the same theatre in *Dick Whittington* (1915-16) she sang "Keep the Home Fires Burning" and "Take Me Back to Dear Old Blighty." Among others she favoured "Mademoiselle from Armentieres" and "I'm Better Off in My Little Dug-out." When mechanised tanks made their sinister entry into the war, she even sang an "uncommonly clever" song about them, "The Tanks That Broke the Ranks Out in Picardy."[9] She was never solely a comic singer and did full justice to many a sentimental ballad including Richard Whiting's "Till We Meet Again." It was her mission to do as much as she could to cheer the boys; "I wish I was a boy, and I should be in France," she once remarked during the conflict. Although she never made the leap to revue, she did star in the musical *Watch Your Step* which toured during the spring and summer of 1916. Boasting a large company of eighty complete with glamorous chorus line, the show, by Harry Day, was based on that at the Empire, London of the previous year, which itself was a version of Irving Berlin's famous Broadway hit of 1914. Lily played with her customary zest and drew much praise for her singing and dancing. She was back to panto duty as Jack again in *Jack and the Beanstalk* at the King's, Edinburgh (1917-18) in which she was billed on the posters as "Edinburgh's Favourite Boy." Nellie Wallace appeared as the dame in that production, which was presumably not a happy experience for either of them.

After the war she continued to appear in pantomime, but they gradually became less significant. She played opposite George Formby, Sr. in *Jack and Jill* at the Coliseum, Glasgow (1919-20), and again the following season at the Empire, Newcastle. It was while appearing in that production that Formby's long shaky health gave grave cause for concern. He took a bad turn one night and went to his dressing room. Greatly worried, Lily went to see him, and he confided to her "I shall not play in this panto again." He died a few days later. They were great friends and she said that he was the greatest comedian she had ever worked with. "I have known him for years," she reflected, "and it is terrible to think how we will miss his wonderful personality."[10]

Oswald Stoll attempted to renew interest in pantos by ensuring that they stayed a fixture in the calendar of his variety theatres. He tried to inject some showbiz glamour, and his productions tended to resemble revues, for instance he relied on American numbers and chorus lines. Among Lily's later ones were the Wylie-Tait production *Jack and the Beanstalk* at the Sheffield Empire (1922-23) which provided a "sumptuous" spectacle and attracted good houses. She made a lively success in the much-trumpeted *Aladdin* at the Wood Green Empire (1923-24). She was a polished performer who had by then played in about twenty-three pantos over a thirty-year period and knew her craft intimately. However, by the mid-1920s, the season had become so short that pantomime was no longer a worthwhile or paying proposition, and the great days of an old institution were soon only a memory. By then she had already escaped its confines and found at last her true vocation on the music hall stage.

(III) Lily in Bloom

> "Miss Morris, moreover, is a painstaking artist: she studies her types closely, and her work shows that she pays great attention to detail. There is, in her inimitable character sketches, a ring of truth which brings them well within the region of great art."[1]

It was at the height of the Great War that Lily introduced some of the distinctive character songs for which she became famous. From then on, she developed her particular and abiding art through the work of some leading writers including Harry Castling. By then she was in her thirties and had considerable stage experience behind her. It was as though all the years in pantomime and travelling the length and breadth of the country's Music Halls had prepared her for what she was destined to do. She had outgrown pantomime and was not content to continually play the same roles forever. Moreover, panto was in decline. Many thought she was largely wasted as a Principal Boy or Girl, which gave her little room for inventiveness. Only a few saw her real potential, one of which was her mother, as Lily once remarked: "My mother often used to say to me: 'You have not found your proper line yet,' and she was right."[2] She was always a natural clown in real life, and began to prove it in the period after the war when she truly found her metier.

Her way into the character songs was in her mode of dress. She altered her appearance principally with the clothes she wore, which were a key to the character she was playing. Normally a smart dresser, she donned unflattering garb and tied her long red hair in a topknot, so that she could affix eccentric-looking hats to it. One of her first character songs was "Don't Have Any More, Mrs. Moore." In the guise of a nosy neighbour she gave an exhortation to the profligate poor not to compound their misery with too many children, husbands or drinks. After all:

> "The more you have, the more you want they say
> And enough is as good as a feast any day
> and "Too many double gins gives a lady double chins."

For each song she became a different personality, as for instance in "Why Am I Always the Bridesmaid" in which she came bounding onto the stage in a shapeless frock and a hat adorned with lilac and sweet peas tied in pink ribbon, wearing heavy boots, and carrying a tattered bouquet of flowers. Using the stage to the fullest she would then proceed to tell her desperate tale, all the while expressing herself with funny gestures and finishing with a priceless dance in which she hitched up her skirts, kicked her legs up and twirled them around at the knee:

> "I had a good chance a week or two past
> And took my young man home to tea
> Mother got playful and gave him a pinch
> And pinched my fiancée from me
> Being a widow she knew what to do
> No use for me to complain
> Then they got married today if you please
> I was only the bridesmaid again.
>
> *Why am I always the bridesmaid*
> *Never the blushing bride*
> *Ding, Dong, wedding bells*
> *Only ring for other gals*
> *But one fine day*
> *Please let it be soon*
> *I shall wake up in the morning*
> *On my own honeymoon."*

The outlandish outfit of her bridesmaid character was inspired by a neighbour whose clothes were always too large for her.[3] She tended to take about a month or so to become comfortable with a song after which her interpretation of the character developed naturally. She essentially approached her craft more like an actress than a pure comic. "I am very fond of character acting," she once reflected, "And it will be observed, too, I do not make-up as much as some artists do. I never put red on my nose. It is not necessary, for I get my character parts over by the clothes I wear."[4] It was a hallmark of her work that she never over-emphasised but was far more subtle with her characterisations, so that they were affectionate parodies with their roots in observation of real life rather than mere caricatures. Everyone had met someone like Mrs. Moore or could identify with the ever-hopeful but deluded constant bridesmaid of an uncertain age. She sang many numbers about matrimony; either the perils of making the wrong choice or the ignominy of being left on the shelf. There were lots of salutary tales of recalcitrant grooms in such as "At the Church Door I've Been Waiting" and "Turned Up." At one point she decided "I'm Going to Be an Old Man's Darling." At other times she was spoilt for choice of suitors, as in "Which of the Three?"

> *"I don't know whether to wed the dark one or the fair,*
> *Or the one with the little moustache and ginger hair.*
> *The dark one is tall, the other four foot eight,*
> *The ginger one is bandy, so he can't be very straight.*
> *Who is it to be? Which one of the three?*
> *It's keeping me awake at night*
> *So, I'm keeping friendly with a policeman*
> *In case they don't turn out all right."*

Often, she thought it was just as well to take love where one found it, no matter how unorthodox the arrangement, as in "Because He Loves Me":

> *"Why does his wife wear bits of string?*
> *While I wear garters with diamonds in*
> *Why? Because he loves me.*
> *Why, when his wife gives me the sack*
> *He throws her out and takes me back?*
> *Why? Because he loves me.*
> *I have to lather him each morning when he shaves,*

During her career Morris sang hundreds of songs, both sentimental and comedy numbers. "I Wonder if You Miss Me Sometimes" (1910).

> *I pile the lather on in little waves*
> *Why does he sit in the chair and blush,*
> *When I tickle his chin with the lather brush?*
> *Why? Because he loves me."*

This number was memorably rendered in raucous fashion in a scene in a pub by Dora Bryan in the classic *A Taste of Honey* (1961). She later recorded the song which was released on her album *Dora*. Morris tended to steer clear of *double-entendre* although some of her material was decidedly in

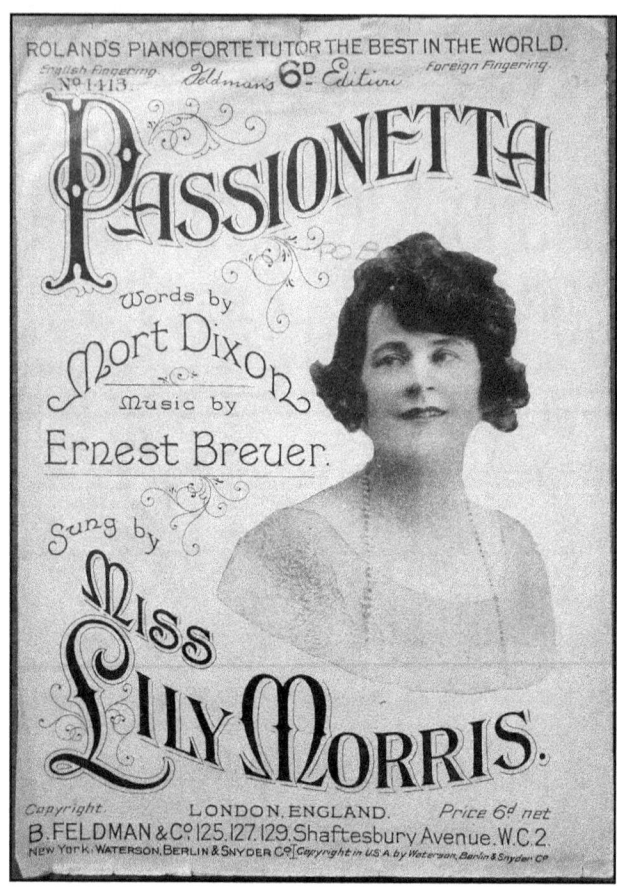

"Passionetta" (1923).

the Marie Lloyd mould such as "Keep a Little Bit of Something in the Larder." By and large she eschewed anything suggestive. Her songs often had a basis in relatable domestic situations and provided social comment. For instance, "What are You Going to Do About Selina?" which, shorn of its comedy trappings, puts the philandering male on the spot,

> *"What are you going to do about Selina?*
> *What are you going to do about the girl?*
> *You told her a lot of Tommy rot*
> *You broke her heart and it's the only one she's got.*
> *What are you going to do about Selina?*
> *Every day Selina's getting leaner*
> *You've been buying strings of pearls*

*At Woolworths for other girls
So what are you going to do about Selina?"*

"What's to be Done?" was the tale of a young man who longs for a life of adventure at sea, much to the chagrin of his prospective father-in-law who makes him face up to his responsibilities:

*"'Cause what's to become of the ones you leave behind yer?
And if we wants yer, where are we going to find yer?
And if Priscilla's lonely, who's to hold her hand,
And who's to buy me beer and baccy and take me down the Strand?*

Lily possibly in Dick Whittington at Glasgow where she was always popular.

> *And who's to buy her clothes, and powder for her nose?*
> *And Obadiah m'lad, let me remind yer,*
> *If you fall in the sea and a shark eats you for tea*
> *Well, what's to become of the ones you leave behind yer?"*

Many of her characters were fond of a tipple and enjoyed themselves with like-minded souls who loved to have a good knees-up. It was all harmless fun:

> "I had a little drop with Martha
> And another little drop with Kate
> Two or three pals and me went to celebrate
> I danced round Archie's organ
> And jigged the Lost Chord too
> The old bloke's hand I went to shake
> But kissed his monkey by mistake
> God Save the King is a marvellous thing,
> But a little drop of gin will do."

One of her best was her *paean* to inebriation, *The Old Apple Tree*, a joyous drinking anthem while the world debated prohibition. In this, she and her friend Phebe decide to sign the Pledge but before they do, they have a final drink or two for old times' sake:

> "Just as I felt a bit merry and proud
> I lost little Phebe somewhere in the crowd
> I looked in the King's Head; I looked in The Queen,
> But no, not a sign of that puss could be seen.
> Thinks I, 'She's gone off. Yes, she's gone for a walk
> But I couldn't find her in the Duchess of York
> So I went in the Old Apple Tree
> And there she was looking at me
> She'd a sailor's hat on and was singing a song
> About 'sailors, beware of the sea.'
> So I joined in the gay harmony
> And we sang like two birds on a tree
> But two policemen about both escorted us out
> Through the doors of the Old Apple Tree."

"Don't Have Any More, Missus Moore" written in 1917 was probably Morris' most famous and popular song.

Her earliest recordings date from 1919 on the Pathe label, with later ones on Regal and Columbia, up until the 1930s. Some of her songs have featured on various artists compilations but there have been relatively few albums devoted solely to her. Many of the titles she never recorded would nonetheless still find resonance today. Surely everyone could easily relate to "I Don't Want to Get Old" and her defiant "I'm As Old as I Look, and As Young as I Feel." At times she favoured those tangential questions that only Music Hall was asking such as "How Does a Fly Keep Its Weight Down." That was written by Harry Castling, who had coauthored several of her songs including her biggest hit, "Mrs. Moore." It was one of the last by Castling, who by that time was sadly on his uppers, and who died the following year (1933). She favoured other regular writers including Thomas McGhee and Herbert Rule who wrote "None of Your Nineteen-Fourteen Tricks with Me" among others. Some of the old composers were prolific writers whose work was tried and true and she returned to them year after year. For instance, "Don't Leave Me" which she recorded in 1923 was by the veterans Charles Collins and Fred Leigh. She had been singing Collins' songs since she was a child. This charming but seemingly throwaway number has all the elements that make a good Music Hall song. A catchy tune with a singalong chorus, it told the tale of Adolphus Brown and his journey back from the club one night after one too many. En route he gets into conversation with an old iron post, who he implores to

> "Carry me up the stairs,
> You can say me prayers,
> And put me in my little bed."

Delivered by Lily with her inimitable verve and skill this becomes a minor gem, complete with distinctive trombone note on the line "Mind the doorstep!" It was all so good natured and even the children could sing along. She also sent up Music Hall itself and the kind of songs she had been singing for so long in "Tiddley Hi":

"Years and years a number of years ago they used to sing, Songs, perhaps, of doubtful quality, still they had an air of jollity."

One of her most engaging ditties was her hymn to those unsung heroines "The Wives of Commercial Travellers":

> "I've been married now for many a day
> To Billy a traveller in ladies underwear
> He gets lots of experience he's so much on his own
> But who is it sorts his samples out the day that he gets home.
>
> *Why the wives of Commercial travellers*
> *Faithful and true, lonesome and blue*
> *He tells me a tale, I'm supposed to roar*
> *He doesn't know I've heard it from the traveller next door*

Right from Monday up till Friday
We talk to ourselves to stop from yawning
Now the cat has gone that way, comes home for an hour to stay
Then goes off away again on Monday morning."

It is hard to imagine anyone else but Lily singing this type of material, but it is full of observation and is so distinctively and quintessentially British in its dry humour that it encapsulates much of what has been lost in the years since.

(IV) American Sensation

"A jolly, peppy redhead, she puts her character songs across with consummate artistry."

– "New Palace, Chicago" The Billboard, 1928

By the 1920s Morris brought thirty years of experience to bear and reached the acme of her art. It was the age of the witty and sophisticated Revue and music-hall with its breezy vulgarity was decidedly on the way out. However, the public still flocked to the shows of the best performers who brought the salt of real life that the glamorous but hollow revues lacked. After the death of Marie Lloyd, Morris suddenly found herself in the limelight as never before, rediscovered as a comedienne in her own right, and made several highly successful tours of the United States and Australia.

In 1923, the drama critic of the *Manchester Guardian* observed her whirlwind effect on a typical audience and wondered aloud why he had never heard of her until now; "She took at the very outset the complete control of the audience which only a highly endowed and experienced artist can hope to establish. She had them whistling and singing: at the end of three songs she had them shouting for more, and had to come before the curtain and make a speech."[1] She reached the height of her popularity in the decade and was even acknowledged by Chance Newton in his *Idols of the Halls* who wrote that she was "one of the cleverest of variety soubrettes."[2]

In 1924-25, she first toured the United States for the Keith circuit, which proved to be a turning point in her career. She began tentatively, following Houdini on the bill at the cavernous Hippodrome, which had a capacity of 5,200. Sometimes her act seemed to run slower than that which Americans were used to because of the time between costume changes. For instance, to begin with she sang six songs with three comedy costumes and an evening gown. On the advice of Jack Lait, she cut the number of songs out in her middle turn to four and speeded up on the change. She soon gained in confidence and found the right tempo.[3] For her final number she appeared in evening dress which was a marked contrast to her usual comedy attire. Fashion-followers even commented on her frocks and one was described as "an azure blue crepe gown trimmed in striped silver cloth."[4] Her vigour captivated audiences from the first and her lively renditions of her songs proved a decided hit. So much so that a prominent New York producer offered her a revue of her own. She reluctantly had to turn his offer down because she had already made commitments to tour Australia and for a series of engagements back home. The twelve-week tour of America could not have gone better. At times she was referred to as the Sophie Tucker of Europe. Lily won over the critics; Robert Speare for one wrote enthusiastically

> "She is ... one of the funniest women on the stage, with a humour keen without vulgarity, a feeling for lyric values without posing as a great singer, a dashing style of happy dance and mimicry ... Originality withal, a most magnetic personality and diction! Oh boy! Every word and syllable she utters is a joy to the ear. The best Vaudeville artist London has sent to us for many a year."[5]

Her act was such a sensation that she began her second tour only a matter of months later in July 1925, this time for eighteen-weeks. She and Archie toured the country and received an enthusiastic welcome wherever they went; "The Americans are a great people," reflected Archie, "and they extended the glad hand right royally, as they do to most Britishers."[6] Lily had cancelled some of her home contracts in order to undertake another U. S. tour so soon, something for which she had to pay a large forfeit. However, the generous remuneration in America made it worth her while. She was touched by the warmth and courtesy she received in the country and again stayed at the National Variety Artists' Club during her sojourn in New York.[7]

Lily Morris: Why am I always the Bridesmaid? • 47

The famous Hippodrome in New York, where many of the great vaudeville stars appeared. Lily made her awestruck debut following Houdini on the bill in 1924. It was the first of four highly successful American tours that she undertook with husband Archie up until 1928.

In 1925-26, she toured Australia, and was just as well-received there as she had been in the United States. She took over from Ella Shields as the headline act at the Tivoli in Sydney and later Melbourne. She expressed a desire to do a special show for the newsboys of Sydney and later did a matinee for five hundred poor children of the city, who all joined in the choruses of her songs. It was a real treat for the youngsters who gathered at the Congregational church on College Street and from there marched on to the Tivoli theatre. Her five-week stay at that theatre was the longest run for a visiting artiste in six years. Among her song successes down under were "Why Did You Have Your Hair Bobbed, Mary?" and "There Ain't No Flies on Auntie"[8] The latter was a catchy number recorded by the Happiness Boys, among others. She especially enjoyed singing it because it gave her ample scope for adlib humour in its rhyming couplets.[9] Her act went over so well in the country that she had some imitators including a Russian singer, Rayna Carbette, who presented her own version of her songs. Personally, she was badly affected by the great heat in Australia, but despite it the houses did solid business. She and Archie were impressed by the great consideration shown to them by theatre managements during their stay, and she spoke of returning to the country in future, but in the event she did not do so.

She was constantly in demand to return to America. Managers did all they could to entice her back. They offered to double her salary, and Lily frankly admitted that was the great incentive for her, as it was for many other British artists. She told them; "Money…speaks all languages, and if you like to make it worth my while, I will come back." They agreed, and she was impressed by how well they promoted her; "I was advertised in letters as big as myself, with life-size pictures," she recalled. She went over big in the country despite her initial wariness about whether audiences would understand her quintessentially Cockney humour. Americans were quick on the uptake, and they responded to her verve with equal enthusiasm; she was usually required to sing about six songs with encores. She was so successful at the Palace that she was given the rare honour of being kept on for a second week. In Hollywood she and Archie met many famous film stars including Charlie Chaplin and Tom Mix.[10]

In December, 1927, she returned once more to the United States for another twelve-week tour beginning at Keith's, Boston.[11] She played many theatres in and around New York including the Fordham in the Bronx, and several in New Jersey including Union Hill, Prospect and the State Theatre. On all these tours, she was a decided hit across the country—with the exception, she admitted, of Kansas City, which she called the most difficult audience she had played to in recent years. "They seemed as if they simply would not laugh," she commented, but was at a loss to understand why.[12] That aside, headline-writers declared she was a riot, and even allowing for hyperbole her tours were a success by any standard. There was something about her exuberant, self-deprecatory style that contrasted neatly with the slick and polished acts that audiences there were so used to seeing. At the same time, many considered that Vaudeville itself was in decline, while the spirit of Music-Hall was, it seemed, in rude health. This was illustrated best perhaps by the all-English bill which Lily headlined at the Palace in 1928. She was not singing blues or jazz numbers or impossibly romantic sentimental ballads. It was her costumes and characters that captured their imagination and the way she had of putting across her songs with "a swing and a dash which is distinctly her own" that appealed to them.[13] It was in essence her Englishness which they appreciated. She never Americanised her act, but her cheerful Cockney ditties about the temptations of drink and work-shy husbands seemed to strike a chord, nonetheless. Surprisingly, a favourite song was "Only A

Working Man" which, despite its references to staples of British working-class culture found favour:

> "I wake him every morning when the clock strikes eight
> I'm always punctual, never, never late
> With a nice cup of tea and a little round of toast
> The Sporting Life and the Winning Post
> I make him nice and cosy, then I toddle off to work
> I do the best I can
> For I'm only doing what a woman should do
> 'Cos he's only a working man."

A selection of the many songs she sang: Above "Who Does the Lady Belong To?" (1915)

"Turned Up" (1924).

This song had universal appeal, and when she performed it at a Royal Command show, it was observed that King George V "sang and beat time with his cigar." She twice appeared in the annual spectacular, in 1927 and 1931. In 1927 she was, by common consent, the hit of the show. H. Willson Disher noted; "Directly she appeared there was a stir in the Royal Box, the King leaning towards the Queen and the Princess Royal with some comment or other of pleasure."[14] She had them all singing along in no time at all and in 1931 she proved such a hit that her turn overran and almost ruined the running order.

Such was her skill that she was able to present the spectacle of a drunken woman on stage at the height of Prohibition in America. At that time, the perils of drink were being widely discussed and various temperance groups had political influence. She was so disarming and there was no sourness in anything she did, so it was impossible to take offence. As Maitland Davidson commented; "Drunken women are often nearly as repulsive on the stage as off, but such is the art of Lily Morris that she shows as just a genial feminine Silenus, with the leer left out, the kind of woman bus conductors call "Ma", and all the jollier for having had several over the eight."[15]

Morris enjoyed her tours immensely, she felt that it was easy for a successful artist to stay in their home country and become complacent and to get stuck in a rut. For her, travel certainly broadened the mind and gave her new perspectives. She admitted that one of the only drawbacks was the sheer amount of work involved. In Britain, Sunday was a much-needed rest day for performers, but in America it was one of the busiest days in the theatrical week and she was required to do several shows on that day. Understandably, she declared this too trying, because, as she pointed out, everyone needs time to recharge. Nonetheless, she was surprised just how well she had been received by audiences there. She felt that being a solo turn also helped, because in the United States most acts were in small companies and there were few solos. By the end of the decade she was being scouted by Warner Bros. to appear in some talkies. She found the idea appealing and realised that it would be a boon to her career. However, at the time she was unable to take up the offer because she was booked solid for two years at a stretch on the variety circuit. Her American tours had been a great personal triumph for her, and she achieved far more in those five years than many other artists did in a lifetime of trying.

(V) A Great Artiste

> "She set us singing the refrains of her songs and evoked the gallery boy's shrill whistle—that hall-mark of approval in London theatres."[1]

By the 1930s, Lily was one of the most beloved entertainers in Britain and widened her popularity with several film appearances. She became a stalwart of the BBC's variety output on radio and was one of the first artistes to be seen on television. After retiring with the beginning of the war, she made a comeback nine years later in a valedictory tour with the *Thanks for the Memory* company that brought her a new lease of life and won over another generation of fans.

She made her screen debut in *Elstree Calling* (1930) for British International Pictures. Among the four directors listed was Alfred Hitchcock. Essentially a variety bill strung together by a tenuous story, this was important for her personally in that it recorded for posterity two of her best songs, "He's Only a Working Man" and "Why Am I Always the Bridesmaid?" However imperfect these stage-bound scenes are they nevertheless give an insight into how she might have been in her act. She appeared in several shorts for Pathetone Weekly, singing two splendid versions of her most famous numbers, "The Old Apple Tree" (1931) and "Don't Have Any More, Mrs. Moore" (1932). After that, her film career went into abeyance for a couple of years before she eventually returned in the feature film *The Radio Parade of 1935* (1934). She sang two numbers, the first was "What's the Use?" The second song was a duet with Nellie Wallace, "I'm Not What I Used Ter Be" in which the two great comediennes appeared as charwomen. Although they famously did not get along, this latter number had both humour and pathos and was widely considered the highlight of the film. The potential of the two old timers was realised by the studio bosses, who thought they were such a success together that they ought to be pared again in a series of films built around them. Unfortunately, this idea never came to pass, perhaps for the obvious reasons of clash of temperament.[2] In *Those Were the Days* (1934) Morris sang "My Old Man (Said Follow the Van)" which was always associated with Marie Lloyd, but which Lloyd never actually recorded. Morris was announced as co-star with Gordon Harker in the British Lion production *The Singing Kettle* but she was replaced by Binnie Hale in the film which was later released as *This is the Life* (1934).[3] Several critics, including James Agate, felt that the big screen did nothing to enhance the old-time music-hall artists such as Morris. On the contrary, they felt the medium detracted from their art, rendering them ghost-like. It was the spark of live theatre before an audience that gave the music-hall its life and spontaneity. That was crucially lost on screen and was why some of the great variety acts of their time, such as Morecambe and Wise for instance, could never make the leap to cinema. Lily was heard on radio from 1932 in the regular shows *Music-Hall* and *Vaudeville*. Among others she featured on: *Radiolympia* (1934), *Famous Music-Halls* (1938) and *Hail, Variety!*

Publicity still of Lily around the time of the Arthur Askey film *I Thank You* (1941), after which she retired from the business for a few years.

(1938) which was devoted to the art of the Cockney comedian. She was one of the first people seen on television shortly after its inception in 1936 in *Starlight* (1936), *Cabaret* (1937) and *Dancing Through* (1937).

Lily's parents had the good fortune to witness first-hand much of their daughter's highly successful career. Her mother died in 1921 just as Lily was entering her best years. Her father died 25 September 1933, at Finchley Road, Golders Green, in his 81st year. He was buried at the Old Southgate Cemetery.[4] Archie and Lily also lived on Finchley Road, almost opposite Gertie Gitana and a short walk from Golder's Green station. In the early 1920s they drove an elegant Italian Scat car (25.9). Lily was an enthusiastic cyclist in her youth and her real love was flying. Archie was devoted to her and he never missed seeing her act. Clarkson Rose recalled:

> "Archie and I always foregathered for a quick one, but towards the end of that refreshment I used to see Archie's eyes wandering and his ears almost flapped as he listened for a certain strain of music. 'Ye'll excuse me now, Clarrrkie,' he'd say, 'but I'm going to see a good act.' And in he'd go, as he has always done faithfully to watch his Lily."[5]

A. C. Astor observed that Archie "watches her as though he had never seen her before…"[6] Lily retained good health for much of her life, but in March, 1934, while appearing at the Lewisham Hippodrome, she collapsed on stage while singing "Mrs. Moore." She was carried to her dressing room and then an ambulance took her home. She always put a great deal of energy into her act and with the long variety tours across the country and added film work it was certainly true that she had been overdoing things.[7] Complete rest was prescribed but after two weeks she was back on stage singing her heart out. She also made another feature, *Variety* (1935), in which Nellie Wallace also appeared. After several years, Morris returned to the screen in the Arthur Askey vehicle *I Thank You* (1941). This time she played a specific character rather than just appearing as a turn, although the character was rather a haughty matriarch that did not suit her well. She came into her own only at the end when she gave a memorable rendition of "Waiting at the Church" in a crowded underground shelter, leading the communal singing. It was a morale-boosting finale to an otherwise tedious film, which sadly proved to be her last.

Morris retired from performing in 1940 and the Arthur Askey film marked her final appearance on screen. From then on, she enjoyed a well-earned rest from the rigours of performing and constant touring. She was still heard on some wartime BBC broadcasts including *Sing Song* (1940), *Who's Your Lady Friend? The Happidrome* (1941) and *Revolving Stage* (1944). Over the years she received a lot of fan mail, much of it from stage-struck girls, who she invariably advised to stay well clear of a showbiz career.[8]

In 1947, Don Ross organised a nostalgic show, *Thanks for the Memory*, built around the old music hall and variety performers who were still around. He tried to persuade Lily to join the tour, but she said she was happily retired, although would consent to take part if ever a replacement was needed. Nellie Wallace was the principal comedienne but part way through the tour she had to take time off to nurse her daughter who was stricken with cancer. Nellie herself became ill and died in November 1948. It was then that Lily was persuaded to join the show by close friend and neighbour Gertie Gitana, Ross' wife. At her first show at the Shepherd's Bush Empire on 24 January 1949, Lily admitted to being nervous for the first time in her entire career. She later reflected that after a couple of weeks of nerves she settled down and began to enjoy herself. "It's more like a family party than a show," she commented.[9] Although not intending or seeking to return to the boards full time, this valedictory show gave her something of a new lease of life. At the Wood Green Empire in January 1950 when she sang "Don't Have Any More, Mrs. Moore" observers were pleased to note that she "can still trip lightly across the stage." The show was unashamedly nostalgic and distilled the merry essence of music hall in a way that had not been done before or, arguably, since. Those who had been young when Ella Shields and G. H. Elliott were in their prime loved to reminisce and think of their lost youth and the world they left behind. One thing the show did do was create interest in some of the greats of the profession, among whom the ranks were dwindling. Morris was also celebrated on the radio programme *Good Old Timers* (1950) along with George Robey. By the time of her last appearance on a variety bill, she was one of those who was already being impersonated by a whole new generation. She put as much gusto into her act as she had in her heyday and stayed with the show for over a year. Sadly, in March 1950 shortly before her planned appearance that night at the Croydon Empire, she collapsed at her hotel. Her condition was described as being "fairly comfortable" but she was no longer able to take part in the show.[10] She never fully regained her health thereafter. Her husband Archie died 17 August 1952 at the age of 83 and Lily passed away just a few weeks later on 3 October 1952, three days after her seventieth birthday. In her will she left £22,508, most of which went to her surviving sister Catherine Moncrieff "in the hope she will remember my beloved husband Archie and I and will derive help and happiness therefrom."[11] There were other small legacies including one of £300 to friend and fellow singer Dolly Harmer, the partner of Wee Georgie Wood.[12] At the auction of her furniture, paintings, photos and effects most interest was generated by her piano on which she played many of her songs, which realised over £1000.[13]

There are several compilations available featuring Morris. Above is the cover of the Windyridge CD *Why Am I Always the Bridesmaid?* which features many of her most popular numbers and includes a rare live recording from the *Thanks for the Memory* stage show in 1950.

Lily Morris was one of the last of the line of great Cockney personalities who once proliferated in music hall. In many ways she was the embodiment of that indomitable spirit of her people, the essence of which came to the fore during the Blitz on London: resilient, resourceful, ever-cheerful, practical and yet sentimental withal. Her songs about home and families, get-togethers and knees-ups summed up the working-class experience at a time when life was hard, and leisure was valued because it was rare.

Her influence lived on more in her spirit rather than in any specific artist. Ever since her heyday there were numerous tribute acts to her. The Welsh-born singer Tessie O'Shea nicknamed "Two-Ton Tessie" often used to sing her songs. O'Shea had a similar larger-than-life persona, and her famous hit "Nobody Loves a Fairy When She's Forty" was one that Morris would surely have loved. Curiously, Lily has not featured in any great detail in many books about music hall and variety. Perhaps this was because she was associated with pantomime for so long and only came into her own as a variety artist after the Great War. It was said of her that she always left her audiences better than she found them. She deserves more recognition for her long years entertaining the nation and I hope this small tribute plays a role in elevating her to her rightful position in the Music Hall firmament.

See discography and list of credits on page 223.

Billy Bennett
(1887–1942)
Almost a Gentleman

"Mr. Bennett sends the art of the music hall spinning back into its original track, but with a new oddity of twist. His turn is English burlesque at its best."[1]

(I) SOLDIER BOY

Billy Bennett was the archetypal music hall comic, for whom the word rubicund might have been invented. Famously Queen Mary's favourite comedian, Bennett was a great absurdist who delivered his parodies of high Victorian verses in a distinctive *tenor robusto*. His style was essentially that of the old-time comics which he brought into the modern age with great success; he enjoyed a good career on the halls and was also a popular radio and recording artist who appeared in several films. Practically the missing link between the pre-war era of Dan Leno and the television age of Morecambe and Wise, his abiding influence was acknowledged by later generations of comedians and still informs the essence of stand-up comedy today.

William Robertson Russell Bennett was born in Glasgow on 21 November, 1887, the son of John Russell Bennett and his wife Catherine. William had two sisters, Kate and Maggie. Bennett senior was a comedian who had a double-act with Charles Martell; they were known as Bennett and Martell, "The Original Lunatics." In later years Stan Aubrey filled in for Martell, and later still, Tom E. Hood. They were sometimes billed as "the fantastic and wild humourists" and legmania artists. They proved a popular team in pantomime, for many years they appeared at Drury Lane in the productions of Charles Gulliver and George Black. In 1895 they played the robbers in *Babes in the Wood* at Leeds, in which Billy recalled his father was voted the most popular pantomime artist of the season by readers of local paper *The Owl*.[2] Later the duo developed a knockabout act in various sketches. One of their big successes was "The Shipwrecked Mariners" routine in which they played a bosun and first mate.[3] Billy told a possibly apocryphal story that as a three-year-old he got lost in Wakefield one day and found his way to a police station. The sergeant asked who his father was and Billy replied that he was a lunatic. Alarmed, the policeman watched in astonishment as Billy acted out his father's stage routine in front of him.[4]

Much of Billy's early years were spent in Liverpool where the family lived at 25 Martensen Street, Edge Hill. He had fond memories of his childhood days in the city and the surrounding country; "When I was a boy," he recalled, "we used to take the penny ferry from Liverpool to Birkenhead, come on our pushbikes along the coast to Chester, picnic along the banks of the Dee—and then go home again by the shortest route!"[5] As a boy he attended the Earle Street council school where he had his first captive audience one

Almost a Gentleman: Publicity photo of Billy Bennett in his iconic stage costume, c1925.

Christmas when some of the boys were asked to entertain the class. He surprised everyone, especially the teacher, when he stood up and did a recitation that sounded so wonderfully prescient about his future career;

"Haul in the anchor, throw out the sail,
Never tie a knot in a bulldog's tail.
As long as I remember I never shall forget,
To use an um-ber-ella when it comes on wet."[6]

John Bennett was keen for his son to follow the family tradition, and as a boy of thirteen, Billy was trained as an acrobat with a troupe. He began his stage life as the back end of either an elephant or a donkey depending on who was telling the tale. He grew to hate the knockabout life of a tumbler and instead became a clerk of a marine insurance firm. After three years he left that office and by the age of seventeen in 1905 he joined the cavalry, the 16th Lancers, as a farrier. He already had some military experience because he had previously spent time in the Volunteers regiment. However, he did not enjoy army life to begin with and realised he had gone out of the frying pan into the fire, but his father insisted he stay in to learn his lesson. Billy suffered a number of accidents during his service. For instance, at Colchester in August, 1905 he was assisting in bringing a forage wagon from the stables when a wheel of the wagon got stuck in the mud. In attempting to assist in freeing the wheel he slipped on a stone and the wagon went over his foot. Luckily, his foot was only badly bruised but not broken. His early army record seemed promising if he wished to be a career soldier and by November, 1907, he rose to the rank of Lance Corporal (unpaid). However, almost a year later he reverted to the rank of private at his own request. He went absent six days in 1909 but afterwards re-joined the regiment. In 1910 he was involved in another accident while on manoeuvres on Salisbury Plain. Pursued by the 18th Lancers he was galloping over a ploughed field when his horse fell and rolled over him. In the process he suffered a broken rib. The ensuing court of inquiry ruled that the accident was not his fault.[7] His first period of service with the Lancers ended in February, 1911 when he was requested to leave the army by his father who wanted him to join his double act after his partner, Martell, had retired through ill health. Martell, or rather Tom Hood, continued his career as a solo act under the name George Antill.[8] Bennett senior sent a letter to his son's commander explaining that his partner wanted to dissolve their partnership but that they had been booked for the Drury Lane pantomime *Jack and the Beanstalk* for five more weeks, and requesting that Billy could take Martell's place.[9] The commander acquiesced and thus Billy began his theatrical career. By that time almost the whole family was earning their living on the stage; young Billy, his father and both sisters were comedians. However, he did not stay long in his father's act and was keen to establish himself as a comedian in his own right. He had been writing his own material for some time and even before he left school, he wrote parodies for the comedian Fred Curran and contributed most of the material used by Gilday and Fox, Yiddisher Comics.[10]

In July, 1911 Billy made his solo debut at Barnard's Palace of Varieties, Chatham, Kent.[11] His success was by no means instantaneous and one night he fared so badly at a Wakefield theatre that the manager threw him out. After that he got a job with a sketch company as a "knockabout waiter."[12] He was spotted by manager Harry Slingsby who brought him to his theatre, the Tivoli in Hull, and gave Bennett his first professional engagement. He was booked for the pantomime season with Harry Russell. Slingsby recognized Bennett's potential and sent him to London for a trial.[13] Frederick Blanchard recalled his first sight of the young Bennett in the autumn of 1913 in a South London music hall:

> "A few bars of music and on came a healthy young lad wearing a misfit evening suit, an extravagant facial make-up and a wig, in a vain attempt to make himself look older than his years. Without any preliminaries he kicked off with a screaming burlesque on "Rag-time Cowboy Joe," and in less than two minutes the audience were at his mercy and I realised here was a diamond—a very rough diamond it is true, but a diamond, nevertheless, that only required polishing to make it into a valuable property."[14]

Bennett followed Blanchard's advice and toured the smaller halls for a year gaining valuable experience and building up his reputation. By the spring of 1914 he had made such an impression that he was signed up by the V. B. O. (Varieties Booking Office) Ltd., and booked solid for the next three to five years. His tour of the prestigious Oswald Stoll circuit began that May. Unfortunately, world events were already conspiring against Bennett's burgeoning career and when war was declared on 4 August, 1914, he was one of the first to be mobilised the following day, on account of being on the reserve list. He was playing at Coventry at the time when his tour, and seemingly his promising future, was cut short.¹⁵ In September, he took out an advertisement in *The Stage* and, in a perfect parody, stated that he was on active service and "Fully booked on the Bully Beef and Biscuit Tour—Direction—Lord Kitchener"¹⁶ In the months prior to being posted, Bennett often entertained in the barracks and at charity shows. For instance, in Co. Kildare in April, 1915 he "fairly brought down the house" at a show given in aid of the Newbridge Nursing Association. He sang "Just as the Sun Went Down" and found particular favour with J. W. Rickaby's old favourite "They Built Piccadilly for Me" which proved to be one of the biggest hits of the night and brought him forward for encores.¹⁷

Bennett was a soldier for much of his early career and spent four years in France during WWI. Excerpt from his *Budget No. 4* showing him at the time he re-joined his regiment in 1914.

In May, 1915, Billy was sent, with the British Expeditionary Force, to France, where he spent almost four years. For much of the war he was with the Machine Gun Regiment. He once claimed that he served at the battles of Ypres, Loos, Somme, Arras, Perrone and Cambrai among others. He also said that he variously acted as cook, batman, signaller, shoe-smith and scout during his army service. Sometimes, he incurred minor disciplinary infringements; for instance, in November, 1917 he was charged with being drunk in the field and given seven days field punishment No. 1.¹⁸ He was confined to barracks when he was late on parade the following year. He said that he was wounded and gassed at Etaples after which he joined the Shellfire Concert Party, forming a double act with Mark Lupino. While in France, Bennett was reunited with an old friend when Captain Harry Slingsby of the R. A. F. happened to be stationed nearby and heard Bennett's act at a tent show one night. All rank was forgotten as Slingsby "immediately dashed in and greeted the trooper in a manner that caused the others to gape in astonishment and admiration."¹⁹ Bennett was demobbed in February, 1919 but not officially discharged from the army until March, 1920, after a total of fifteen years' army service. Some of his wartime exploits are not supported by the available records. Despite claims that he won the Military Medal, the Distinguished Conduct Medal and the Belgian Croix de Guerre, the available records only list the 1914-15 Star, the British War Medal and the Victory Medal. He loved the *spirit de corps* of army life and reputedly had a tattoo of the regimental insignia emblazoned across his chest. He loved to recount tales of his adventures in the war, such as the time he was company cook. It was a job that required skill and the ability to improvise, such as when he came across what he thought was a coarse French flour with which he proceeded to make some puddings, but then discovered the flour was in fact cement! He recalled "During the terrible retreat early in 1918, when French villagers fled before the oncoming Germans, chickens, rabbits and pigs were left behind at our disposal if we wanted them—and we took care the Jerrys did not get any—and I can tell you I had a busy time cooking them."[20] He made many lasting friendships and was loved and remembered by all ranks, as illustrated by an encounter with his commanding officer, General, then Colonel Gough, many years later. Bennett was surprised that he remembered him, and recalled the many times he came up before him and how "The cells in the old guard room at South Cavalry Barracks were a second home to me." Gough was grateful for the many favours Bennett did for him, such as the time he did a turn for King Alfonso of Spain in the regimental concert party. Despite the odd periods spent in the guardhouse, Bennett left the army with an exemplary record.[21]

(II) THE MAKING OF A GENTLEMAN

Bennett soon began to re-establish himself after the war, his by-line then being the tag of "The Real Trench Humourist." One of his first shows after leaving the army was at the Tivoli, London, in April, 1919. He still appeared in khaki as often as not and much of his material was geared towards the same crowd who had laughed in the barracks, with jokes about Sergeant-Majors, the rising price of beer or complaints about army food prevalent. His audience consisted largely of ex-servicemen who responded heartily to his act who knew exactly where he was coming from and understood all the slang terms in a typical routine:

"When I got back to barracks I was late for dinner. All they had left me was a drop of jippo in the dixie, and that was full of sand, so when the Orderly Officer came round I made a complaint. I said: 'This stew is full of sand, Sir.' He said: 'What did you join the army for—to fight for your country?' I said: 'Yes, Sir, not to eat it.' So I went down to the cookhouse scrounging a bit of buckshee scoff. The Bobajee gave me a bit of steak. I said: 'Is it tender?' He said: 'As a woman's heart.' I said: 'Well, swop it for a couple of rissoles.'"[1]

He was mooted to play the lead in Arthur West's Welsh war comedy *Taffy in Hunland,* but the production never came to fruition, perhaps due to fatigue about army subjects in the post-war period.[2]

In the autumn of 1919, he joined his first revue, a tour of *As You Were,* for the noted impresario Charles B. Cochran, known as "Cocky." The show had already run for thirteen months in London and the countrywide tour lasted almost another year. Bennett had a leading part as a war profiteer who gets fed up with the fickleness of women and via various pills and potions is whisked off to different ages such as a Park Lane mansion in 2018 to the court of Louis XIV and the time of Helen of Troy. Theatre critics dubbed it "a fantastic revue, full of wit, and humour."[3] Despite being Bennett's first musical revue, he warmed to his role and played to effect opposite comedienne Sybil Arundale. *The Era* commented "Billy Bennett worked hard and most successfully as Sir Bilyon Boost, his droll 'make-up' and quiet, natural and humorous style being excellent."[4] Another observer wrote; "Billy Bennett is the principal laugh-provider, and there are few dull moments whilst he is on the stage. Miss Arundale and he play up to each other splendidly, with the happiest results."[5]

In November, 1920, Bennett scored as the manager of a shop in Fred Karno's burlesque revue *Red Hot,* originally known as *Ideas. Red Hot* was rather cryptically sold as "A story of a Girl, A Vow, A Colour and a Fortune." Karno was a hugely influential figure in the history of comedy, famous not only as the discoverer of Charlie Chaplin and Stan Laurel, but many others including Will Hay and Max Miller. He was revered by younger comics, including Bennett, whose parents had known him since the time he was a young acrobat when he had stayed at the same boarding house. Karno fondly recalled the time Mrs. Bennett mended his Sunday best striped trousers and curled his hair "in the accepted fashion of all

Sheet music for "Buck-Shee" (1920). In army parlance anything buckshee was free.

true acrobats."[6] *Red Hot* was a typically zany Karno production with some bits of inspired nonsense; in one scene Bennett had himself delivered as a parcel to save on the train fare. He learned a lot from playing with the Karno troupe about the mechanics of farce, and of ensemble playing. Principally a solo turn, his sociability gave him a natural facility to adapt to a packed and frenetic stage. It was no surprise that king *farceur* Ben Travers listed

Bennett as one of his favourite comedians. When *Red Hot* finished, he concentrated on his variety stage career, honing his act. The music hall stage was filled with hopefuls all striving to be noticed, but Bennett from the start had something else that set him apart from the rest. He had his own unique style that he developed. He changed his approach—along with his sartorial style—after an experience in a Dublin theatre. At that point, he still dressed in khaki to deliver his act, and entered to various martial airs such as "Tipperary." In light of the civil war in Ireland and the antagonism that would have ensued, the theatre manager advised him to alter his music, dress and some of his material. He took the manager's advice and ditched the army uniform. In Liverpool he came across an old dress suit which gave him his new appearance. The outfit was complete with boiled shirt, cummerbund, a large red handkerchief and hobnailed boots. He had retained the army boots, but adopted the would-be stylish man-about-town in a frock coat with plastered down hair and black sagebrush moustache that became his trademark style. His rise was swift, and within a matter of months he was topping bills across the country. By October, 1922 he adopted the tagline "Almost a gentleman"—a perfectly apt description of his persona and style suggested by Archie Parnell. Bennett was truly one of the first post-modern comedians. There had been many parodists before, but there was something different about the way he presented his material which pricked the balloon of pomposity and reverence for the Victorian era of sentimentalism.

Throughout the 1920s he embellished his solo turn and widened his repertoire; he appeared in pantomimes, revues and plays. He occasionally joined with others in sketches, for instance with Theo Ward in *Masterpieces* and Charles Austin in *Poor Old Parker*. A feature of his act during the 1924 season was "The Wager" with quick-change artist Owen McGiveny. In this, McGiveny challenged Bennett to match his feat of playing all the characters in a burlesque of *Oliver Twist*. Bennett rose to the challenge, aided and abetted by others on the bill. A version of the routine had proved a great success in New York a couple of years earlier with the double-act Wheeler and Wolsey, and was described as "The Loudest Laugh of 1924." In 1924-25, Bennett co-starred with Susan Kellogg in a tour of *The Rainbow*, a lavish Albert de Courville production described as a super revue, which was reputed to have cost about £30,000 to stage. One of the biggest outlays was on the costumes which were all made in Paris by Max Weldy. Some of the settings included scenes in the Far East and Versailles. There was some topical humour with a satire of the recent spectacular discovery of Tutankhamun's tomb in "When the Egyptians discover London." The show boasted a 48-strong chorus line and was hyped as "an orgy of beauty, melody and fun." For some it dragged in parts, but most critics were agreed that Bennett provided the largest measure of the fun, especially in the scene "Pharaoh Among the Ruins of London" and in his rendition of the song "In the Rain."[8]

In 1925 he played Old Bill in 'Ullo, a revue by Bruce Bairnsfather based on the characters in his popular Great War cartoons. With his red nose and walrus moustache, Bill was the embodiment of the dogged, phlegmatic spirit of the ordinary soldier in war, with a kind of gallows humour that suited the situation. One of his most fondly recalled cartoons featured the redoubtable Bill and his pal stuck in a trench on the Western Front with shells bursting overhead and the caption, "Well if you knows of a better 'ole, go to it." On account of his appearance and experience alone, Bennett was almost Bill to the life. He was approached by Bairnsfather, who needed a star name to save his revue, and hopefully recoup the money that he had personally sunk into the endeavour.[9] Ullo had fifteen varied scenes beginning with Bennett as Old Bill in conversation with Nelson at the top of his column in Trafalgar Square. Bill's adventures took him from the trenches of France to diving for sunken treasure in California and ended with the real highlight of him as speaker of the House of Commons. Bairnsfather had a lot riding on the show, and was involved in all aspects of it, including the design of the costumes and posters. Bennett appeared in a pre-West End tour of the provinces in the spring and early summer of 1925. The reviews were positive, describing 'Ullo as "exceptionally bright and telescopic." He received some fine personal notices including one which declared him to be "the life and soul of the production."[10] However, during the run at the Finsbury Park Empire in June, he left the show in order to return to the variety stage and was replaced by Johnny Danvers. In all likelihood, Bennett might have been reluctant to become too strongly identified with one character.

By now a near-veteran of revue, in 1926 he wrote his own, *Out of Work*, based on a layout by Archie Parnell. Surprisingly, Bennett did not star in it because he had written it expressly as a vehicle for his friend Charlie Higgins, an upcoming comic who displayed much of the instinctive Bennett wit. They met when sharing a bill at the Alhambra at which time Higgins was part of a double act, St. Juste and Higgins. Bennett was immediately impressed by Higgins' comedy character work and enjoyed watching his act night after night from the wings. It was this

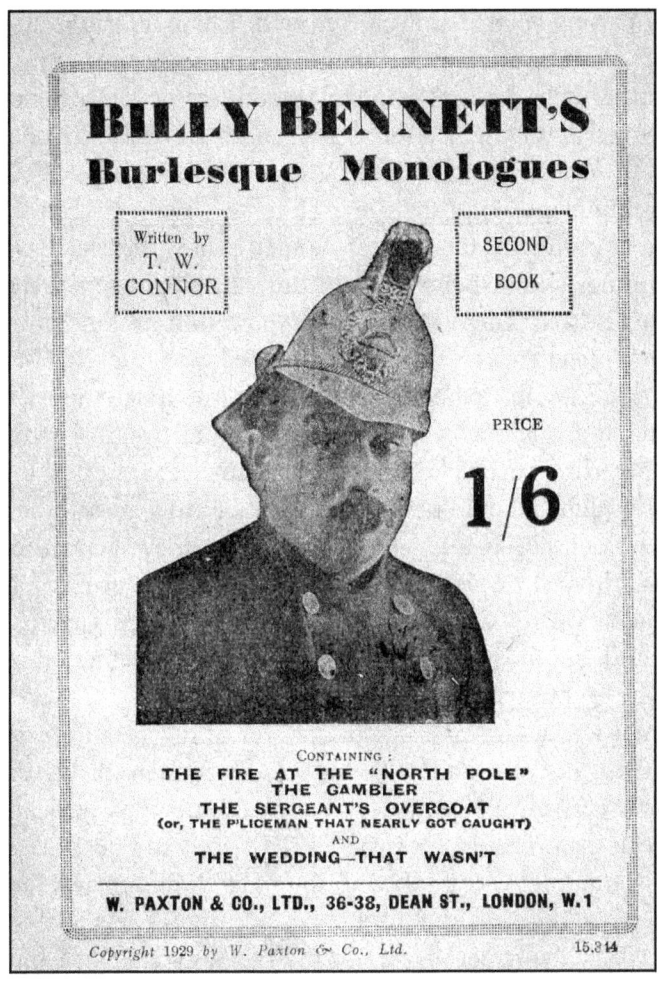

A series of Bennett's burlesques were issued between 1919 and 1942 and are now collectable items. Above: *His Second Book* (1929), written by T. W. Connor who contributed material to a variety of artists.

turn that inspired him to write the revue, although he confessed that he was so pleased with the finished result that he was tempted to star in it himself, but that was just not possible because he was booked up on the variety circuit for many years in advance. *Out of Work* proved to be a highly popular revue which toured extensively and made Higgins' name. (See Charlie Higgins)

In the summer of 1926, Bennett toured South Africa, with great success in most places. An exception was in Pretoria where his act was received in stony silence and greeted with polite applause after he had finished. He later construed that the reason for this was that the audience were mostly Dutch speakers who had not understood a word he had said. He liked to tell a story against himself of another experience he had in the city when theatre prices were raised just for his visit. Some local dignitary at his hotel informed him that he used to be able to get into the Grand theatre for two shillings but that for Bennett's show the cost had increased to two shillings and sixpence, "And I don't think you're worth the extra tanner," he retorted. Thereupon, Bennett gave him his tanner or sixpence back, after which he was feeling rather pleased with himself. "But imagine my surprise," he said, "when I went to leave the hotel about an hour or so later, to find a queue two hundred strong all waiting for tanners."[11] He was forced to curtail his tour on account of a sudden unspecified illness. Although he could have been treated locally, he said he preferred to return home to be treated by the doctors he knew. Unfortunately, this meant that the rest of his intended world tour did not happen. He had been booked by Percy Crawford to tour the Tivoli circuit in Australia and New Zealand, but those plans were abandoned and Bennett never toured either of those countries.[12]

Bennett was a shrewd judge of material and was seldom tempted to stray far from his root audience. He was a uniquely British humourist whose earthiness and absurdity would probably not have been appreciated by European theatregoers, for instance. He wisely did not attempt to visit France; although he was booked to tour the United States, he didn't go through with it—for health reasons. His admirers knew well the culture that he was parodying because it was their own. In 1928 he was signed up by the prestigious Shubert circuit for a three-year contract in the United States, beginning with a starring role in the musical *Good Boy* due to open in September at a salary of £250 a week.[13] He left Britain for the big adventure at the start of August, but when he arrived in New York spent only a few days in the city and then sent a telegram to his mother saying "Doctors Have ordered me home. B. P. [High Blood Pressure] through the heat." He did not even attend the rehearsal.[14] Another report stated that it was a misunderstanding on the part of the manager.[15] He later explained that he found the heat unbearable; "The rooms were just like Turkish baths," he related, "I had only landed an hour when the heat began to affect me; my ankles began to swell. Rehearsals did not begin for another week, and I thought I should get acclimatised. On the fifth day (Sunday) I could hardly hobble along, and I was due to rehearse the next day. I went to a doctor and he said I had blood pressure through the heat."[16] After that he booked his passage home. He was still afflicted on the return journey. He arrived back in Southampton on a Saturday and by the following Monday he was playing his familiar haunt of the Holborn Empire to riotous laughter.[17] *Variety* commented somewhat backhandedly that he "would have been sure-fire in the States twenty years ago."[18] Bennett expressed the hope of visiting America in future, but never again in the summer. In the event he did visit the country on other occasions but he never actually played there. He maintained that artists were not

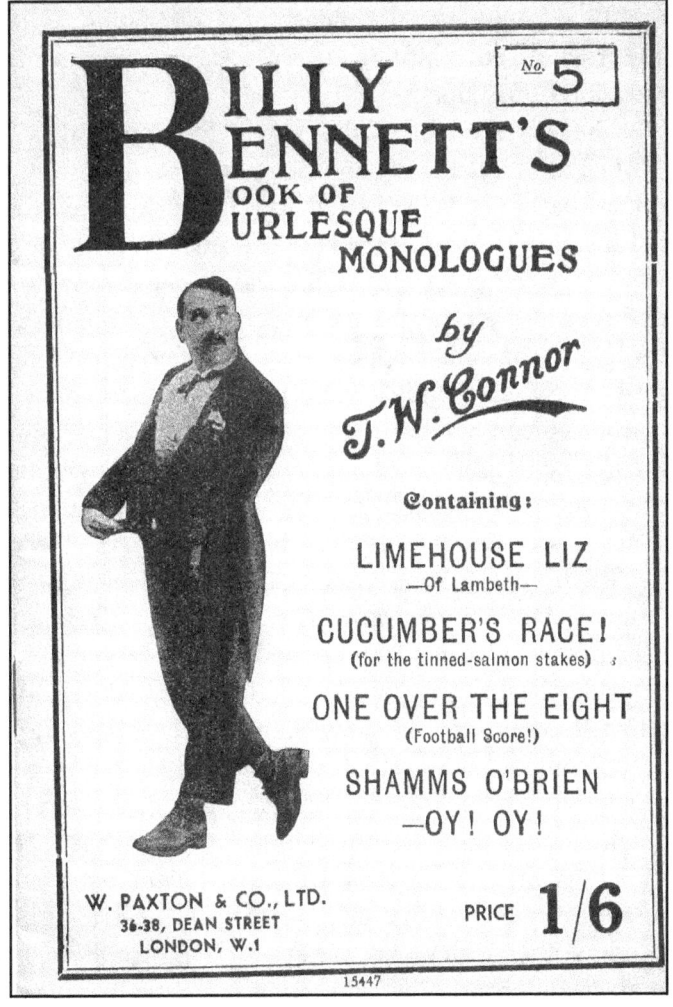

No. 2 in the series of Bennett's Burlesques (1930)

sufficiently well paid there and that the chief form of entertainment was a cabaret-style show which did not suit his type of comedy. There was, for him, nowhere comparable to the variety theatres of Britain.[19] His humour was probably far too British to have taken off to any extent in America, and his truncated South African tour was his only attempt to establish himself outside of the British Isles.

(III) A Versatile Artist

During the 1920s, Bennett consolidated his reputation as a singular Music Hall turn and a successful revue artist. He also made his recording, broadcasting and film debuts.

In 1928 he was the star of the Vivian Ellis musical *Will O' The Whispers* (April to June) at the Shaftesbury. Several songs from the show by the popular baritone "Whispering" Jack Smith were released on the HMV label including "Miss Annabelle Lee" and "When Day is Done." Smith and Bennett were the crux of the show, one providing romantic melancholy and the other the broad comedy. He was for many a welcome presence with his constant reappearances in different guises, as a cod ventriloquist, a conjurer and a mind-reader. He scored perhaps his biggest hit as Napoleon in a burlesque with his almost 'Josephine' played by Margaret Yarde. Bennett also engaged in cross-talk with Smith in a 'Whispering' routine. Music and comedy were balanced out, with several set-piece musical scenes including an ambitious big-scale ballet of George Gershwin's "Rhapsody in Blue." Among the songs which Bennett sang was "Is Variety Dead?" The answer was a resounding no as long as he was on stage. The following year Bennett joined a similar revue show, *Coo-ee*, at the Vaudeville Theatre, Strand, with Stanley Holloway, Claude Hulbert and Dorothy Dickson. In the show, Bennett played several different characters including a London cabbie with an emaciated horse but was at his best when he came closest to his usual act. In the second half he appeared in drag, along with the other actors, and also as a lettuce. A lively, unpretentious and entertaining show with an excellent cast, Bennett came in for his share of plaudits. *The London Mercury* described him as the star turn and another reviewer commented; "His rich, hearty, vigorous humour is always appropriate whether in big music hall or in an intimate revue such as *Coo-ee*."[1] In between revues, Bennett was on home ground sharing bills with all the other music hall artistes of the era with whom he really belonged, prominent among them George Robey and Lily Morris. He once appeared in an affectionate *homage* to the bygone days of music hall in *Melodies and Memories* at the Alhambra. Of the "Pleasure Gardens Scene" H. Willson Disher wrote: "The chief joy of this is the unexpected appearance of Gladdy Sewell, in bloomers, and Billy Bennett, wearing the inglorious forerunners of plus fours while wheeling the tandem to inspire the strains of 'A Bicycle Made for Two.'"[2] He acted as compere for the American pianist Melville Gideon's *Charivaria* at the Empire, and caused widespread mirth as Romeo opposite Dorothy Dickson as Juliet in a send-up of the famous balcony scene from Shakespeare's play.

The post-war years were a time of irreverence when the old certainties of the Victorian era seemed not only outmoded but faintly ludicrous. After the Battle of the Somme and the wholesale slaughter of Passchendaele nothing much seemed to matter. It was as though the axis of everything had shifted irrevocably. The First World War changed everything and above all people questioned their leaders and the status quo. Everything from state religion to popular entertainment had to fall into step with the new world order. The songs of the war had reflected the change; from the urgent recruiting patriotism of "We Don't Want to Lose You (But We Think You Ought to Go)" to the bitter irony of "Take Me Back to Dear Old Blighty" was a major leap in three years. At the same time music hall itself had become respectable since the seal of royal approval had been bestowed by the Royal Variety Performance. That desire for respectability had undermined the essence of the old spirit of the halls as the people's entertainment. Bennett straddled both the old and the new. Whether in a spectacular musical revue or a traditional variety bill he stayed essentially true to the character he created and which endured in the popular imagination as the archetypal music hall comedian.

In the days when people had to entertain themselves, recitations and monologues were hugely popular. Some of the old favourites included "The Shooting of Dan McGrew" which was among Bennett's repertoire. One of his most inimitable recitations was "The Green Tie of the Little Yellow Dog" based on "The Green Eye of the Yellow God" which sounded as though it was written by Kipling, but was the work of J. Milton Hayes. It was written in 1911 and was often performed by Bransby Williams among others. The work was popular with satirists, and George Robey had also done a parody called "The Green Fly on the Little Yellow Dog." Like Bennett, Hayes had spent time in the military and wrote the verse in five

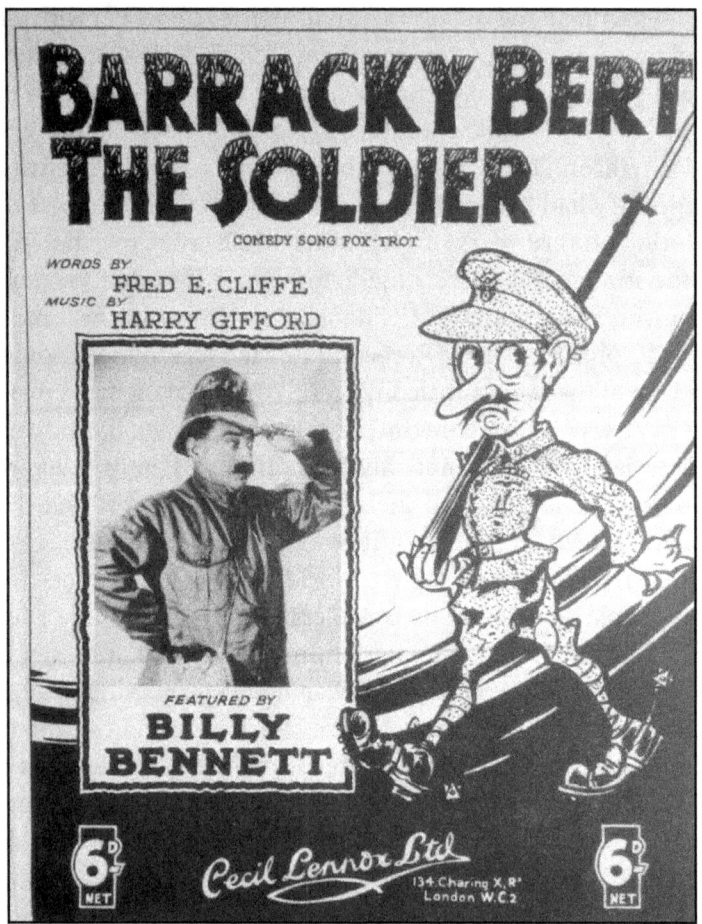

Bennett continued to sing comedy songs about military life long after he was demobbed. Above: "Barracky Bert" c1926.

hours with a clear plan of what he was trying to do. Hayes took exception to Bennett's appropriation of his original and tried to get an injunction against it. Hayes claimed the first four lines of the parody were largely the same. Eventually a settlement was made out of court.[3] Bennett was adept at choosing those recitations which, with their mixture of portentousness and sentimentality were ripe for parody. The apotheosis of his art in this vein was represented by "The Charge of the Tight Brigade" a parody of the Tennyson classic and the high Victoriana school, which also included sly comments on the war, its aftermath and the nature of jingoism; It began "In fifteen charabancs rode the six hundred," and continued:

> When they'd scored fifty goals,
> Postmen delivered coals,
> Boy scouts climbed up their poles,
> All waving sausage rolls.
>
> Navvies in camisoles
> Went to their better 'oles,
> Back, back to draw their doles
> And buy silk pyjamas."

Tellingly, the original line from Tennyson's poem "Someone had blunder'd" was retained. This line, as the original poem, was inspired by a contemporary report of the battle in *The Times,* which largely put the blame for the rout on the shoulders of the commanding officer. The same inherent criticism was just as relevant in the wake of the First World War as it was for the Crimean war, if not more so. Bennett's parody chimed in with the irreverence of his generation for the age that Tennyson and Kipling represented. While poets Ezra Pound and T. S. Eliot were struggling to break free of the long shadow of the Victorian poet laureate, Bennett cut to the chase with his inspired burlesque. Similarly, he sent up Kipling's ever-popular *Road to Mandalay*:

> "There's a pub three miles behind us
> And we've passed it on the way
> Come you back, you British soldiers
> There's a Scotsman wants to pay."

He was equally derisive of the crooners of the 1920s and 1930s as evinced in his parody of a love song "I'll Be Thinking of You."

> And when the birds are softly cooing
> I'll be thinking of you
> When I'm on the road to ruin
> I'll be thinking of you
> When the sun goes down in splendour
> I'll be feeling very tender
> Where you trapped me with a fender
> And my dreams came true."

Bennett's Burlesques No. 5.

His best material was that which encapsulated his earthily surreal world view, such as "The Only Girl I Ever Loved":

> "The only girl I've ever loved was Rosie
> She used to be a dancer in revue
> So I went to the Hall and asked for Rosie
> The stage-door keeper said, 'I'm telling you,

'Rosie doesn't dance here any more
They had a gas escape at number four
We heard a loud explosion and poor Rose was blown to bits
One ear came down in Rugby and in Crewe the part that sits
We found one leg in Bradford so we know she'd done the splits
But Rosie doesn't dance here anymore."

Such a ditty encapsulates much of his unique appeal and also shows why his humour would not travel well. Even if Detroit and Maine were

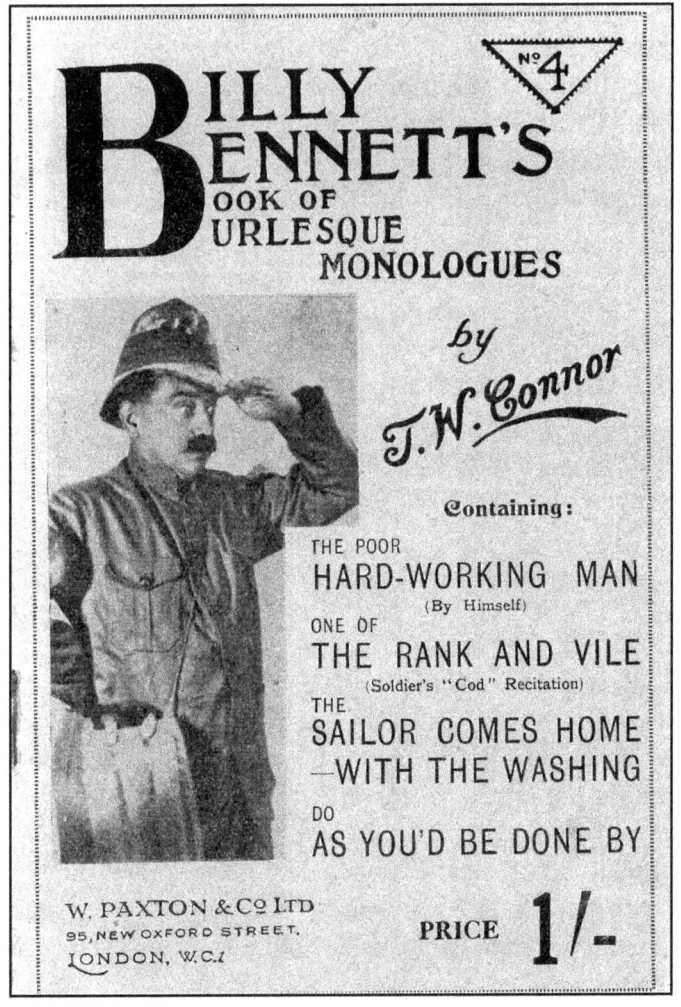

Bennett's Burlesques No. 4.

substituted for Rugby and Crewe this song would unlikely be appreciated outside the British Isles. Some of the songs were written by T. W. Connor, and others including Percival Langley, but all Bennett's patter was his own; "I write my own stuff," he noted, "though many listeners send me lots of so-called gags, particularly after a broadcast. A thousand letters a week is no uncommon thing for me and each is answered carefully."[4]

He made his BBC debut in 1927 and although traditional red-nosed comics were not the order of the day at the corporation, he was so popular and his art so entirely his own that he was a notable exception. He made his first screen appearances in short films from the late-1920s onwards including the nine-minute long *Almost a Gentleman* (1928) made by the pioneering De Phono sound-on-vision process. There were several silent shorts for Pathe, and some talkies, including *Pathe Magazine No. 35* (1929) in which he did a cod-ventriloquist act drinking a glass of water while singing "Show Me the Way to Go Home." In *Unnatural History* (1930) he gave an absurd lecture on the natural history of bats, and concluded with the advice "For any more information about bats please consult Mr. Jack Hobbs."

(IV) The Royal Command Comedian

> "Like a successful boxer, he delivers an attack before one has had time to recover from the preceding one. The result is roars of laughter."
>
> – *The Stage*, 30 June, 1925

Bennett was a big draw for royalty, ever since his first Royal Command Performance in 1926, for King George V and Queen Mary, which first made his name and raised him to star status. Observers noticed that the Queen did not laugh so much that night at the other acts, until he made his appearance, after which she never stopped. He told, with a straight face, of his father who was in hospital after breaking his fingers while cracking jokes to a deaf-mute. His quips about parsimonious Scotsmen and his rendering of "A Soldier's Farewell to His Horse" found favour.[1]

"I swam out to Sydney, on my floating kidney,
And then, back to Alsace Lorraine.
When I stepped on the pier, the wife shouted 'I'm here,'
So I jumped in the water again."

On his second appearance two years later, his mother was in the stalls. As he related, "She told me afterwards that she almost died of fright lest I should forget my words, and that she repeated them as they fell from me, to the amusement of her neighbours"[2] In all he appeared at four Commands and on his third appearance in 1933 at the Alhambra he was awarded a gold watch.[3] Of that evening's show an eyewitness wrote "Her Majesty leaned forward in her box so as not to miss any of Billy's gags, and laughed unrestrainedly at them, at times removing her lorgnettes to wipe tears from her eyes, so great was her mirth."[4] The Queen appreciated his assured, quick-fire delivery of such throwaway lines as "I went into a restaurant yesterday and I said to the waiter 'Do you serve crabs here?' and he said 'We serve anybody, sit down.'"[5] The following year his turn was one of his briefest, but he still hit the mark.

The cachet of being Queen Mary's favourite comedian must have attracted a lot of business his way. His bill matter sometimes reflected his elevated status; after his first appearance he was known as "The King's Comedian" and by the time of his final turn in 1934 he became "The Royal Command Comedian." That year he was the only single act on a bill with over 200 artists, which clearly demonstrated the changing times and emphasised that single turns were becoming a rarity. Bennett kept the flag of individuality flying in an age of increasing conformity. He concentrated on domestic jokes as he noticed that the Queen particularly liked those. "Both the King and the Queen are a wonderful audience," he once remarked.[6] The Royal family has long been known to appreciate earthy humour and there was something about Bennett's particular brand of playful nonsense that struck a chord with all walks of life. As Stanley Holloway observed, there was never any side to Bennett and such sincerity endeared him to a great many people who welcomed his lack of artifice in an age of increasingly apparent falsity. Holloway also referred to Bennett's streak of amateurism, but there was nothing remotely amateurish about his approach to his craft. On the contrary, he was an incredibly hard-working professional. As one of his employers once observed;

"Whatever he tackles always seems to have the same result—music hall, cabaret, revue, pictures, radio and records, are all equally successful, and this I attribute to the thoroughness with which he goes about his work. No slacking or skimping with Mr. B., but coat off and full steam ahead at each performance. I have watched him with interest on innumerable occasions and at places as far apart as the Poles. Shoreditch to Mayfair is nothing to him: he makes them rock in an East End music-hall and then goes to an exclusive West End club and repeats the operation on the cream of society."[7]

Bennett was often considered an anomaly in his age, a throwback to the old days prior to the war. The leading critic Vernon Woodhouse considered him the only comedian of his time who truly belonged in the same class as the greats of Music Hall.[8] When quizzed about the secret of his success, Bennett replied simply; "I succeed, I think, by a good make-up and by good songs and patter. With these, and a confident heart, I can, under ordinary circumstances, generally succeed in being funny."[9] Bennett maintained that he never suffered from nerves, but the bandleader Henry Hall, who once shared a dressing room at a Royal Variety show with him, recalled in his memoirs that Bennett was "as nervous as a kitten before he went on ... and then the minute he was on the stage gave the performance of his life!"[10]

In November, 1930, Bennett joined with James Carew in a parody of a minstrel act, as Alexander and Mose. They had a series on the radio and took the show on the road, although it was not revealed for some time that Bennett was in fact Mose. He still appeared on the same bill in his usual character during this time. Even by then a burnt-cork minstrel-type routine would seem to have been decidedly passe, but their cross-talk act, based on the American style, proved surprisingly popular. The idea had first occurred to Bennett's agent Archie Parnell while he was laid up in hospital, and was inspired by the success of Amos 'n Andy, who were big wireless stars in America.[11] Carew had once been with a minstrel troupe. The exposure on radio gave Alexander and Mose a ready audience and they also recorded a few sides of patter. They formed a concert party with other artists and took their show on tour in 1931. This proved a resounding hit. The Times declared: "Messrs. Bennett and Whelan have a lot to do, and they do it not only with technical ability, but with an air of enjoyment which communicates itself to the audience and endears them to it."[12] When Carew left the act in 1932, he was replaced by the veteran Australian actor Albert Whelan. After Whelan decided to do other things, the act disbanded.

Throughout the 1930s Bennett appeared in many revues, and in 1934 had much success in the fifth consecutive *Crazy Month* at the Palladium. Later that year he was the star of Jack Taylor's super revue *King Folly* during the Christmas season (1934-35), which also toured. A colourful, big-scale extravaganza with a large cast, this consisted of some fourteen scenes, eight involving elaborate built-up sets. *The Stage* praised the production as a worthy successor to John Tiller's entertainment, declaring, "This beautifully mounted and dressed show is the best of the series that Jack Taylor has produced."[13] Bennett scored in all his scenes, especially as the unlikely idol of a temple in the Chinese-inspired episode "Jardin Exotique," and in the "Sparks and Marcers" parody of Marks and Spencer. He was also a welcome presence between scenes, popping up both in his Alexander and Mose routine, and solo. The ambitious show featured members of the Royal Ballet, including leading soloist Anthony Dollin, who recalled feeling rather like a fish out of water in the world of provincial variety. Of Bennett he wrote "His humour was broad, but it made 'em laugh."[14]

Bennett made his big screen feature debut in *Radio Parade of 1935* (1934) which was effectively a variety show strung together by a weak story. The same was true of both *Soft Lights and Sweet Music* (1936) and *Calling All Stars* (1937). Better by far was *Almost a Gentleman* (1938) which was built entirely around him. He played a night-watchman who is mistaken for the boss of a firm of toffee makers. Stalwart character actress Kathleen Harrison did sterling service as

Publicity photo of the off-stage Bennett.

his wife, and Gibb McLaughlin was prominent in the supporting cast. The film was made at the Nettlefold Studios at Walton-on-Thames. *Almost a Gentleman* managed to avoid the decade's insistence on hordes of dancing girls *a la* Busby Berkeley. Instead it was a thoroughly British product with moments of slapstick and the memorable sight of Billy being vamped by seductive French *femme fatale* Marcell Rogez. One pen portrait of the film described it thus; "Robust, good wisecracks—snappy monologues, a long succession of gags…"[15] The following year he featured in the engaging Ealing period comedy *Young Man's Fancy* (1939). Anna Lee was the star and Bennett appeared attired in the uniform of a Hussar. It had a good cast and did decent business, but if anything, Bennett just wasn't in it enough. As the *Motion Picture Herald* commented; "Billy Bennett, in an all-too scant role as Miss Lee's military impresario is a Victorian W. C. Fields with an English accent."[16] The picture was nominated for the Mussolini Cup as Best Foreign Film at the Venice Film Festival that year, the last before the war. It was unfortunate that he did not make more films and perhaps, had he lived, he would have come into his own as a film comedian as time went on.

In the late summer of 1936, Bennett donned Pierrot garb once more and joined his friend Clarkson Rose in his perennially popular *Twinkle* pier show at Eastbourne. For much of 1938 Bennett joined forces with popular singer Leslie "Hutch" Hutchinson in a tour of Charles L. Tucker's *Variety Roadshow*. The revue had a nautical theme, and Bennett acted as compere. Hutch was the star of the first show, and the two provided a complete contrast. The combination of Hutch, with his smooth, romantic and sophisticated singing style which captivated all the females present, and the breezy, honest vulgarity of Bennett, proved a big draw. Hutch even accompanied Bennett on one of his numbers in a shipboard cabaret scene. The two stars co-wrote the music and lyrics with Max Wall.[17] Owen McGiveney also revived his wager routine of 1924, which was of sufficient vintage by then to seem new. Upcoming comedienne Hilda Baker had a spot on the programme. In the follow-up version of the show later the same year, Hutch was replaced by popular heavyweight xylophonist Teddy Brown.

Bennett found big musical comedy productions were hard work but enjoyable and rewarding. He also relished the camaraderie of an ensemble show. He felt it gave him new perspectives on his solo turn; "It freshens one up enormously to have to learn a part and to portray a character," he once reflected.[18] Being a single act involved a prodigious amount of work, he revealed, and was much harder than being part of a show because everything was down to the individual. He worked out a lot of material for his act, about two thirds of which he discarded.

The entertainment business was changing and he managed to adapt his old-fashioned approach to it. He was called on to appear in smart West End cabaret shows such as those at the Paradise Club in Regent Street, which at that time was the place to be seen and he went over well. As one witness remarked; "Billy Bennett fits into the new cabaret at the Paradise like the proverbial glove. Unlike Tommy Trinder, he does not attempt to argue with his audiences, but delivers his material with a thrust, and there is no doubt of its effect, judging by the reaction of the hearty laughter which ensued."[19] He found audiences varied considerably when doing his stage show. He said that those in Newcastle, Manchester and Cardiff were the quickest to appreciate his act but found most difficulty in some towns such as Coventry where, he commented "they don't seem to be able to follow my quick line of patter."[20] One of his worst experiences occurred in an unnamed provincial town where the audience took him *literally*.

(V) THE ART OF COMEDY

> "Let it be said of Billy Bennett that he raised every night in the week to the level of Saturday night, gave his audience infinite amusement, and never uttered a word at which sensible people could take offence."
>
> – James Agate

Bennett found great success as a recording artist, mostly with the Columbia label from 1926 onwards, and had a few releases on Regal and Regal Zonophone. His latter-day reputation rests to a large extent on his records.

Although widely popular in his day, he did have his detractors, who just could not see the joke and considered him too traditionalist or simply too vulgar. Others felt that his recorded output failed to work because he needed to be seen on stage to be properly appreciated. This view was long promoted by record reviewers in *Gramophone*, one of the leading music publications of the time, who remained largely unconvinced by him. In flat contradiction to their view, a contemporary critic wrote "Having seen him I can vouch for it that he loses none of his mirth in recording."[1] In 1978, many years after his death, a compilation LP was released by Topic Records. Topic was founded in 1939 as an offshoot of the Communist Worker's Music Association, and from the 1950s onwards was in the vanguard of the British folk music revival. The songs of music hall were effectively the twentieth century urban music of the ordinary folk. The Billy Bennett record, naturally entitled *Almost a Gentleman,* gathered together most of his best-known work and sold well thanks in part to being played extensively by John Peel on his Radio One show, thus bringing the great comic to the attention of whole new generations. Peel commented on the parallels between Bennett's surreal lyrics and those of John Lennon.[2] Interestingly, Lennon was said to have been inspired by Bennett to attempt to write a witty book of his own; the result was *How I Won the War.*[3] In 1997, the Bennett record was re-released as a CD with five extra tracks.

One of his best tracks was "My Mother Doesn't Know I'm On the Stage" which played on the low reputation of actors and actresses:

> "Sometimes she sees the powder on my clothing
> And then it's such a nuisance to explain
> If she thought it was powder, she'd go crazy
> Of course, I have to tell her it's cocaine.
>
> The day she saw me out with Gladys Cooper
> She started shouting murder and police
> And would have caused a dreadful scene in public
> So I told her that the girl was Crippen's niece."

The actor Colin Firth recently sang a far different version of this song, which testifies to the strength of the original lyric. The reissue of *Almost a Gentleman* includes the classics "Don't Send My Boy to Prison" and "She Was Poor but She Was Honest." His rendering of these two songs of social comment complete with boozy chorus backing seems strangely at odds with the heartfelt sentiments of the lyrics, and yet somehow apt. His treatment shows how he was perhaps more of a post-modernist than he is thought. His genius was such that we will never know if he was being serious or not.

Among those numbers not committed to record were "The Cheese it Stands Alone" "Stay Out of the North" and "Hollywood, Hollywood, City

Bennett spent his formative years in Liverpool and was a perennially popular figure in the city. He regularly appeared at the Empire, a great theatre which was built in 1866 as the Prince of Wales and is still going strong today.

of Sin" in which latter he managed to rhyme Lillian Gish with "Chips and fried fish." Most of his work was not topical, and then only in a tangential way such as "The League of Nations" in which the League

> "met in Berwick Market,
> To discuss on which side kippers ought to swim."

He was one of the first British comedians to introduce the "Boom, Boom" device, the last line of a verse that pointed to the obvious gag. This was taken up by many later comics, especially Morecambe and Wise. Bennett relished the play on words, as in "The Foreign Legion":

> "I went for those Riffs in their little short shifts,
> And I gave them two biffs with my boot.
> If you biff a Riff he'll run back to his wiff
> In a jiff with a rift in his lute."

His material might appear resolutely politically incorrect for today's sensibilities, but the key thing was the spirit with which he presented it. There was no malice in anything he did, it was all pure fun and absurdism.

Surely none but the most po-faced could take exception to "Street of a Thousand Lanterns":

> "When the bar was closed and Limehouse dozed,
> Uncle watched and Aunt kept nix
> They saw the young man called Hugh Pi Kan
> Showing Wong Wong his box of tricks."

He once gave an insight into the art of comedy, about which he knew more than most, with some pointers for aspiring comics. A fundamental rule was never to laugh at one's own jokes "even the heartiest scream from your listeners should not bring a semblance of a smile to your sphinx-like countenance," he wrote. He stressed that the keyword was sincerity: "You must apparently mean every word you utter, and as your lines become more ridiculous you must become more serious, even to the point of appearing indignant with the audience for daring to laugh at you!"[4]

Some of his material was obvious, but the sheer silliness was appealing, viz. "Sobstuff Sister":

> "But Sally stood out in the pictures
> Yes, Sally stood out like a star,
> But one night she cussed when her shoulder strap bust
> And she stood out a trifle too far."

Or "She's Mine" his paean to his girl who is a little on the plump side:

> "I thought she looked grand as she swam in the foam
> But a sailor said, 'Crikey, the fleet's coming home.'
> He stuck a harpoon in the captive balloon
> And pulled her ashore with his line
> The crowd stood and cheered as she lay soaking wet
> One said, 'It's a whale or a porpoise I'll bet.'
> I said, 'No sir It's only a girl men forget
> But it's mine, all mine.'"

His inspired sense of the ridiculous informed everything he did, and showed a singular imagination at work. It is hard to think of another artist who could do justice to the curious "If Winter Comes" which followed the "sad fate of a pork sausage through the seasons."[5]

Fourth Souvenir Budget issued c1940.

"The bees are full of beeswax. The Tripods full of tripe.
And the plumbers that I meet are full of plums.
The bus is full of Bustles and the Powder's Fullers' Earth.
But the world will lose its smile if winter comes."

At other times he enjoyed parodying the popular ballads of the day including an affectionate send-up of the sentimental Flanagan and Allan hit "Hometown".

"Hometown, with its coal and slack and cinders,
Where they never wash the winders,
So, when they have a bath on Friday.

> They don't pull down the blind!
>
> Hometown, there's no bathroom done in pink there,
> So they all sit in the sink there;
> They have to wash as far as possible,
> But still they don't mind."

On occasion he even had items in his repertoire of a serious nature. The effect on an audience must have been startling, if not thought-provoking, if he ever recited the poignant "Me and a Spade" about the burial of Nobby Clark, a fallen comrade in arms:

> "Then a hush, and the padre stopped talking,
> I crumpled and knelt down - and prayed.
> Then I rolled up my sleeves, so did Padre,
> And we took it in turns with the spade.
>
> Then he said, 'Now we'll get back to billets,
> To the rest that we've needed for weeks.'
> He gave me his flask and I moistened my lips,
> We'd already moistened our cheeks.
>
> We arrived at the billets at sunset,
> Reported on evening parade.
> This time there wasn't no Nobby—
> Just the Padre, and me and the spade."

(VI) Echo of Laughter

> *"[Bennett] was full of the incongruity of Music Hall and was the personification of it."*
>
> – W. MacQueen-Pope *The Melodies Linger On*

Bennett was by all accounts just as funny off-stage as he was on, with a ready wit. He was a good mixer and an inveterate storyteller who loved nothing more than socialising with his fellow professionals.[1] During the war he entertained the troops on radio and continued to appear in variety and revues until his sudden and untimely death after collapsing on stage at the Opera House, Blackpool, in 1942.

He was an enthusiastic and much-valued member of numerous clubs including the Savage Club and the Grand Order of Water Rats. As an after-dinner speaker he was *sans pareil*. He was a one-time president of the V. G. S. (Vaudeville Golfing Society) and enjoyed himself at many an annual V. G. S. dinner, often providing the cabaret. One memorable night he joined with friend and fellow comedian Norman Long as "Dirt and Lazy" in a "joyous burlesque" of Gert n' Daisy.[2] Golf was his favourite sport, but he also took occasional shooting holidays in Scotland.

One of his closest friends, who had known his father, was Fred Russell, who once wrote of him: "He was not only a genius of comedy, but a man of noble attributes, not the least being generosity, understanding, and faithfulness in friendships."[3] Stanley Holloway wrote that Bennett was "completely ingenuous and lived a well-ordered life."[4] A confirmed bachelor, he referred to himself laughingly as "God's gift to lonely women" and was apparently never short of female company; the only proviso was that they were out of the house by the time his daily help arrived the next morning at 11am. He was naturally humorous, and told many stories against himself such as the time he was in the middle of his act when a woman carrying a bunch of flowers walked down the central aisle of the theatre and handed the flowers to a stage manager to give to him. Imagining he had some secret admirer he desperately tried to find out about the mystery woman. It transpired that she was a flower seller and rather than waste the flowers she had left at the end of the day, she thought she would give them to him.

Bennett's family remained important to him. Both his sisters had careers on stage; it was a precarious life, especially for actresses. He supported them during his lifetime and left all his money to them in his will. He was a shrewd businessman and by the time of his death had amassed a small fortune of £38,000, which surprised many of his fellow performers. His sister Kate said that he made most of his money in after dinner speaking which was always lucrative, and he seldom turned down an engagement.[5] He worked tirelessly, and it was not unusual for him to appear in five shows in one night—two each at two London theatres and a radio broadcast.[6] Invariably he banked everything he earned and had few real luxuries. He knew his worth and was once involved in a much-publicised dispute with the BBC over his fee. They offered him £1 a minute but he demanded more. "I am sorry the matter has been made public," he commented at the time, "and I can't help thinking a better offer could have been made." The BBC responded by saying "We offered Mr. Bennett £20 for a 15-minute turn, and we considered it a fair offer for his services."[7] He was a doyen of the corporation's variety output, especially on the perennial *Music Hall*, and in the early months of 1939 he was given his own 30-minute show, *Almost an Academy*. The series of six programmes was recorded at St. George's Hall with the resident BBC organist Sandy Macpherson providing accompaniment. A typical episode was a nonsense lesson conducted by Professor Bennett entitled "A Musical Spelling Bee." He did not exclusively work for the BBC, and was also heard on the *Rinso Music Hall* programmes on Radio Luxembourg and Normandy.[8] He produced a series of about half a dozen collections of his monologues. *Billy Bennett's Budget of Burlesque Monologues*, published by W. Paxton & Co. of Dean Street, London which appeared between the mid-1920s and the early 1940s. These booklets are now highly collectible.

Bennett's mother was by all accounts a formidable lady; he described her as his best pal. She would often sit in the front of the stalls and assess how the act was coming across. She was quick to defend her son from any and every perceived slight.[9] His father also accompanied him to social functions, especially those by the V. G. S. He had retired from the business before 1914 and moved to Brighton where he died in 1936 at the age of 68.[10] Billy retained links to Liverpool and especially his old school on Earle Road, which he regularly visited over the years, giving out prizes on Speech Day. He gave sound advice to the boys; "You'll never get anything without hard work," he told them.[11] In 1932 when he was appearing at the Pavilion theatre a short walk away from the school, he invited the old boys to the show as his guests, including his old teacher, Mr. T. H. Allen.[12] Like many of his fellow players, he supported a number of charities.

He developed a fondness for travelling by car and by aeroplane. In the 1920s he enjoyed motoring in his Austin Six. Later he drove a Titan De-Luxe and was once prosecuted for dangerous driving in Southampton, for which he was fined £5 plus £2 costs.[13] He had a yen to sample the thrill of air travel in what was a new age of discovery. For instance, for an engagement at the Royal, Dublin in October, 1933, he chartered an aeroplane which left from Heston airport in Middlesex at 10 am and arrived in Dublin at 12:30.[14] In the 1930s he visited America again and travelled over six thousand miles by plane, including a trip over the Grand Canyon at an altitude of 11,000 ft. During his stay in the U. S. he visited the

Hollywood studios and was escorted around the MGM lot, where he saw the last few shots of *Saratoga*, the final film of Jean Harlow, and watched Spencer Tracy and Luise Rainer making *Big City*. He wrote to his old friend Clarkson Rose, "There are heaps of erstwhile vaudevillians hanging round Hollywood hoping for the best." He went on "The cops have closed the strip-tease shows in New York, but in Los Angeles and 'Frisco they are still going strong, and it's an ideal family entertainment providing your lady friend belongs to another family."[15] On another visit he wrote that he went to see Jack Dempsey's house which was "very ornate and splendid" and mentioned that he was hoping to catch a baseball game.[16] His visits to America became annual events during the decade, until 1939, in which year he postponed his trip because of the death of his mother. His mother died on 26 May that year and he received a great many condolences from his friends.[17]

With the coming of the war he appeared in shows for the troops and was a regular broadcaster. He continued to appear in revues, such as *Black and Blue* at the Empire, Liverpool, in which he played a chief air raid warden alongside singer Frances Day. His other main entertainment was in pantomime and he co-starred with Arthur Askey in the long-running *Jack and Jill* at the Prince of Wales, Birmingham, 1939-40.[18] During the darkest days of the war in May, 1940, Bennett helped keep up morale with *Present Arms,* at the Prince of Wales Theatre. The music was by Noel Gay with lyrics by Frank Eaton. The typical wartime frolic teamed Bennett with Max Wall and gave the latter many opportunities to display his inimitable walk. According to one reviewer, Bennett contrived to appear largely as his old familiar self "bursting out of a bright blue suit and breaking occasionally into his peculiar and characteristic poetry recitations."[19] James Agate wrote: "Mr. Bennett, in a bowler hat and a blazer which has a suspicious M. C. C. look about it, is not at all a gentleman and manages to murder the French language and the rules of scansion with equally magnificent aplomb."[20] The show proved popular and ran until August.

Bennett joined other acts with ENSA and took part in a series of munition-drive concerts for factory workers, some of which were broadcast by the BBC.[21] Later that year he joined Tom Arnold's variety roadshow *Enough to Make a Cat Laugh,* alongside other favourites such as pianist Charlie Kunz. Bennett was also a mainstay of Arnold's follow-up presentation *Boys and Girls of the BBC,* which proved a hit across the country in 1941. This starred Hutch again, and Cyril Fletcher, an up-and-coming young comic. Fletcher remembered Bennett's kindness to him; not only did

The Bennett record Almost a Gentleman was issued by Topic in 1978 and brought the great comedian to the attention of a whole new generation when John Peel played tracks on his radio show. A CD version with extra tracks was released in 1997.

he help him with his radio material but gave him valuable advice on how to improve his stage act.[22] One commentator noted that Bennett "cuts an incredible figure as a fairy queen in the closing burlesque."[23]

He was a regular on forces broadcasts during the war, including the revue *On the Dot* (Oct. 1939), *Top of the Bill* (1940), *Friday: First House*, *The Happidrome* and *Old Mother Riley's Christmas Party* (Dec. 1941). He also took part in special entertainments aimed at particular sections of the service; for instance, in *Ack-Ack, Beer-Beer* for the men in anti-aircraft, balloon Barrage and Searchlight units. An interesting programme was the *King Pins of Comedy* in which he was interviewed by Wilfred Pickles. One of his final appearances was in a supper time cabaret show, *Cocktails, Kippers and Capers* (April 1942). He continued to be heard on *Music Hall* until 2 June 1942.

In the 1940s his health began to give cause for serious concern. He had suffered periods of recurring ill health over the years, ever since his early days. In 1920 he had to undergo an operation which kept him away from touring for a month, and another operation cut short his South African tour in September, 1926.[24] There was also the problem with high blood pressure which had manifested itself at the time of his abortive tour of the U. S. In 1935 he had an accident when he hurt his leg at the Empire, Sheffield. Three weeks later the leg became poisoned and took some time to heal. In July, 1940 he feinted in his dressing room; rest was the prescribed cure on that occasion.[25] In March, 1942 he was topping the bill with Forces' Sweetheart Vera Lynn at the Stoll Theatre, Kingsway. After a few weeks, he began to feel unwell and from the end of

April, he was unable to take any further part in the show because of illness and another comedian deputised for him.[26] Undaunted, the following month he signed up to play in George Black's *Vanities* at the Blackpool Opera House. He appeared twice at the opening night performance on 23 May, but had a heart attack soon afterwards and was unable to appear again. His place was taken by Billy Dawes. Bennett had rented a house in Blackpool for the season where he stayed with his sisters. Sound recordist Joe Batten happened to be recording Reginald Dixon at the Blackpool Tower organ at the same time as Bennett was at the Opera House. Batten recalled in his memoirs; "We had heard that he was in bad health and I had been charged by members of the Savage Club to find out what was wrong. I called on him at his house in South Shore, and was told that he was very ill indeed. I asked to see him. But when I went into his bedroom, he was unconscious and I came away without speaking to him. He died ten minutes after."[27] Billy Bennett died on 30 June, 1942 at the age of only 54.

Bennett left a big gap in the world of British entertainment and was greatly missed. He received much after-praise from all ranks of society including leading comics such as Ken Dodd and Morecambe and Wise, as well as the intelligentsia. He was mentioned in the autobiographies of figures as diverse as the actor Ray Milland and the much-loved cricket commentator of *Test Match Special*, Brian Johnston. Playwright John Osborne was a fan, and even called his second volume of memoirs *Almost A Gentleman*, which also served as the title of a memorable episode of *Hancock's Half Hour*. Critic James Agate wrote several times in appreciation of him. At the time of his death he wrote what has become the comedian's lasting eulogy:

> "Bennett will live in the annals of music hall. Nobody who saw him is ever likely to forget that rubicund, un-aesthetic countenance, that black, plastered quiff, that sergeant-major's moustache, that dreadful dinner-jacket, that well-used dickey and seedy collar, the too-short trousers, the hob-nailed boots, the red silk handkerchief tucked into the waistcoat, the continual perspiration which was the outward and visible sign of a mind struggling for expression—these things will not be forgotten."[28]

See discography and list of credits on page 232.

Charlie Higgins
(1892–1978)
"It's Good, Isn't It?"

"Higgins is an individual comedian of unusual talent."

– R. B. Marriott, 1934[1]

(I) DOUBLE-ACT

Among the variety comedians of the 1930s only a relative few encapsulated the old spirit of the Music Hall before the trammelling effects of the First World War took their toll. One such was Charlie Higgins, hardly a household name, and yet he reached the heights of his profession in the inter-war years. Popular on stage, record and radio, his racy absurdity still sounds surprisingly fresh and can raise the spirits today given the chance.

Charles Robert Higginson was born at 3 Whalley Street, Manchester on 23 July, 1892, the son of Robert and Sarah Higginson. His father was a carter and yard man at an ironworks in Ancoats. Charlie originally worked in a cotton mill but as a youth he harboured ambitions to be a clog dancer and joined a local juvenile group. It was a demanding discipline to learn, as he recalled; "My tutor used to go into the room below and if he heard a false beat with the clogs he used to come upstairs and knock holes in us."[2] With two others he formed a trio and they appeared at church concerts and other entertainments. At one Band of Hope meeting they began singing "Genevieve." However, it was in the wrong key, an octave higher, but Charlie gamely tried to sing it in a high-pitched voice, which amused his two friends so much they left the stage to him. The audience laughed heartily and he was called for an encore. That experience decided him to pursue a career as a comedian. At a Sunday morning concert at a private club next-door to a chapel, he gave his turn but no-one clapped. Instead they stood up and held their arms aloft. He panicked and fled the stage, thinking that he had been a flop, but the stage manager ushered him back on and assured him "Go on, you're a triumph. That's their way of showing appreciation." He later discovered that hand-clapping was forbidden in the club so as not to disturb the services in the chapel next-door.

With the outbreak of war in 1914, Charlie joined the 1st Battalion King's Liverpool Regiment, and during his service years he became the doyen of concert parties and camp entertainments. This further convinced him to make comedy his profession. He already had some experience in variety and had reputedly played the Hippodrome before the war. It was while serving in the Liverpool Regiment that he met pianist L/Cpl. Robert Charles St. Juste, who was already an established professional entertainer. St. Juste had been on the variety circuit since before 1910, and his mother was also a Music Hall artiste. From 1913, he joined in partnership with Hal L. Miller as Miller and St. Juste. They had much success at the London Coliseum and across the country with a song and cross-talk act under the billing "Two Boys and a Piano." The act disbanded around 1916 by which time St. Juste had joined the Liverpool Regiment and Miller the Royal Navy Air Service. In 1918, the King's Battalion was stationed at Cork, in Ireland and in September that year a concert party toured the country, of which both St. Juste and Higginson were prominent members, although not as a double act. Two years after the Easter Rising, Ireland was still in a state of ferment and the British army were in effect an occupying

Signed publicity photo of Charlie Higgins by Broadcast records, c1930.

force. Although soldiers must have been despised, the brief tour was surprisingly successful. The troupe was made up of ten men and three women, including two double acts and a trio. All the men had been professionals in civilian life, and one of the singers, Dorothy Roche, had been with D'Oyly Carte.³

After the war, the King's Jesters took their show on tour and in April, 1919 they first appeared in London at the Victoria Palace. At that time, Higginson was still using his real name and was a solo act singing the hit

Rare sheet music for "Where the Cross Eyed Claras Grow" (1920), a typically offbeat number by St Juste and Higgins during their years as a successful double act.

"K-K-K-Katy" to great effect. *The Stage* noted that he "scores a distinct success with a highly humorous study of a Tommy who is fed up with a soldier's life…"[4] Shortly after, the two Charlies joined forces; Higginson shortened his name to look better on variety posters and they were billed as St. Juste and Higgins, in the process adopting the name of the King's Jesters. They embarked on a provincial tour under this sobriquet and proved popular. However, one night on 15 May, 1919, after a show at the Sheffield Hippodrome, they were arrested for desertion from their regiment. The local police had received a telegram from Aldershot saying that they had been absent since 2 May. They showed their documentation proving they had been demobilised, but to no avail, and were taken away under military guard. They still had some time to serve and more documents to pass through before they could finally be free of the army, which famously did things in triplicate. Higginson's case was heard on 30 July and St. Juste's the following week. The upshot was that they spent the next few months seeing out their remaining time before they were formally honourably discharged on 11 November, 1919, a full year after the Armistice.[5]

After that six-month hiatus they soon picked up where they left off on the halls. They continued to call themselves "The King's Jesters" and were described on posters as "The Entertainers Who Entertain." Both were attired in immaculate evening dress and by all accounts made a lively and popular team. In addition to being a pianist, St. Juste was a noted siffleur who could harmonise in two keys and imitate birds. His speciality in the early days was "The Whistling Blacksmith" to which he accompanied himself. For his part, Higgins sang, danced, lolled on the piano, told jokes and played different characters. They wrote their own sketches, including a military burlesque "Misery and Co." in which they worked in some of their experience of war. Another sketch involving a man being kicked by a mule proved a real winner. Higgins often finished the turn with what was known as his "tearaway" dance. They did send-ups of the prevalent vogue for sentimental American ballads such as "That Kentucky Home of Mine." Typical of their approach in this line was "Where the Cross-Eyed Claras Grow" which transposed the sensibilities of the Deep South to the wilds of industrial Lancashire:

> "You talk about your blue-eyed Sue –
> About your pink eyed Marys too
> But down Wigan way there's the sweetest girl I know –

It's one-eyed Flo.
I've packed my other sock
And to-night at twelve o'clock
Down in the dell where the cross-eyed Claras grow
I'm gonna go…"

Higgins would then launch into his patter "Talk about your Blue-eyed Marys in Pennsyltucky—you see our Black Pudding Berthas in Bolton.

"My House is Haunted (By the Ghost of a Beautiful Girl)" from 1920 was written by the prolific Worton David under the pseudonym Wynn Stanley, whose songs were sung by many other music hall stars.

We've got 'em skinned..." This number, like some of their others, was co-written by Wynn Stanley, a pseudonym for Worton David, a prolific composer who founded his own highly successful music company.

St. Juste and Higgins favoured such typical 1920s nonsense ditties like "They'll Never Know Me in Old Dahomey" and "Every Time I Kissed Her She Would Start to Sing." At times they even sang topical tunes, such as "Wembley" for the British Empire Exhibition of 1924. St. Juste composed his own songs including "A N'egg and Some N'Ham and an N'onion" which was the hit of Easter, 1925 at Blackpool. Higgins often sang this in his solo act years later, and it was also favoured by other performers including Clarkson Rose. Their act had widespread appeal and they rose up the bill. At the Theatre Royal, Dublin in 1924, a reviewer declared; "St. Juste and Higgins with a piano supplied ragtime and other cheerful numbers in a manner that proved them to be versatile comedians."[6] A leading critic commented; "St. Juste and Higgins are a resourceful pair; the drollery of the one and the sibilant capacity of the other make capital entertainment."[7] By then they had reached perhaps the peak of their popularity as a duo, having built up their reputation and worked together for six years. It was shortly afterwards in the autumn of 1925 that they broke up their partnership and went their separate ways.

(II) Solo Turn & Revue Artist

> *"While performers [who have made a living] out of wig and false nose are learning to ape the ways of West Kensington, Charlie Higgins arrives with a voice that advertises his birthplace and clothes that are in a state of civil war."*[1]

Higgins joined a travelling revue called *Magnets* at the Hippodrome, Devonport, which toured the midlands and provinces and later moved to the famous old Alexander, Stoke Newington. He changed his style, discarded the evening-suited image and began to make his name as a character comedian in low comedy. He was widely lauded for his role in his first revue as a genuine find with a striking individual style all his own.[2] At Coventry the drama correspondent described how he displayed his natural comic and character-acting ability; "He occupies the boards for the major portion of the time, but his humour does not lag, and his final joke makes one laugh as heartily as his first. He takes on many roles, and proves a success in them all. As a desert queen he creates roars of laughter, and as a policeman looking for promotion, he is an equal success."[3]

In 1926-27 he toured extensively with the *Out of Work* revue which was written by his friend and golfing buddy, Billy Bennett. Having watched his act each night from the wings, Bennett was inspired to write it expressly for Higgins as principal comedian. The story centred on Basil Bitters (Higgins) who is sacked from his job in a store and tries half-a-dozen other jobs with disastrous and hilarious results. Bennett had first met Higgins when they shared the bill at the Alhambra, London, the year before, when Bennett first proposed the idea to him. Higgins was initially cautious but as soon as he saw the script was enthusiastic. Bennett co-wrote the book with Frederick Blanchard, and Higgins had some input on the music side. The comic element was naturally to the fore, and he appeared in eight of the fourteen scenes. Apart from the twelve Hudson chorus girls and their acrobatics with a skipping rope, Higgins was the heart and soul of the two-hour show. Bennett was at that time on the up-and-up, having become a royal favourite and the attachment of his name also increased attention on it. Higgins won some glowing press notices and the revue made his name. The *West London Observer* remarked; "Right through the show he works the humorous side practically single-handed, sings a number of songs, plays the banjolele, and displays an ability which stamps him as a good all-round laughter-provider."[4] One of the most popular of the sketches was "The Navvies Jazz" in which he sang and danced with a gang of road-menders, which he later recorded. *Out of Work* was considered a "merry and bright show throughout" and Higgins was praised for his comic ability in many guises, whether as a sandwich-man, toy salesman or bath chair attendee.[5] An episode in a lingerie shop prompted "roars of merriment."[6] In all his scenes critics were agreed that he displayed his off-the-wall humour with "a special gift for rhyming patter."[7] *Out of Work* was a long and demanding show which required great stamina of its star, because he was on stage practically the whole time, and on the road for the best part of two years.

In 1928 he toured with a number of revues. In the summer months he was with Albert de Courville's spectacular *The Show World* which had seventeen different scenes. Higgins played in many of them as entirely different characters. He provided most of the comedy, interspersed with musical numbers from the other cast members. Some of his standout scenes included "The Magic Hat" in which he played a put-upon husband who turns the tables on his termagant wife, and "Getting a Drink" a brilliant essay in exasperation. Among his song hits were two by Ted Waite, "When I See an Oyster Walk Upstairs" and the satirical "Mr. Waterhouse's House." This latter with its singalong chorus provided a comment on poor housing conditions and a social system that was still in thrall to the Victorian Poor Law, long before the advent of the Welfare State:

> *"After Mr. Waterhouse's daughter's house*
> *Comes the picture house, the public house, the slaughter house*
> *And in case you want to know,*
> *The last house in the row*
> *Is everybody's house*
> *'cos that's the workhouse."*

At the Hammersmith Palace a reviewer described his effect on the audience; "The humour of Charlie Higgins is quaint and subtle and from the rise to the fall of the curtain his efforts to amuse are so pronounced that audiences are loathe to part with him. Whether in the guise of hen-pecked husband, a boat man, an inmate of an asylum or collector at a railway station, he extracts every ounce of comedy in the various roles he undertakes."[8] He came out with rapid-fire gags and showed great interpretation in his song "The Porter's Blues." However, it was not so much what he said that endeared him to audiences, as the way he said it.[9] A leading critic observed that he "so often heightens his comical effects by adding a twist of melancholy to them."[10] The show was another personal triumph for him. In the autumn he joined *La Revue Artistique,* which lived up to its name including a corps de ballet and host of romantic songs sung by T. C. Fairburn's Opera company. Such high art mixed surprisingly well with the low, and Higgins provided the comic interludes in between. He showcased several more of his unique character sketches including "The Shoeblack," "Truth Will Out" and "The Dipsomaniac." In his advertisements he was keen to establish the routines as his own invention which implied that he must have had some imitators using his ideas.

He continued to develop his own distinctive solo act on the music-hall stage. He adopted a ludicrous outfit, consisting of plus fours with socks and suspenders showing, brown boots and bedraggled tails that almost reached the floor. He had a penchant for daft headgear and his trademark was a silk topper which was a size too small. He picked up the hat in Piccadilly market one morning while his wife hid in embarrassment. He would often enter to the strains of "With Me Gloves in Me 'and and Me 'at on One Side." His approach was refreshingly anti-modernist, bringing the joyous spirit of a previous age into the slick but increasingly uniform Art Deco world. This individuality was greatly appreciated, and set him apart from many of his contemporaries.

Like fellow Lancastrian George Formby, Higgins also played the ukulele, but unlike him he could play the guitar, and even introduced a xylophone into his routine at one stage. He had been used to working as a double act and often had an assistant to bounce off the jokes and unanswerable riddles. His stage partners included Matt Leamore and Wilbur Lenton. One of his most popular foils was Bert Bray who made a droll but stolid straight man, against which the Higgins' buffoonery was especially effective. A snatch of typical dialogue was captured on record:

> Charlie: If there's ten women standing under one umbrella in Manchester, how come they don't get wet?
>
> Bert: Why?
>
> Charlie: Because it isn't raining. He's proper daft. They're two-a-penny everywhere.
>
> Bert: What are?
>
> Charlie: Halfpennies. He's a proper ninny.

Often his bill matter was "A Fool if He Only Knew It." Later he was remembered for his catch-phrase "It's good, isn't it?" which he often used in the middle of his songs, such as "Charlie Makes Whoopee".

> *"Oh, dear Belinda, me guiding star,*
> *"I'm at yer winder with my guitar."*

In 1930 he made a successful tour of South Africa, and returned with several stories, apocryphal or otherwise, such as the meeting he had with a Zulu tribal chief who only wore a loincloth and bought a hat and umbrella, but not to wear; he insisted on putting the hat on the end of his umbrella which he hoisted aloft. Shortly after his return, Higgins was touted as the star of a series of short comedy films with the prospect of a starring role in a feature film if they were successful. However, the shorts would appear not to have been made after all.

At that time his star was in the ascendency and he was a solid supporting turn who also topped the bill at the major variety theatres alongside such stars as Max Miller. Unlike some northern comedians, Higgins was equally at home in the south and patrons of many London halls welcomed him back time after time. At the Brixton Empire for instance, a reviewer declared; "That talented purveyor of nonsensical matter, Charlie Higgins, meets with no difficulties at Brixton, where his comic powers are always relished and his cheerful vein of fantasy is freely evident in his snatches of droll ditties and other laughable ideas."[11] Higgins was popular on the radio and became a highly successful recording artist in his own right. He released a string of small records, 8" or 9" instead of the standard 10" or 12" for the Broadcast label which was only extant between 1928 and 1934. These sold for a shilling and were available at a number of outlets including W. H. Smith. They are highly collectable today, fetching anywhere from £5 to £10 each, some of the rarer ones are over £25. Some of those songs were re-released on the same label, also on Unison, and as 10" records on the Rex label. An excellent compilation of his songs is *All Poshed Up* by the always-reliable Windyridge. Available as a CD or download, the 26-tracks cover most of his known output.

There was more than a touch of fellow Formby in Higgins' style of humour:

> *"When swimming at Blackpool I felt full of loathing,*
> *Some sly, dirty dog had pinched all me clothing,*
> *I saw the lot go—collar and bow,*
> *And me little short shirt and me tanner yo-yo.*
> *On the seashore bleak and sandy*
> *Not a rag or stitch was handy*
> *I was worse than poor old Gandhi*
> *With me bag full of nuts and a sweet in me mouth."*

The characters he portrayed in song were often a variation on the seemingly gormless Lancastrian type who is not really as daft as he looks. Many reviewers caught on to his spirit of playful absurdity. One critic wrote of him: "His humour is broad and vegetable. It depends for its success on his engaging and infectious hilarity. It is successful. There was loud laughter in the audience all the time he was on the stage."[12]

His songs were incredibly catchy with a bouncy rhythm and rendered in a typically breezy style. Most were written by William Hargreaves, once the husband of Ella Shields, for whom he wrote his most famous song "Burlington Bertie from Bow." Among his other numbers were "Give My Regards to Leicester Square" and "I Know Where the Flies Go." Among Higgins' most popular recordings was the engaging "I'm a Daddy at 63":

> "Sixty-three, sixty-three,
> One of the boys at sixty-three
> All the women I try to please
> Bouncing them playfully on my knee
> In the park after dark
> Wearing my astrakhan…"

He often presented a familiar northern type of the seemingly insignificant little man, cowed by his domineering wife, but who still has an eye for the ladies "Show me a skirt and I'm full of beans." The character was a familiar one from the days of Frank Randle. This was typified by "Daddy at 63" and more so with "Jolly Old Uncle Joe" who is "Sixty-five and full of bedevilment" and his father who is "96 and still up to his tricks." He had great fun with the verbal repartee of two bickering neighbours in "Mrs. McGrath and Mrs. O'Rafferty." Some of his numbers had a different tone, for instance "When the Jolly Good Times are Booming Later On" which seemed to owe a lot both in style and content to Leslie Sarony's big hit "Ain't it Grand to Be Blooming Well Dead" from the same year. Higgins' song might almost have been an alternative anthem for the Depression, parodying the mantra of the politicians assuring the public that good times, like blue skies, were just around the corner:

> "When blinkin' trade has uplifted blooming things
> We'll have a harp and a lovely set of wings."

Elsewhere he offered endearingly daft homilies such as "Never throw stones at your mother, Throw bricks at your father instead." His cheerful nonsense included such gems as "Running Up and Down Our Street" and "Mother's Walking Round in Father's Trousers." His oeuvre was bright and breezy but shot through with an elusive wistfulness. He sang affectionate parodies of the old-time romantic ballad in "Down in the Fields Where the Buttercups Grow" and "Where the Violets are Blue." He related his misadventures on a continental holiday in "Charlie in Spain":

> "A Spanish miss, so dark and slender
> On her guitar was playing a Spanish plink-a-plonk.
> I threw a kiss, so sweet and tender;
> She threw a wet tomato and hit me on the conk…"

The Empress, Brixton, where Higgins was always popular in his act and in panto. The theatre was opened in 1898 and rebuilt in the Art Deco style in 1930. In its heyday it played host to most of the greats of music hall and variety, but suffered a similar fate to many of the old variety theatres. It became a cinema and later a bingo hall but despite local opposition was demolished in 1992.

One of his recordings, "Charlie Makes Whoopee" was banned at the time, because it happened to mention the Rector of Stiffkey, who complained to the record company and successfully petitioned for the record to be withdrawn. The Rector of Stiffkey was famously struck off and defrocked for consorting with prostitutes. He ended his days in a circus sideshow in Blackpool where he was gored to death by a lion.

In 1933-34, Higgins returned to revue, and was part of Lawrence Wright's *On with the Show*, a lavish adaptation involving a big cast and some 21 scenes based on the long-running entertainment that had proved so popular at the North Pier, Blackpool for several seasons past. In one section Higgins played a bumbling Lancastrian type visiting London; other scenes in which he was involved included a family day out at the seaside and a soldier routine. The scale of the show presented problems and by the time of the opening night just before Christmas, 1933, the company had only had three days in which to rehearse. Despite those early difficulties, audiences warmed to the revue and a critic concluded that it was "one of the most gorgeously presented shows of the kind ever seen in London, and no expense appears to have been spared in any particular."[13]

In between his appearances in revues and as a solo act on variety bills, he often appeared in pantomime either as a dame or as leading comic. He toured with various other big radio favourites of the time including Tommy Handley in *Radio Revels*. In one of those tours in 1936 he played a beleaguered hospital patient in Clarkson Rose's sketch "Cold Comfort" with Clapham & Dwyer and the Waters sisters. Higgins was heard on the BBC in the long-running *Music Hall* and in 1936 broadcast live from the Northern Hotel, Portrush. With the arrival of television, he popped up in several episodes of filmed variety shows such as *Variety* (1937), *Cabaret* (1938) and *Comedy Cabaret* (1938), none of which survive today. Between May and July 1939, he toured America with his wife, but it is not certain that he played any engagements.

He continued to entertain during the war years boosting morale, and at Christmas, 1939 he proved a hit at the Empress, Brixton in *Red Riding Hood*. The local reviewer declared; "Charlie Higgins is a picturesque Dame Trott, a sophisticated rather than a traditional pantomime dame and his appearance never fails to produce the laughs expected of him. He gives a clever, full-flavoured impersonation of the old lady in all his scenes and established himself a prime favourite with the audience."[14] He had fun in *Sinbad the Sailor* (Hippodrome, 1941-42) which gave him ample opportunity to air his popular ditties such as "In the Waxworks

Late at Night." In February, 1940 he was one of fifteen Carroll Levis' "Discoveries" (an ironic description considering he had by then been in the business for over twenty years). Two years later Charlie was the headliner in the touring revue *Yankee Doodle Comes to Town* (1942), a lively show which proved popular across the country. This was an Anglo-American production aimed at welcoming the visiting U. S. servicemen who had recently entered the war. The title role was played by a lesser-known American vaudeville artist, Trixie Maison, supported by the Yankee Doodle Lovelies chorus girls.

Once Higgins found a successful formula, he tended not to alter his material substantially. Audiences demanded his old favourites and he was keen to satisfy them, but he still managed to keep his act entertaining. His acting ability coupled with his naturally ebullient spirit meant he retained his love of his work which he once revealed he cared about immensely. As he explained; "When I sing about buttercups in a field, or when I am having a scare in the waxworks, I make myself feel the emotions I portray; I often believe for several minutes together that I *am* with the buttercups, and I *do* feel scared by the eeriness of the waxworks. By pretending very seriously that my act is a real and present happening, new every time I do it, I can continue to give it that freshness and spontaneity which is essential."[15]

He worked less after the war but continued trouping and was still receiving good notices in pantos. For instance, he caught the attention as Simple Simon in a northern tour of *Red Riding Hood* (1946-47), of which a correspondent declared; "He bubbles over with good spirits and speedily gets on good terms with the youngsters."[16] He was popular too in *Mother Goose* at the Newcastle Palace (1949-50), alongside the veteran Ella Retford; and as Idle Jack in *Dick Whittington* at the Shepherd's Bush and Hackney Empires (1950-51) which, unusually, featured a woman, Iris Sadler, as the dame. In a distinct sign of the times, that show used more American material including novelty songs from the hit parade. Higgins was seen less thereafter but remained a supporting act on variety bills up and down the country until the early 1950s. In the summer of 1953, he toured with *Variety Revels* and retired shortly after. One of his last appearances was in October of that year at an annual charity entertainment for the Caxton Convalescent Home, Limpsfield, Surrey, on a bill that included rising stars Benny Hill and Harry Secombe among others.[17]

Charlie married Florence Margaret Rogers at Lambeth in 1921. She was born and bred in Lambeth, one of four daughters of Arthur Rogers, a china packer and warehouseman at the East India Dock. Florence, always

The Charlie Higgins CD, All Poshed Up was released by Windyridge in 2009 and includes all his known output. His wonderfully bright and breezy irreverence showed the true spirit of music hall well into the 1930s.

known affectionately as 'Floss', was also an actress, and the couple had a daughter Alitia. They lived for many years at 25, Newcombe Park, Mill Hill, N. W. 7, where Floss's family also stayed. Charlie remained a great raconteur in later years and often entertained at local and family get-togethers. He maintained a keen interest in collecting records.[18] After a long and happy retirement, Charlie died on 5 February, 1978 aged 85.[19] His widow died in August, 1987 aged 89.

Higgins is seldom if ever mentioned today. Perhaps this is because he did not change his material in the mid-1930s and his style was essentially of the old-fashioned kind. He came close to topping the bills at that time, but in the following years slipped down the batting order and because he never made the leap to films or television, he failed to become a household name. Nonetheless, he was a fine artist in his own right who deserves to be recalled from the mists of time. I first became aware of him thanks to the broadcaster, the late Frank Wappat, who used to have a show on BBC Radio Newcastle. Wappat played several of Higgins' songs and I was immediately struck by their breezy *joie de vivre* that seemed to encapsulate the lost spirit of the halls. His songs stand up strongly today as fine examples of the later variety artists who brought with them the true character of a time gone by. It is hard to resist the pure merriment of his endearing world. In the words of his opus "All Poshed Up":

> "When the roll is call up yonder
> It's a cinch I'll never reach that happy land
> Charlie Peace and Crippen sure to think they've been a-trippin'
> When they see me walk behind them with me daisies in me 'and."

See discography and list of credits on page 237.

Alfred Lester
(1870-1925)
"Always Merry and Bright"

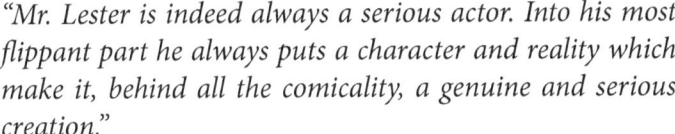

"Mr. Lester is indeed always a serious actor. Into his most flippant part he always puts a character and reality which make it, behind all the comicality, a genuine and serious creation."

– The Spectator, 1924

ALFRED LESTER WAS a lugubrious comedian who avoided the jolly idiot approach and perfected the persona of the ultimate pessimist. It could be argued that he channelled the underlying fatalism of Music-Hall into his stage characters, although much of that outlook was decidedly his own. He found his greatest popularity in Britain on the revue stage from the Great War up until his sudden death in 1925. If he had been reincarnated as a film comedian it would have been one in the Buster Keaton mould. Unlike Keaton, Lester is almost completely forgotten and liable to remain so. However, he was a good example of a different type of comic approach and one who successfully straddled the music hall and revue stage, pointing the way forward for others.

Alfred Lester was born Alfred Edwin Leslie on 25 October, 1870 in Preston, Lancashire, the son of Edgar Alfred Leslie and Annie (nee Ross).[1] Both his parents were actors, as well as his paternal grandmother, and even his elder sister Kate. Alfred, Jr., aged five, always known in the family as Alf, made his stage debut in about 1875 or 1876 as Little Willie Carlyle in *East Lynne*. Alfred senior was a fine comedian in his own right

Alfred Lester as the lost policeman in *The New Aladdin* at the Gaiety in 1906. This role and his sketch The Scene-Shifter's Lament brought him to the widespread attention of London theatre audiences, after years of bit part acting and provincial tours.

who had made his reputation at the Royalty and St. James's theatres. He died of consumption on 21st April, 1876 aged 32, and was buried in the cemetery in the town. A well-loved figure in theatrical circles, he was known for his personal generosity. There were several benefits organised to help the young widow and children, which netted £104 16s. 6d. Annie's own state of health was described as poor at that time. She was forced to abandon the stage and made ends meet by taking in lodgers and found work as a needlewoman and seamstress. As soon as daughter Kate was old enough, she was put into service. By 1881 the family were living in Albion Terrace, Hendon, Middlesex. Mother Annie died in 1886 at 43 and three years later Kate married George Toplis, an electrician.

When Alf was about fourteen, he was helped out by the actor-manager Charles Wyndham, who had known his father. Wyndham gave him a job in the box-office of the Criterion Theatre. Alf still dreamed of being an actor, however, and after four years working there, he approached Wyndham hoping he would give him a small part in a production, but Wyndham refused. Alf promptly gave in his notice and tried to find stage work himself, doing the rounds of theatres and booking agents' offices, all to no avail. In desperation he took out all his savings and decided to try his luck in America. He only had a little money so he worked his passage as an assistant steward on an oil tanker. The sixteen-day passage was a trial for him amid the smell of oil and the rolling sea which, combined, made him feel nauseous. When he reached New York, he did a flit and made his way to several theatres where he tried to get an audition without any success. He later reflected "My preconceived idea of storming the States with the wonderful ability of the great 'English Boy Actor' somehow didn't materialise, and at the end of ten days I was glad to steal back to the old oil tank, plead forgiveness, and work my way home."[2] Many years later he reflected with feeling that he could still smell the acrid engine oil.

On his return to London he was back to square one trudging the streets until he managed to find a job through an agent in the Euston Road, to whom he had to pay a commission. He was understudy to the Demon King and Abanazar in *Aladdin* at the West London, Edgware Road, for which he received 18s. a week. He was taken on by George Thorne as a character comedian and toured the provinces in many productions including *Our Boys, Betsy, Arabian Nights, Boots at the Swan, Ici on Parle Francais,* and played Conn in *The Shaughraun*. He was in various repertory companies and toured extensively in any kind of role he was given in such offerings as *Black-Eyed Susan, Life and Honour, The Colleen Bawn* and *Ingomar*. One of his avowed favourites among all his roles was that of the villainous Cardinal Richelieu in *The Three Musketeers*. He gained some attention in a congenial part in *The Lights o' London* at the New Ealing Theatre in August, 1900. A reviewer wrote; "Mr. Alfred Lester at once got on friendly terms with pit and gallery by his rendering of the part of Philosopher Jack, and his first appearance as the proud proprietor of a combined ice cream and 'tater' barrow in the Borough was productive of much amusement."[3] He later essayed other roles in the same play. He did well as the brooding ex-convict in *The Bank of England* (Dec 1900) and began to show more aptitude for comedy as Jibbs, a Costermonger, in a provincial tour of *A Woman Adrift* (1901). Among other standouts he contributed a fine character sketch as a bird-fancier in *The Romany Rye* (October, 1901) and as Spider Jack in *The Rich and Poor of London* (Dec. 1901) at the Theatre Royal, Leicester. In June and July, 1902, he branched out and ran his own stock company at the Theatre Royal, Chesterfield along with Sidney Cranston. They put on *Nell Gwynn*. He had a similar season at the Royal, Cardiff in the summer of 1904. It was around that time that he started writing his own material and finally got his big break to show what he could do in his sketch "The Scene-Shifter's Lament" which he debuted in April, 1905 in *The Officer's Mess* at Terry's Theatre. The idea first came to him during a tour of Ireland in *Romany Rye* when his character was supposed to be cast adrift alone on the wide ocean. As he bewailed his fate, the audience started laughing, and the more he anguished the more they laughed. He eventually realised why they were laughing, when he saw the wrong scenery had been dropped in by an incompetent scene-shifter who had put in a park scene instead. From this, Lester developed his idea of a stage-hand who thinks he could play Hamlet better than the professional actors. The sketch caught the public imagination and he visited other houses with it. Manager and impresario Alfred Butt happened to see him perform the sketch at the Crown, Peckham and signed him up at once for the Palace. Lester's appearance in *The Palace Review* that September rocketed him into the front rank of comedians and he was afterwards in much demand. That Christmas he played the dame in *Dick Whittington* at Kennington, opposite Vesta Tilley.

Lester successfully made the leap from music hall to revue. He is seen here as Nix, the Bosun, with Jean Aylwin as Anita in Havana at the Shaftesbury in 1908.

Flushed with his new-found success, Lester made a more concerted effort to make a name for himself in the United States. He started a tour at Proctor's Theatre on Twenty-Third Street in New York in 1906, with his "Scene-Shifter" sketch. Unfortunately, his efforts met with little enthusiasm. The correspondent of *Variety* was, like much of the audience, somewhat nonplussed by his turn. Lester realised that his act was just not getting across the footlights and decided to curtail his tour, cut his losses and return to England. His material was not at that point strong enough to get over, or his dry humour was just too alien for anything other than a British audience. In October that year he made a further impression as the Lost Policeman in *The New Aladdin* at the Gaiety theatre. The show had a big build-up but some expressed disappointment at the finished result. However, *The Times* singled out Lester for praise, declaring his character sketch to be "a delightful piece of genuinely humorous acting."[4]

Lester as Peter Doody the hapless jockey in *The Arcadians* (1909) which was widely considered to be his best role and secured his reputation as a character comedian.

He consolidated his reputation as a revue actor-comedian of note as Nix the Bosun in *Havana* (April, 1908) at the Shaftesbury. That was a prelude to his greatest success at the same theatre as Jockey Peter Doody in *The Arcadians* which he played for the best part of two years (1909-11). His highlight was the song "I've gotta motter—always merry and bright." There were several versions of how it all came about. According to one author, producer Robert Courtneidge had no confidence in Lester for the role from the start. Courtneidge was known as an intolerant and demanding employer and decided to dismiss Lester. Another witness said that when first offered the role, Lester could see no merit in it at all, and during rehearsals became so anxious that he took off to Devon saying he could do nothing with the character. Courtneidge enticed him back, and even bowed to his resolve to give him a song to sing. The result was "I've Gotter Motter" the idea for which emanated from the play's text. Courtneidge recalled; "Lester took the song perfectly seriously, and even got the musical director to coach him in the high notes."[5]

Throughout his years of consistent success in revue, Lester pursued an equally successful parallel career in Music Hall. After finishing one show he would go across town in the time-honoured fashion of many of his fellow

Lester as Doody in a scene with Phyllis Dare in *The Arcadians* at The Shaftesbury (1909).

professionals and do his sketch turn several times on the variety stage. As if that wasn't enough work, he would sometimes entertain in pier shows at south coast resorts, especially Brighton at the weekend. He worked on his own sketch ideas and used the work of other writers and in June 1911 at a gala performance at His Majesty's Theatre, he scored a hit as the constable in *The Critic*. Then came his stint as a doleful waiter in *A Restaurant Episode* at the Coliseum, and he gave the same sketch at the Royal Variety Performance at the Palace Theatre the following year. Others in his series included his gasfitter who becomes *The Amateur Hairdresser*, and *Longshoreman Bill who never goes to sea*.[6] He mined a rich seam of character in *The Village Fire Brigade*, *A Labour Candidate*, *The Broker's Man* and *The Sundowner*. In some of these he was assisted by Buena Bent, and several were recorded. The rules about sketches in music hall had by then been relaxed somewhat. In the early days, anything vaguely resembling a play or even an excerpt from a play was banned by the powers-that-be to demarcate the limits of what could be done on a variety stage and make sure it was separate from the legitimate stage. This was one reason why double acts were not as common in Britain. Short sketches were just acceptable as long as they did not include more than two actors. Lester's character sketches were gems of observation which drew on his acting skills as much as his comedic abilities. These sketches have been seen as influential in comedy and some authors have noted the similarities between Lester's incompetent fireman idea and Charlie Chaplin's short *The Fireman* (1916).

Lester in typically lugubrious mode in a publicity photo that traded on his stage persona.

Despite the shortness of the sketches they were nonetheless trying to do, in fact, more so than a play. This was brought into sharp focus when Lester was called as a witness in the case of Will Evans, who was sued by his employers for claiming he was exhausted and that the Music Hall had ruined his health. Lester testified along with several other actors and Variety players about the conditions they had to contend with, which they all agreed were detrimental to physical and emotional health. The veteran Seymour Hicks said the strain of performing to the best of one's ability was difficult enough, but in a typical music hall it was much harder. Hicks commented; "It was a great strain—especially if one had not much confidence in oneself—and no artist really had." On one occasion he lost his voice entirely because of the thick pall of smoke overhanging the auditorium, which he said sometimes almost knocked one over. Added to that there was the constant chatter in the galleries and most of the audience constantly lighting their cigarettes, cigars or pipes. All those who were called in the case agreed that there was not the same level of stress in a play as there was for a single turn in a music hall. When he was called on to testify, Lester said that he did four turns a night and found it extremely hard work; he also talked about how difficult it was not to become mechanical.

The illustrious Gaiety Theatre was built in 1864 and flourished as a music hall for many years. It later became the home of musical comedy but was badly damaged by bombing in WW II and demolished in 1956.

Doing *The Arcadians* was not stressful, he added, but his fifteen-minute music hall sketch *The Fireman* he found utterly "exhausting." In his statement he talked of the difference between the quality West End theatres and the halls in the suburbs and provinces; "The atmosphere was different; the audience was more restless; there was the striking of matches and there was more movement in the music-hall. The artist had to make his humour more obvious and broader. He had to use his voice more. One had to depend on oneself alone. Tobacco-smoke at the outlying halls was very bad."[7] The smoke would certainly not have done Lester any good and most likely contributed to his illness. Of course, the vast majority of the population smoked then. They were used to open fires and smoke from heavy industry. The London smogs were famous and this was long before the Clean Air Act. The health dangers of smoking were not known about until the 1950s if not later.

DOYEN OF REVUE

He continued his run of successful roles as Vodka in *The Grass Widows* a jolly comic opera at the Apollo with Jack Buchanan and Dorothy Minto. Lester then joined Cicely Courtneidge and Jack Hulbert in *The Pearl Girl* 1913 at the Shaftesbury. After 100 performances the comedy element was strengthened and by then Lester had worked up his part as Byles the man of all work, a Spanish servant and amateur gondolier. He was given another song, "a burlesque of the Spanish love song of the fiery order" of which he made the most.[8] In 1915 he produced the *Simpson Stores* sketches at the Coliseum, which ran for the duration of the war.

His biggest hit in wartime was his role as Oliver Bing in *The Bing Boys are Here* (1916-17). This well-beloved revue caught the national mood and the need of the time and provided an escape from the realities of life. Lester co-starred with George Robey and Violet Loraine in one of London's biggest attractions. It was as much as anything the contrast in styles of the two comedians; Robey ever-optimistic by nature, unperturbed by anything, Lester worried about everything. The hit of the show was undoubtedly Robey singing with Loraine "If You Were the Only Girl in the World" which immediately caught on. All three stars were united in "Another Little Drink Wouldn't Do Us Any Harm" which was among those songs from the show that was later released on the Columbia label.

His friend and fellow actor Richard Ferris once shared "digs" with Alfred and remembered that he was always dogged by ill-health but remained a kindly soul who thought of others; "He was neither young enough nor fit enough to join the army in the war," recollected Ferris, "but I should think he spent hundreds of pounds in parcels to his actor friends at the front. He never forgot when Christmas came 'round!"[9]

In July 1917, Lester began in *Round the Map—A Musical Globe-Trot,* which was in some ways an extension of the Bing Boys and even reunited him with co-star Violet Loraine. There was of course no Robey, and this time Nelson Keys was the foil to Lester who played several characters. It was in this show that Lester sang the famous, if not infamous "The Conscientious Objector's Lament."

Programme showing Lester as Oliver Bing with George Robey as Lucifer Bing in *The Bing Boys are Here*, 1916-17, one of the great morale-boosting shows of the war. Lester and Robey made the perfect double act and became good friends.

> "Send out the army and the navy
> Send out the rank and file
> Send out the brave old Territorials,
> They'll face the danger with a smile
> Send out the boys of the old brigade
> That made old England free
> Send out me brother, me sister and me mother
> But for Gawd's sake don't send me."

The song was known before the war began at which time it was said to have been written by a Gordon Highlander. The lyrics relied on the famous British sense of irony, but there was much discussion in the press in 1914 as to the effect it might have on morale, and some even suggested it would give succour to the enemy. Regardless of all that, the men at the front took up the chorus with gusto. By the summer of 1917 the time was exactly right for cynicism and it proved a decided hit which he recorded with great success. The increased exposure of the song led to a High Court case concerning authorship. Dave Burnaby and Gitz Rice were listed on the sheet music but one Harry Lamb claimed that he had written it. Lamb said he composed the similar "Send Out the Boys" in Dundee in 1910.

Among Lester's other popular songs were "I Do Like to Sing in the Barth" and Rule and Holt's "Ours is a Nice 'ouse, Ours Is":

> "Of all the fathers in the world, there isn't one like our's is
> Some desperate people hold up banks, he holds up
> public houses
> We fiddle for a living and the police have their suspicions
> But though we keep on fiddling we are none of us
> musicians.

In March 1918, he was offered a leading role in Andre Charlot's revue *Flora*, but turned it down. In August that year he appeared as Hu Du in *Shanghai* at Drury Lane. In November, 1919 he played George in *The Eclipse* at the Garrick, for Charles B. Cochran. This gave him a droll song all about the "various people he would like to kill, sung with a distinct enunciation which would put to shame much greater singers."[10] Teddie Gerard was a stylish contrast to Lester's character and much of the comedy was built around the two. The run of successes continued into 1920 with a warmly-received revival of *The Shop Girl* at the Gaiety. The original 1894 production had starred Seymour Hicks and Ada Reeve. Of the revival, Lester was judged "the outstanding feature of the evening" as Miggles the shopwalker in a London emporium. Many considered it his best work since *The Arcadians*.[11] There followed *Pins and Needles!* with Edmund Gwenn at the Royalty. Once more, Lester felt uncomfortable in his role to start with, but this time he never really warmed up to it. It did not help that during the run of the play he was afflicted with an attack of lumbago and had to withdraw for a while, although he duly returned. Despite his problems, critics felt that he worked well with Gwenn in their episode together.[12] That year Lester made another appearance for Cochran in *The Fun of the Fayre* at the London Pavilion. Among the cast was Evelyn Laye, the doyen of light musical-comedy, and a young Clifton Webb. One of Lester's best songs from *The Fun of the Fayre* was "Germs" which was published around the same time and which he also recorded. The song suited his lugubrious persona admirably, being at once ironic and ultra-pessimistic:

> "*Some little germ is going to find you some day*
> *Some little germ will creep behind you some day*
> *Then he'll send for his germ friends*
> *And all your earthly trouble ends*
> *Some little germ is going to get you some day.*"

The song was covered by a number of artists including, many years later, Phil Harris, when it was rechristened "Some Little Bug." Lester was one of many who sang "Yes! We Have No Bananas" surely the most ubiquitous and annoying song of 1923. In the same year he also recorded "I Love Me" (from the revue *Rats!*) which was covered to great effect by Clinton Ford. *Rats!* at the Vaudeville took a while to settle down, and much of the comedy devolved to Herbert Mundin, a character actor who later took his talents to Hollywood and is especially remembered for two performances in particular, as 'Barkis is willing' in *David Copperfield* (1935) and Much the Miller in *The Adventures of Robin Hood* (1938). He died in a car crash at the age of 53. *Rats* was more a collection of sketches of varying quality rather than a revue; Lester's impersonation of a harried stationmaster worrying about the future rail plans was deemed one of the highlights. He was to have appeared in *Phi Phi* at the Pavilion, but after a dispute with a fellow cast member during rehearsals he left the show.[13]

In the meantime, he continued his series of sketches and made a hit as *The Night Porter* at the Coliseum in 1922, which one critic declared was "humorous both in conception and execution. It is not often that so excellent a vehicle is found for the display by an individual comedian of his peculiar talents."[14] He relished the opportunity to demonstrate his character-acting ability further as the old showman in *The Punch Bowl*, widely considered as one of his best roles. His "quiet, offhand, irresistible humour" was to the fore. After the first night the papers were full of praise, but one headline knocked him back. The *Evening News* proclaimed "Alfred the Almost Great." George Alltree recalled; "Lester came rushing into my office with the *Evening News* in his hand. 'There's a dreadful thing to say about me,' he said. It took me nearly an hour to convince him that it was meant as great praise, not condemnation."[15] The show went along well and Lester blossomed as the old timer. A teenage Hermione Baddeley also appeared in *The Punch Bowl*. She was just starting out on her career, and recalled Lester's kindness and profound influence on her in terms of the art of comedy and especially timing.[16]

Unfortunately, his health began to break down. He was ill during the first weeks of 1925 and had to take a little time out from the show, but he appeared again from February until Easter. By then his cough was much worse, and he started coughing violently on stage. At first the audience thought it was part of the act. His condition grew worse and he was advised by his doctor to go and stay in a warm climate. Consequently, he left the show reluctantly and his place was taken by Robert Hale.

Lester travelled by sea to Morocco where he spent several weeks. He also visited Tangier, and his condition was apparently greatly improved. He was keen to return to London and complete a full year in *The Punch Bowl*. He began the journey back by boat to the port of Algeciras in Spain with two friends. They all stopped off in Seville, where Lester witnessed a bullfight, but he could not bear the cruelty to the horses, and left the stadium hurriedly. On the train to Madrid, which was packed, he caught a chill. When he arrived in the city, he visited the famous Pedra Art Gallery. While in the gallery he became ill again and his health broke down completely. His friends procured an English doctor and he was taken to the Anglo-American Nursing Home. There he remained a few days and appeared to be rallying; so much so that one of his companions travelled on to Paris. Then Lester took a turn for the worse and died suddenly on 6 May, 1925, aged 55. The causes of death were given as pneumonia and Encephalitis Lethargica. This latter is a disease that was unknown before 1917 and began in Vienna, spreading across much of Europe and North America from then on until the early 1930s, affecting many thousands. The flu-like symptoms included drowsiness, double vision and lack of muscle coordination. It induced a deep lethargy in patients who sometimes slipped into a coma-like state, hence the common name Sleepy Sickness. Some died in a short time, others lingered for many years and in some cases their personalities were altered. The cause remains unknown. His body was embalmed and was sent to London via Bilbao. He was cremated and the funeral service took place at the Kensal Green cemetery before a large gathering of friends and fellow professionals.

George Robey, who had worked with Lester for so long on *The Bing Boys Are Here,* was shocked by his sudden death and paid warm tribute to him;

> "He was one of the dearest fellows I ever met in the business… In his individual and private life, he was one of the sweetest and finest fellows off the stage—kind and sympathetic, modest and quiet. He was a most generous soul and did much benevolent work privately among his fellow professionals. No one will ever really know the amount of good he did in the world."[17]

In his will, Lester left the substantial sum of £37,779 8s. 5d., most of which went to his sister and her family. Despite his wealth he retained the frugal habits of his early years when he must have suffered great want. For instance, he used to keep half-smoked cigarettes for later, and always travelled by the number nine bus back to his house at Ladbrooke Terrace in Holland Park. He could well have afforded to use a cab but such never occurred to him. It was difficult for friends to induce him to take a holiday, but he did sometimes travel to the continent, particularly France and Italy. A sensitive man, he loved animals and was devoted to his old terrier Lady. In his will he left several bequests to animal charities including the R. S. P. C. A. and the Canine Defence League. His other charitable legacies were to the Music Hall Benevolent Institute and the Actor's Orphanage Fund among others. He was a fastidious eater, and one of his friends recalled the time he showed the waiter exactly which cuts of meat he wanted at an upmarket West End restaurant.

Had he lived Lester may well have gone on to achieve his long-held ambition to become known to an American audience. He was due to play in Andre Charlot's revue in New York in November, 1925, at a salary of $1,500 a week.[18] In the event his place was taken by Jack Buchanan, who proved a big hit alongside fellow British entertainers Gertrude Lawrence and Beatrice Lillie. It proved a springboard for success for Buchanan, who some people felt resembled Lester physically but whose suave personality was the complete opposite. Other plans were scuppered, such as those of Sydney Blow who wanted to write a play for Lester, a project which they discussed at length before his untimely death.[19] Perhaps he might have made it onto the big screen in time with his filmed sketches.

Some of the songs Lester made popular are still sung on occasion, especially those of the Great War, such as "A Conscientious Objector" and "Goodbye-ee." However, the man himself is largely forgotten today. There is little film of him, only a short clip from Pathe newsreels which shows him in character as the old showman in *The Punch Bowl*. His influence is harder to discern in popular culture but there were some later comics who had a similar miserabilist approach, for instance Max Wall and even Les Dawson at his best. Lester's contemporaries rated him highly, Stanley Lupino called him "a comedian of the classic type." Lester knew exactly how he wanted his comedy to be; "I don't want lines about graveyards from authors, I want really cheerful lines," he once declared. "It is by delivering cheerful things as if I were speaking them at a funeral that I get my effect." There was an immense amount of competition among comedians and it was necessary to have something which made one stand out from the crowd. He stood out because he was different to the vast majority of comedians in his time who went for the age-old approach of the constantly-smiling clown. Pathos had always been integral to comedy, as the ultimate sentimental comic Charlie Chaplin knew only too well. Although Lester may not have introduced the deadpan form of comedy, he was one of its finest exponents and he pointed the way for others to experiment with what was funny and helped to redefine the meaning of truly idiosyncratic music hall comedy.

See discography and list of credits on page 241.

Tom Foy in Dick Whittington at the Theatre Royal, Hanley, 1907-08.

Tom Foy
(1866-1917)
"The Fool of the Family"

"Tom Foy is a comedian of inexhaustible resource."

THE MUSIC HALL contained several comics who specialised in regional characterisations from all over the British Isles. Among these a relative few were from Yorkshire. With the exception of Dickie Henderson, and later Sandy Powell, the county was not known for its comedians, in stark contrast to its neighbour and rival Lancashire. One of the most popular in his day was Tom Foy, who was ironically a Lancastrian of Irish extraction, but who perfected his presentation of a Yorkshire dolt in the early years of the twentieth century. He was especially remembered for his stage act with an intelligent donkey, and for the many sides he recorded for the Zonophone label.

Thomas Foy was born in Manchester in 1866, the son of John Foy, a tailor, and Catherine (nee Shanley). As a boy Tom went to St. Anne's school in Manchester, but the family later moved to Halifax. He always longed for a life of adventure, and at the age of fifteen he had the notion to run away to sea. However, his father got wind of his scheme, fetched him back and gave him a thrashing. Tom had a natural facility for sketching and was apprenticed as a sign writer, at his father's insistence. Some reports state that he later set up in that business in Sowerby Bridge. However, he once said that he tired of sign-writing after three months and joined a travelling circus as a scene-painter; "I began to like circus life, and was determined to become a clown," he recalled. "Those were times! Up at four in the morning, and never in bed before one o'clock." He worked variously as a lightning cartoonist, a cowboy and bucking pony rider. He practised his tumbling at Shrogg's Park in Halifax. At one time he had a minstrel act, but finding he had no make-up one night went on as an Irish character and proved popular. "Eventually I made my debut as a full-blown circus artiste," he recollected.[1] While touring Ireland he met Ernestine Matthews, of the famous Matthews clan of acrobats. She was billed as "The Queen of the Carpet" and "The World's Most Famous Lady Tumbler." One of the leading lights of The Seven Sisters Matthews her family had toured America in the 1860s and 1870s when they were hailed as "England's Most Famous Gymnasts." They played in the San Francisco Circus and Roman Hippodrome as well as P. T. Barnum's (1873-74).[2] Tom and Ernestine married at Everton in 1898. They developed an act, together with one of Foy's brothers, as The Three Foys Three. They were based in Liverpool and later toured. They began to work out choreographed routines which were essentially circus acts. Sometimes they were joined by two more Foys and billed as The Five Foys. Their sketch "The Excursion Depot" made its debut in the mid-1890s, and the troupe toured extensively with it for almost a decade up until the mid-1900s. The knockabout routine utilised the family's acrobatic skills coupled with Tom's natural dry humour and winning personality, which inevitably pushed him to the fore. He wrote most of his own material and they worked the sketches over a surprising number of years, touring the country and revisiting some theatres many times. In 1901 he introduced "Keep Off the Grass" (1901-03) which played more to the group's acrobatic prowess. One of his most successful sketches was "The Yorkshire Lad in London" which lasted for five years (1904-9). This was followed by another five years with "The First of April" (1909-14) the premise of which was a marital mix-up. It was with this sketch that Foy introduced a donkey into his act. The grey donkey was first spotted by Ernestine on the back of a cart belonging to a hawker in Bristol. Tom had an instant rapport with the highly alert animal, which he named Jack. He was one of several pets that Tom kept. Audiences immediately took to the donkey and the inventive way in which Foy interacted with it as an integral part of his act. Jack responded to his voice and could pick him out in a crowd. There was an old adage about never working with children and animals, but the sheer novelty of the idea made his act a big draw. Besides, the animal was often considered the brightest thing on stage and a natural performer. As one eyewitness wrote; "Tom Foy's animal is a well-trained, stubborn, but withal intelligent moke gifted with a real sense of humour."[3] Soon the donkey became so associated with him that he also made his way into pantomimes.

Like many of his sketches, "In Trouble Again" (1914-16), *sans* donkey, also had a wedding theme, but a more farcical and involved story of misunderstanding. Although it was popular, many wondered where the donkey had gone. Hence, Jack made a welcome return in "Hunting Trouble" (1916-17), which sadly turned out to be Foy's final routine. Most of his popular routines made their way onto disc in an adapted format, thus preserving the essence of his act for posterity. He was a prolific recorder, mostly for the Zonophone label between about 1910 and 1917. These form a highly collectable series, fetching anything between £10 and £30 depending on scarcity and condition. Most of these

Tom Foy and his donkey, Jack, c1909. The donkey became an integral part of his act and he seldom appeared without him.

recordings appear on the excellent Windyridge compilation CD *Donkey and Me*. His quaint observations sent up the archetypal Yorkshireman who measures everything by how it relates to "God's Own County." For instance, "I've Been to America" in which he declares artlessly "It's bigger than Yorkshire." He goes on to explain how they talk through their noses in New York but in York they talk through their hats. He presented the figure of a shy and foolish chap with his own way of looking at the world. Many of his sketches were concerned with matrimony, either marital mix-ups or the idea that he might be conned into marriage. Being a canny northerner, he thinks of all the possible pitfalls and concludes that getting spliced is too expensive so he decides "I'm going on me honeymoon mesel' and get married when I come back!" On "The Yorkshireman in London" he explains how he is trying to find someone; "I've been tramping all over London all 't'morning, and nobody knows him." On these recordings he was often assisted by his company, including a well-spoken gent, who made a fine contrast to Foy's brogue. This may well have been the character referred to as the Colonel, although no actor's name was given. On other tracks Foy satirised the village gossip on "I'm Not One That Wants to Says Owt." Although most of the sides are patter, he sometimes sang songs that suited him such as "Much Obliged to Me" and "The Fool of the Family." There were only a few who presented specifically Yorkshire characters on stage in a similar vein, one other being Jack Lane "The Yorkshire Rustic."

Foy was a pantomime regular from the latter years of the 1890s onwards, either as chief comic or dame, and won many admirers for his lively turn as Widow Twankey in *Aladdin* at the Rotunda, Liverpool (1899-1900). In this he not only showed his athleticism with the Five Foys, but his own unique drollery. He also sang a number of songs and even utilised his lightning cartoonist skills. He was praised for his character work as Mrs. Wilkins in *Peter Wilkins* at the Royal Princess's, Glasgow (1901-02). It was a rare outing for the panto which had only been performed once previously at the same theatre in 1889-90. One of his biggest pantomime successes was *Cinderella* at the Gaiety, Manchester (1903-04), which teamed him to great effect with the laconic Malcolm Scott as one of the ugly sisters. It was on the advice of Eugene Stratton during that production that Foy decided to try his luck in London where he proved a hit at the Oxford that effectively made his name in the capitol. Thereafter he was the life and soul of *Little Jack Horner* as Simple Simon at the Theatre Royal, Nottingham (1913-14). One of his highlights was a scene in a restaurant in which the diminutive Foy staggered "across the stage under a towering pile of plates."[4] He played Idle Jack in *Dick Whittington* many times and of his performance in Belfast (1914-15) a correspondent wrote; "He is all the more effective because of his restraint and the consequent unexpectedness of his jokes and witticisms."[5] One of his most fondly-recalled performances in panto was as Billy Buttons in *Cinderella* at the Royal Opera House, London (1916-17), which starred Ella Retford, Fred Emney and the Egberts. The presence of the donkey on stage with the tramp-like figures of the Brothers Egbert and Foy gave the panto a distinctly Beckettian look. That production had a tragic opening when Emney as the dame badly injured his spine on a slide used for a slapstick gag. He was operated on, to no avail, and died a few days later.

Foy was apparently as funny off stage as he was on, with a generous spirit and a naturally friendly persona that remained unaffected by the trappings of fame. He did buy a large house in Brentwood on the proceeds

Foy made many recordings between 1910 and 1917 for Zonophone, most of which appear on the CD *Donkey and Me* by Windyridge. Above: Label of "The Yorkshireman in London" (1912) which was among my grandfather's collection of records.

of his earnings, but readily gave his time to charitable causes. During the war he took part in many entertainments for returning troops, for instance in November, 1916 he gave a matinee for wounded soldiers at the Birch Hill Military Hospital in Rochdale.[6]

Just as his career was going well, Foy suffered a heart attack and collapsed on stage at the Argyle, Birkenhead on 23 July, 1917. He was unable to continue in the bill and went home to Brook House, Brentford. He died there two weeks later on 7 August at the age of 51. A highly popular figure in the profession, there was a remarkable presence at his funeral which was conducted by his cousin, Father Frank Foy. He was interred in the Roman Catholic section of Brompton Cemetery. His widow Ernestine continued to perform his last sketch, "Hunting Trouble" for a while after his death, but with muted success. She survived her husband by forty years and died on 26 November, 1957 aged 87.

I would never have heard of Foy had it not been for a record of his among my grandfather's collection. I know he got it second hand and it was always one of his favourites. The cultural value of those recordings increases as the years pass, providing a priceless window into a lost world. Tom Foy may not be known by all but a few, but he deserves his place in the pantheon of popular entertainers because he was a genuine humourist with an act that was all his own and contributed in his own unique way to the fabric of his era.

See discography and list of credits on page 243.

Vivian Foster
(1867-1945)
The Vicar of Mirth
"Yes, I think so!"

"We are all here on earth to help others; what on earth the others are here for I don't know."

– "The Parson Addresses His Flock"

ON THE FACE OF IT, the music hall would hardly seem to be the place to achieve success with a subtle act that relied solely on words in the guise of a vicar. Against the odds, Vivian Foster was highly popular in the first half of the twentieth century. He satirised the kind of self-serving man of God who was all-too familiar to the audience of the time. Although his humour might seem charming and innocuous now, he ruffled some feathers in the BBC Religious Department in his day, which led to the mysterious curtailment of his promising radio career. By then he was a well-established act on the halls and successful recording artist in his own right. His lasting fame came courtesy of the poet W. H. Auden, who once quoted him, and so unintentionally perpetuated the art that was Foster's life's work.

John Foster Hall was born in Horncastle, Lincolnshire, on 19 May, 1867, the second of six children of the Rev. Joseph Hall, and his wife Sarah Ann (nee Foster). Joseph hailed from Dublin where his family lived on Thomas Street, and had served as a young curate in Dresden. In the early

A rare picture of Vivian Foster, the Vicar of Mirth, c1925. Foster sent up the pompous self-serving man of the cloth in his act on the music halls and became an unlikely star of early radio.

1860s he was appointed to the parish of Gedling, Nottinghamshire. In 1865 at the Holy Trinity Church, Liverpool, he married Sarah Ann Foster, the only daughter of John Foster, the Belgian Consul in Hull. Foster was a highly-regarded public figure in the city and after his death a window in St. John's church was dedicated to his memory.[1]

In 1867 Joseph Hall was appointed curate of Horncastle, and the following year was moved to Shirland near Alfreton in Derbyshire, where he became the Rector. John recalled his childhood with fondness, and the many famous people he met including John Bright, Richard Cobden and other leading political and literary figures of the day; "Although we lived in the country," he remembered, "we seemed to be sought after, and not always from the monetary point of view. I shall never forget, under the weeping willow in the rectory garden, the day Carlyle patted me on the head and made some cutting remarks on the length of my hair."[2]

John won the Rowland Scholarship and went to Derby School, where he stayed from September, 1879 until December, 1883.[3] He was keen on sport, and was a regular in the cricket and football teams. He made a creditable batsman and cricket remained a lifelong love.

His biggest influence seemed to be his father, who he described as "very broadminded and humorous." As a youth John used to assist him in day-to-day things such as delivering the parish magazines, which brought him face-to-face with his father's flock, and gave him an insight into human nature. Early on he showed his skill of mimicry and natural gift for observation. He recollected, "Nothing pleased my father more than my boyish reproductions of his clerical colleagues."[4] His father died suddenly after a stroke in April, 1882 aged 51, at which time John was only fourteen. In the words of his obituary-writer, Joseph Hall was a good orator and a "staunch Conservative" who had often given political speeches. Indeed, he had delivered a "telling" speech at Stonebroom only a week before his death about Ireland and Free Trade. He was a man of principle who stood by the tenets of his faith as he saw them, particularly on the subject of the Burial Act of 1881 which he fought against strongly even after it became law. His refusal to certify the burial of a Nonconformist parishioner led to a court case in which he was called as defendant. Intense worry over the matter was cited as a definite contribution to his sudden demise.[5] He was a popular personality in the locale and it was said that after his death the congregation fell away considerably. Just over a year later a window was dedicated as a lasting memorial to him in the church where he had been rector for thirteen years. The centre light of the east window depicted "the figure of Christ in priestly vestments" with the Virgin Mary at the font. Much of the cost was provided by local J. P. Gladwyn Turbutt of Ogston Hall.[6] One of the children, Lillian, died as a teenager, and in 1885 their mother Sarah Ann Hall died at the age of 49. The younger children gathered around the eldest daughter Ethel who had also been well-educated.

John started his teaching career at Thanet College, Margate. Later he was the headmaster of his own small private school in Onslow Gardens,

London. On 10 October, 1894, he married Sarah Edith Tudor-Thomas at the church of Llanwrtyd, Breckonshire. They had a son, Leslie Foster Hall, born in Margate three years later. From around 1900, John took advantage of the school summer holidays and joined a concert party based in Broadstairs. He proved a natural entertainer and mimic and gained rapid local fame. Soon, he appeared in all kinds of amateur concerts and began using the stage name Vivian Foster. Before long he was playing the music halls. An auditor of one of his early shows wrote that he "is always greeted with loud laughter as soon as he appears on the platform."[7] In 1904 he joined a troupe known as the Bohemian Entertainers, and the following year he was with the Merry Mascot Company based at Crystal Palace. At that time, he was billed as a society entertainer and ventriloquist. With the Mascots he was a Jack-of-all-trades; he entertained at the piano, sang humorous songs and featured in a one-act farce *Sarah's Young Man*. He was described as a "wonderful" ventriloquist, swapping repartee with his dummy Joey. At Brighton, an observer declared that he "displays power and versatility as a ventriloquist and vocalist."[8] It was not until later in the decade that he settled on his vicar character and to begin with he sometimes made use of his ventriloquist skill by interrupting himself during his ecclesiastical discourse by throwing his voice, which made it sound as though he was being heckled from the audience. His character sketch of a parson developed from a skit of a vicar opening a village bazaar, and the accuracy of his portrait obviously hit home with his audience, who recognized the kernel of truth in his satire. He became a fixture on the halls and in 1907 he toured in the support programme to Phyllis Dare. That same year he played a season at the Palace theatre, and later he supported Louise Freear on tour.

He came to prominence with the Grotesques, a follies group which had first been organised by the talented songwriter and actor Vere Smith. After Smith's early death the group continued to tour, and Foster took on the role of the vicar which had once been played by Smith. In 1913 they had a highly successful run at the Palace theatre, and proved such a hit at the Savoy that their initial three-week engagement was extended to three months. Foster was such a central figure of the troupe that after he left, they ran into difficulties. Their employer, Moss Empires, wanted to terminate their remaining contract because "Vivian Foster is no longer the vicar."[9]

He was a busy entertainer during the war years and in November, 1914, headed the cast of *Business as Usual* at the London Hippodrome. A popular patriotic revue in eight scenes, it caught the prevailing mood and included the songs "Are We Downhearted? No!" and "When We've Wound Up the Watch on the Rhine." Albert de Courville and E. V. Lucas were the producers, and there were many familiar names in the cast including Violet Lorraine and Harry Tate. It was with this show that Foster introduced his skit "The Parson and the Sewing Party" which he recorded around the same time. The revue proved such a hit that two tours ensued, one in the north and the other in the south.

The art of the monologue reached its apogee in the inter-war years. The work of Marriott Edgar was made especially popular when brought to life by the great Stanley Holloway on record. Illustrated monologues, Francis, Day & Hunter, c1931.

In 1922 he suffered great personal loss when his wife Sarah died after what was described as a "long and painful illness." She always remained cheerful and was much loved by a wide circle of friends.[10] That year marked his broadcasting debut. He vied with Norman Long as the earliest entertainer heard on the radio. He was a regular voice on the BBC in those early years of the wireless, which undoubtedly augmented his popularity and he became one of the first radio personalities. His unctuous delivery of his monologues, interspersed with his catchphrase "Yes, I think so!" at the most unlikely junctures, proved highly popular with listeners who were used to hearing religious talks for real both on the radio and in their daily lives. It was the heyday of the monologue, when the likes of Marriott Edgar and Gillie Potter were greatly appreciated. Edgar was the author of several classics including "The Lion and Albert" which was such a hit for Stanley Holloway. Potter presented the character of an eccentric English gentleman and wrote some witty monologues that made him on radio. Perhaps it was the inherent British appreciation of literature that made their work so appealing to audiences at that time in history.

Just as Foster's broadcasting career began, he also recorded a number of sides for Columbia. He had made his first recordings in 1915, but most of them were done during the height of his popularity in the mid-1920s. His satire must have hit too close to home because several clergymen complained to the corporation about his act. The BBC religious department concurred with the complainants and Foster was effectively "phased out." When he applied for broadcasting dates, he was forced to undergo a special audition. This in itself was a curious thing considering his unquestioned popularity and after four years of working for the organisation. It transpired that only one member of the panel conducting the auditions was against him, but by some kind of sleight of hand, his broadcasting dates were altered, and so his final broadcast was heard on 11 December, 1926 from Glasgow, after which he was silenced. His merriment was much missed and there were several calls for him to be reinstated. These fell on deaf ears, and it was ironic that the next time he was heard on the radio was twenty-five years later, long after his death in 1951 on a nostalgic compilation show looking back at the history of variety, *These Radio Times*. Robb Wilton had suffered a similar problem when his character of the bumbling Mr. Muddlecome, J. P. was blamed for giving magistrates a bad name and taken off air. Wilton was allowed back in 1937, when hopes were raised that Foster would be given a similar reprieve, but unfortunately, he was not so lucky. It appeared that he was the victim of censorship at the Reithian BBC.[11]

Undaunted, Foster continued to appear on the variety circuit, and for many years afterwards was billed as the famous wireless comedian. For much of 1929 and again in 1930 he appeared in *Once in a Blue Moon* with Richard Teasdale, who had starred in the West End hit musical *No, No, Nanette*. The concert party, organised by Harry Bennet, was described as a new kind of entertainment. They also appeared at the Malvern Festival.

He continued to record his monologues, and his last records were released in 1932. Original releases, which were all on the Columbia label, can be found occasionally, and fetch between £5 and £25 each. All of his known recordings are available on a delightful compilation from Windyridge (see below). He delivered his monologues in a mock-portentous voice, the familiar undulating tone of a sermoniser; educated, pious, superior and aloof:

"I wish to say a few words in defence of us poor parsons. People think we work hard on Sunday and have the rest of the week for enjoyment. We most certainly do work hard on Sunday, but we work still harder during the week. For we have to live peacefully amongst our parishioners. Yes, I think so!"

On record he spoke about marriage, Christmas, and even expounded on the latest dance crazes. His monologues sometimes veered into surreal flights of fancy and he had his own idiosyncratic turn of phrase. For instance, when instructing how to dance the Charleston; "Then the movements of the body are so important. You can learn these by smacking a blancmange and watching its convalescence." His was a subtle, observational humour; deceptively gentle but with a keen insight into human nature and motivation:

"My dear friends, I am very pleased to see your smiling faces. At least they look like faces to me. Yes, I think so! I am sorry that the weather has kept away all our best people."

He expertly conveyed the familiar piety and lack of self-awareness of the clerical figure in public life, emphasised with his deliberate pronunciation of "Wed-nes-day" for instance. His routines used sly humour that could go unnoticed; "I was going down a very poor street with a wealthy lady in her £2000 motor car. I was hopping—hoping that a sad sight would cause her to make a substantial donation. I said, these wretched people have nothing to brighten their lives. And she said to her chauffeur 'Switch on the headlights, and go slowly.'"

The Anglican vicar was always seen as unworldly and easily shocked, and it was not thought possible to discuss certain subjects with him, or even in front of him. The mere sight of a dog collar made people stiffen up—it was similar to the common reaction to the sudden appearance of a policeman. In the First World War he was seen as part of the Establishment and usually a long way back from the front line. On stage, he was long a stock figure of derision, usually portrayed as well-meaning but ineffectual and completely at sea in the real world. Over the years a number of influential voices were raised in protest at their depiction. For instance, by the Exeter M. P. Sir Robert Newman, who once made a pointed criticism of Foster at a public meeting without actually naming him.[12]

After several short films for Pathe, he made his sole feature film appearance, as a vicar of course, in the lesser-known Gracie Fields vehicle *This Week of Grace* (1933). Fields was then at the height of her fame as the most beloved comedienne of Thirties British cinema. Despite the relatively small size of the role he was allotted, at least one reviewer described Foster as "an outstanding feature of the production." The following year he contributed the Foreword to a compilation of religious-inspired jokes and anecdotes, *Humour from Pulpit and Pew*.

He was a natural entertainer who was seldom phased by interruptions or calamities, and insisted the show must go on. Once when the electric lights failed at a pier show and the stage was plunged into darkness, he continued his act with a candle in each hand. Another time he faced down a rowdy crowd of sailors in Plymouth and had them cheering by the end.

In real life, Foster had many friends in the clergy, and he was even known to read the lesson on Sunday in his local church. Clarkson Rose, who had known him for many years, wrote that he was so bound up in the character he played that it "clung to him offstage."[13] He had some bad luck with accidents over the years but always played them down. In April, 1925 he was badly bruised and shaken after being crushed against a wall in Tottenham Court Road by a car that had careered out of control. He spent some time in the Middlesex Hospital after that.[14] A few months later he had the misfortune to be hit by a falling electric light batten while on stage at the Manchester Hippodrome.[15] It took him some time to recover, and when he was eventually able to work again, he had a relapse and was forced to delay his return still further. In the 1930s he suffered recurrent bouts of ill-health which meant his appearances were less frequent, but he never lost his optimism, or sense of humour. One time, when he was having difficulty walking, he wrote to a friend; "The other day … I was just able to toddle to the letter-box near my home in Regent's Park. I was wearing an Old Derbeian blazer. A well-speaking man came up to me, touched me on the shoulder, and said, 'I know that blazer. I was at Eton myself. Could you lend me sixpence?'"[16] He was greatly liked by his fellow professionals. Despite his health problems he continued to play the variety stages of the country up until the early 1940s, and remained a real trouper to the end. As Bransby Williams recalled of one of his final shows; "At Oxford New Theatre, he was far from well, yet assumed a smiling presence on stage, and kept his audience in spasms of laughter. It was the true story of the clown hiding his suffering."[17] Foster died on 21 March, 1945 aged 77 at his home in Golder's Green. His son continued in the business under the name Leslie Glenroy, although few ever realised who his father was.

Others in the music hall had impersonated clerical figures before, such as George Robey for instance. In some ways the type was always an easy target for satirists. Frank Milne (1888-1937) made a speciality of vicars in his *Music Box* entertainment, but Foster was the only one to make the study of the unctuous parson his life's work.[18] Certainly, there has been no one since so associated with the persona. Poet W. H. Auden was fond of quoting Foster's line "We are all here on earth to help others; what on earth the others are here for I don't know." Foster would surely have been tickled that his words should have become immortalised by a leading poet of the age. Encapsulated within it is a pithy comment on the religious mind, the sense of deep irony and the fact that any man of God is only human after all; that he does not necessarily believe the things he says and cannot rise above his own self-interest.

See discography and list of credits on page 244.

The Art of the Female Impersonator

"There is no art so misunderstood among the public as that of the female impersonator. No road to theatrical success is more difficult."

– Bert Errol in interview, 1925

ANY YOUNG MAN who wanted to pursue a career as a female impersonator in Britain at the dawn of the twentieth century had his work cut out. Despite the long tradition of pantomime, it was not something which was encouraged, and before the First World War there were a relative few who made it through to the mainstream. The war loosened attitudes and morals a good deal. Tommies and Doughboys alike dressed as girls to entertain their comrades. Hence there was more acceptance of the female impersonator. However, there was arguably always a residual antipathy to them in England, something which male impersonators did not encounter.

The tradition of cross-dressing is an ancient one that goes back to Greek and Roman times. In the Elizabethan theatre, women were largely absent from the stage and most female roles were played by men. Pantomime itself is a uniquely British tradition that goes back a long way and is of obscure origin. Many of the enduring characteristics of it stem from the medieval mummers plays, in which cross-dressing was an important aspect. Much of the impulse for the plays was the idea of the world turned upside down, which is essentially the basis of pantomime.

Continental Europe had a more relaxed attitude in some regards than Britain, and there were several successful European impersonators, notably the Swedish John Lind (1877-1940). Lind, (previously Lindstrom) began performing as a teenager in ballet dressed as a woman, after which he toured Finland, Russia and Germany with a female partner. In 1904 he appeared at the London Pavilion billed as *?Lind?* Part of his act consisted of impersonations of such figures as Anna Pavlova and Isadora Duncan. He toured the world and found international stardom with his show for twenty years, although he was not well known in his native Sweden. He retired from the stage due to ill health in 1923 and died in relative obscurity in 1940. A similarly successful artist was the Swiss Max Waldon (1868-?), who performed what was described as a "Speciality Transformation Act" that consisted of five changes of costume. A classically-trained dancer with the German Royal Ballet, he toured the continent and also visited America. By all accounts a talented and finished performer, he flourished from around 1899 until 1911, after which he disappeared from the spotlight.

These performers were working at a time of rigidly-defined society roles for men and women. One has only to look at the opposition to women having the vote in the Edwardian era—an opposition moreover which included many women among its ranks. It effectively took a war for suffrage to come about. In the aftermath of the revelations during the trials of Oscar Wilde, it took a good deal of courage for any man to dress as a woman in the 1890s. Even in the tolerant atmosphere of the theatre there was always far more acceptance of male impersonators. Vesta Tilley, Hetty King et al received a degree of respectability for their art, but it was not the same for the men who went the other way. The male impersonators had a considerable lesbian following, so the assumption might be that the female impersonators had a gay following—albeit necessarily closeted. However, contemporary reports stressed that women were the most appreciative among audiences.

Before the war, Malcolm Scott was the foremost female impersonator in Britain. He was more accurately a dame comedian, and his whole approach was that of burlesque. He differed from Bert Errol, whose career is discussed in the following chapter. There were others, notably Kelmsley Scott-Barrie (1883-1918). Scott-Barrie, sometimes known by the initials S. B. was born as Teddy Woolhouse in Leeds and ran concert parties on the Yorkshire coast at Scarborough. He had a degree of local fame at the New Pavilion in Harehills, Leeds, and elsewhere in the provinces. He achieved perhaps his greatest success in pantomime at the Lyceum in London, a performance one critic deemed almost "an Ibsen study." Constantly in financial trouble he frequently could not afford to pay his players and was more often than not in the Bankruptcy courts. During the war he served for three years in the West Yorkshire Regiment and continued to appear in such concert parties as the Pelicans. Sadly, he died of wounds at the age of thirty-six in October, 1918, just a few weeks before the Armistice was signed. Scott-Barrie was considered a serious rival to Scott and Errol, but never developed his act as far and did not achieve their level of fame. He may well have supplanted them in the post-war era, had he lived.

The war was arguably the single greatest event that changed perceptions and attitudes, and led to a flowering of the art. Chief among those who emerged in that time in Britain was Reg Stone (1897-1934). He started his career in the Splinters concert party on the Western Front with its famous all-male chorus line. After the war the group reformed and was popular in revue for twenty years thereafter, until Stone's sudden death at the age of only thirty-six. There followed a number of others, notably Douglas Byng (1893-1987), a popular revue artist and cabaret turn, who thrived on being outrageous.

In his approach, Bert Errol took his cue from the American impersonator Julian Eltinge (1881-1949), who set the template for the kind of polished and respectable act that was acceptable to a wide audience. Eltinge enjoyed worldwide fame and was hugely successful in his lifetime. He was the toast of London in 1906, and became one of the highest paid performers on stage. In addition to his theatrical career he also appeared in several films. Born William Julian Dalton in Massachusetts, he first donned female garb at the age of ten. He made his reputation in plays where he played an all-American boy who was forced to dress as a woman by the demands of the plot. His fame was such that he even had a theatre named after him. However, in his early days he faced problems of his own, not least the forthright opposition of his father, who was horrified when informed his son wanted to dress as a woman for a living, and made him agree to attend military academy for a year. This did not cure his urge to dress in female attire. His father's response echoed that of much of the male population at the time. Some people would always be uncomfortable with the idea. Most took it for what it was, and those certain of their masculinity probably laughed the loudest. Eltinge's act was predicated on the assumption that he could actually pass for a woman, and at the denouement of his routine he whisked off his wig to reveal the truth—to gasps of astonishment from the audience. Off-stage he was at pains to stress his masculinity and impugned any slur on his manhood. For instance, he let it be known that he indulged in such pursuits as boxing. Perhaps he protested too much. His later career arc reflected the decline of the vogue for female impersonation, which reached a peak in the 1920s but had fallen out of favour by the time of his death of a cerebral haemorrhage in 1949 at the age of 59. There were several contemporaries of Eltinge, most of whom adopted a similar approach. One who did not was Bert Savoy (1876-1923), the antithesis of the respectable type of entertainer. In a double act with Jay Brennan he had an avowedly camp style and was said to have been an inspiration for Mae West. He had a similar acerbic, wisecracking humour and used catchphrases such as "You don't know the half of it, dearie." He defied the unspoken convention among female impersonators by staying in character and never removing his wig. In the long run, his approach was arguably far more influential than that of Eltinge. A true pioneer from an earlier period was Burton Stanley (*fl.* 1880s), a male soprano who played the diva in Tremaine's Burlesque Opera Company in the 1870s and later formed his own operetta companies which toured extensively across the United States in the following decades and who also visited Europe.

There was always a fundamental difference between the American and British approach. In the U. S. there was no pantomime tradition and the art grew more out of the burlesque show. The word burlesque evokes different meanings and connotations. In England, a burlesque was essentially a satire or parody. In America it came to be associated with a particular kind of entertainment that was strictly for adults and not feasible for a family audience. This divergence leads it to the present-day situation when a burlesque show is primarily a gay event. It appears that there was more tolerance in the United States than there was in Britain. While it was acceptable for a male performer to appear as a pantomime dame, there was far less acceptance of one who always donned drag. This was especially apparent in the career of Bert Errol, who found great difficulty in England as a young man but blossomed in America, where the atmosphere was more conducive, there were far more impersonators, and a greater sense of freedom to express oneself.

Bert Errol
(1883-1949)
"The Lady (?) with the Tetrazzini Voice"

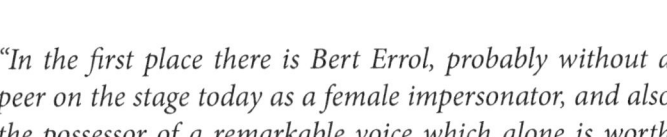

> "In the first place there is Bert Errol, probably without a peer on the stage today as a female impersonator, and also the possessor of a remarkable voice which alone is worth listening to."
>
> – *The Montreal Star*, 1920[1]

BERT ERROL WAS ONE of the few British entertainers who made a highly successful living out of playing a woman. His natural ability to sing soprano and switch easily to tenor formed the basis of his act. Tellingly, he spent the larger part of his career touring America, where he scored his greatest triumphs, and only returned to England in his fifties. He was keen to identify himself as an actor who portrayed female characters rather than as a man trying to be a woman. As such, he sought to link his art to that of an old established tradition of the English stage and distance himself from any taint of sordidness which might be levelled by his detractors in the theatre of his day, appalled at the notion of any man who wanted to wear a dress.

Errol was born as Isaac Whitehouse, the youngest son of Isaac and Elizabeth Whitehouse, in Aston, Birmingham, on 11 August, 1883. His father originally hailed from Dudley in Worcestershire and ran a successful family business as a brass founder and lock moulder, with about twenty employees.[2] Isaac senior was a well-respected figure in the city and had

Bert Errol was the most glamorous of the British female impersonators of his day and had a remarkable voice in which he sang many romantic ballads. Above: Sheet music of "Just Like a Rainbow"

a love of soccer. He was associated with Aston Villa Football Club from 1883 and served as Vice-President from 1891 until his death in 1918.[3]

Young Isaac endured a prosaic upbringing in a suburb of industrial Birmingham, and he followed the family trade as an apprentice brass dresser. He studied chemistry and was expecting to continue his career in that line until a chance encounter with his sister's music teacher changed the direction of his life. He had always displayed a talent for singing since his days as a choirboy at the local church of St. Peter & St. Paul. However, when he reached the age of puberty his voice did not break like other boys. After enduring much ribbing from friends, he finally left the choir in his seventeenth year. What might have been an acute embarrassment to him personally, actually gave him the rare ability to sing soprano, which was his passport to fame. One day his sister's music teacher, Grace Ivel, came to the house to give her a lesson. Ivel heard a beautiful soprano voice singing "Lo, Hear the Gentle Lark" emanating from an upstairs room, and remarked "I never knew you had a sister who could sing." "That's my brother," came the reply. Ivel asked Isaac to sing for her, and he obliged with his speciality, "The Jewel Song" from Gounod's *Faust*. She

Errol in his early career, possibly during his time with the Adeler & Sutton Pierrots at Rhyl, c1908.

was so impressed that she offered to give him free singing lessons for six months.[4] He took his singing seriously, and studied for some time with the renowned tenor Jean de Reszke (1850-1925), who he said was a great teacher, and later with Signor Francisco Cortesi.[5]

He appeared locally in concerts around Birmingham and from at least 1905 began to use the stage name Bert Errol. Around 1907 he made his debut in an Adeler & Sutton concert party at Teignmouth, Devon. It was with that Pierrot show that he made his first appearance as a woman for a short sketch and proved a natural in the role.[6] It was then, he later said, that his real life began. His singing brought him to wide attention; in those days he often sang numbers from the classical repertoire. His voice was his greatest asset, and he found no difficulty in switching between tenor and soprano. One commentator noted that he had a voice "of unusually high range, a cross between falsetto and mezzo-soprano which he uses to splendid advantage."[7] He was often compared to the Italian opera singer Luisa Tetrazzini; hence he was billed as "The Lady (?) with the Tetrazzini Voice." He joined the Harry Reynolds Minstrel Troupe for a year (1909-10). Reynolds was distinctly impressed with Errol's vocal ability and female impressions, but less so with his ordinary speaking voice, which he said at that time was weak and let him down in his stage comedy business.[8] That was something which improved markedly with time and became a strength as he gained in confidence. He made his debut at the London Pavilion in 1909 billed as "The Male Soprano and Double-Voiced Vocalist." Some observers even called him a triple-voiced vocalist, as a tenor, soprano and contralto.

For all his apparent success, he characterised his formative years as a great struggle against an ingrained prejudice for any man who dressed as a woman. He once said that female impersonation was by far the most despised branch of the profession, reflecting the wider intolerance of society at large. He maintained: "The stalls used to sneer and ... the rest of the house was less than polite."[9] In such a harsh environment he worked hard to make his routine pleasing to all and succeeded in finding a receptive audience. To aid his cause he was careful to avoid being vulgar or suggestive. This way he won people over, and in a few short years, a Canadian critic remarked; "His act impresses because of its genuine artistry, and also because it is on the highest plane of entertainment with a wide public appeal."[10]

In June, 1910 he married aspiring dancer and singer Rachel Isaacs, whose father Lewis was a commercial traveller for Lyons Tea. Rachel was always known as Ray, and used the stage name Ray Hartley. Her sister Jennie was also on the stage. Bert and Ray's daughter Betty was born the following year and when she was a teenager, she too joined the act as a dancer.

During the years from 1910 until 1928 Errol made several overseas tours, to Europe, South Africa, Australasia and the United States. His American tours were a great success, and at his peak saw him as a serious rival to Julian Eltinge. Eltinge had made female impersonation acceptable if not popular at that time, with his sophisticated and polished turn. The Danish-American artist Bothwell Browne (1877-1947) was considered more convincingly feminine than Eltinge. Errol was sometimes compared to Browne, to whom he bore a physical resemblance. There were others from England who tried to make a go of it in America, such as Herbert Clifton (1885-1947). He had a similar singing act to Errol, but tended to do more character studies, especially of charwomen. He was successful but eventually abandoned drag and pursued a career as a bit part player in Hollywood.

Errol in vamp mode c 1915.

On his first tour in 1910 Errol was billed erroneously as Errol Burt, and garnered much advance publicity, most of which was apocryphal, such as the tale that he had a devoted following among the cream of society on the Continent and that he had played for the crowned heads of Europe. It was also said that he was the scion of a prominent New York family who had disowned him because of his chosen profession. He drew press attention for the $1000 that was allegedly due in customs duty on his cases of lavish, jewel-encrusted costumes, many of which were said to have come from the estate of the 5th Marquess of Anglesey, Henry Cyril Paget.

Errol wearing a light dress, photographic postcard, published by
J. R. Brunton, F. R. S., of Burnley, c1911 Wellcome Library.

The Marquess, who had died five years previously at the age of twenty-nine, was one of the most flamboyant *bon viveurs* of the British landed gentry, who lived way beyond his means and had a penchant for dressing in exotic female attire. Some early reports even claimed that Errol and Paget were close friends. Errol had already appeared in Paris where he reputedly once traipsed the streets of the city with a lobster on a ribbon.[11] His New York debut was trumpeted, perhaps falsely, as a dancing feature based on Flaubert's *Salambo*, with music by Pierre Gutterb of the Theatre Sarah Bernhardt. He was to have toured for the Shuberts, but when he asked for £100 a week and they offered him $100 instead, he changed his mind. Instead he signed with the Keith circuit. All his American tours did good business, and his 1913-14 tour went so well that it was extended by ten weeks, which meant he had to cancel his British Moss Empires tour that spring.[12] The first few tours lasted six to eight months and the later ones were almost a year long.

During the war, Errol served in the army as a corporal in France (1917-19). According to some reports he had "an enviable war record."[13] He was doyen of "The Gaieties" concert party that included Leslie Henson, who became a famous name in post-war musical revue. The war led to a relaxation of social norms, and to an extent made female impersonation more acceptable, particularly after so many soldiers in all the Allied armies in entertainments across France had appeared in drag. A fanciful writer in the French magazine *L'Illustration* described a show in Paris at which Errol made an impact. Described again as an American, the author of the piece wrote that the glamorous actress Lillian Russell had given him advice on his frocks and taught him how to paint his face. In addition, "324 fine gentlemen" had already proposed to him.[14] Life with "The Gaieties" concert party was decidedly hectic and potentially dangerous. They had their own truck and were required to put on a show at short notice in the most hazardous places, often soon after entering a captured town amid the rubble of ruined buildings, and

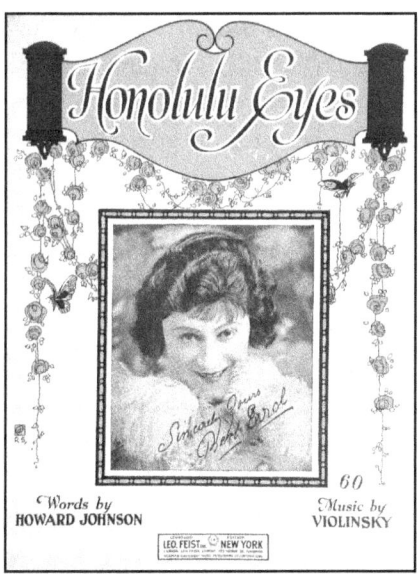

Some collectible sheet music covers of the popular songs that Errol sang which are so redolent of the early years of the twentieth century. Above left: "Honolulu Eyes" (1920). Above right: "La Veeda" (1921).

once in a half-ruined theatre. There was a famous photo of Errol making up surrounded by a scene of utter destruction a matter of hours after the Allied advance.

In the early years of his act he often impersonated then popular opera singers of the day whose names are now mostly forgotten, including Constance Drover and Ruth Vincent. Initially, he continued to favour the operatic songs he had perfected, particularly "The Jewel Song" and "Il Bocio" by Adrini. These became mainstays of his repertoire throughout his career, but he tailored his material to suit his audience and in America bought songs of upcoming composers such as Irving Berlin. He also found success with lightweight romantic ballads including "Venetian Moon" and had one of his biggest hits with "My Hero" from *The Chocolate Soldier*. When he first sang, few questioned he was a woman, although later his stage deportment left the audience in no doubt that he was a man, and he would appear in masculine attire in the second part of his show. When he reappeared as a woman, he would end his act in the usual way by triumphantly removing his wig, in a similar manner to Eltinge. As the tours progressed, Errol called his show "Modes and Manners of…" adding the year to the title. He was in some ways one of the earliest "Transatlantic" artists, who sang sentimental songs about Kentucky even though he had never been there. He greatly enjoyed the social life of the American tours, and made many friends in the country. He once visited Hollywood, where he was invited to a grand ball at Paramount studios. Someone suggested he should go to the local theatre to give them some much needed publicity. He borrowed an ex-fashion show gown from the Paramount wardrobe department for the occasion and was promptly voted the best-dressed woman.[15]

He enjoyed good tours of Australia (1924-25, 1928) and South Africa (1925) and found audiences receptive. He made a successful tour of Germany in late 1927 and was such a hit at the Scala, Berlin, that he was invited again the following year for a longer engagement.[16] In New Zealand it was reported that his show almost started a riot, and the audience just could not get enough of him.[17] He found the expanses of the Antipodes invigorated him and that the air suited his health. He loved to travel and relished the chance to escape from the dreadful English climate, the sheer mundanity of life at home, and the lack of scope for an entertainer of his kind. In Melbourne he reflected "The sky seems farther away here, and one feels one can breathe. At home it seems so much nearer, pressing down upon you."[18] He made his final tour in 1928, for which he renamed his show

"Types and Times" instead of "Modes and Manners." As always, he travelled with his extensive luggage containing almost a dozen big trunks full of gowns.

Errol's act was a family affair, with wife Ray an integral part, as dancer, singer and dresser. She was also on hand to emphasise his masculinity, something that he was keen to do to stop any whispers about his sexuality. He often introduced her at the end of his spot, as if to reassure the audience. His act remained essentially the same over the years and would consist of him singing about four different songs and changing his costume in lightning time; he aimed for 2 minutes 30 seconds. One of the few films that exist of him is *Ringing the Changes* (1922) which shows him doing his quick change. While he was getting changed into the next costume, Ray would occupy the stage in a song or dance routine; in later years daughter Betty also helped out in the same way. Ray picked out all her husband's gowns and designed others for him. She always chose the greatest quality and they were often the most expensive. She would think nothing of buying a dress for £100; one of the most costly was over £300, at a time when the average wage was less than £5 a week. By the mid-1920s, he was a highly paid entertainer, and his frequent long American tours were especially lucrative. His ostentatious costumes were a big part of his act, and he favoured bejewelled gowns of satin, silk, or cloth of silver and magnificent headdresses with huge plumes of ostrich feathers.

Errol publicity photo dated 1920.

Errol had an undoubted glamour, but he called his act "arch entertainment" and was at pains to establish the difference between a *female* impersonator and a *feminine* impersonator, that is, between a man playing a legitimate female character, in a tradition that went back to Shakespeare, and one pretending to be a woman, i.e. adopting feminine

Errol toured the United States many times between 1913 and 1930. Above: Dressed as a bride, Apeda Studio, New York, c1922 Wellcome Library.

mannerisms. In common with most others in the profession he also sought to distance himself from any thought that what he did extended beyond the confines of the stage: "I believe it is possible for a man to impersonate with sane consideration of the female character," he once reflected, "in the same way as he might play the melancholy Dane. Hamlet is not melancholy away from the stage."[19]

When he was younger, he enjoyed sports, especially rowing and golf. However, he had to give them up when one theatre manager happened to remark that he was becoming too muscular in his neck and shoulders. Instead, he developed a liking for the open road and took up motoring.[20]

In the 1930s Errol ceased to travel abroad, and decided to concentrate on variety circuits in Britain. This coincided with the slump in theatre business in the wake of the Wall Street Crash and the subsequent Depression. He realised he was getting older and could no longer convince as a young female. Instead, he turned his attention to pantomime and became a perennial favourite in dame roles, emphasising the comedy

Sheet music of "Venetian Moon" (1920) a typically romantic Errol number.

aspect of his persona. His wife opened a rooming house for fellow artistes, the Errol Hotel in Gower Street, and daughter Betty took her place in the act.[21] The two most regular pianists he used were Reg Fowler and Gordon Stewart.

He had played historical characters throughout his career; for instance, he caused a sensation as Joan of Arc in a Tableau with "The Gaieties" at Lille just after the war. This aspect of his act became more apparent as he got older, when he emulated the approach of Malcolm Scott. He presented a version of Scott's Queen Elizabeth, which he introduced with a song, "Good Queen Bess" and at one point even purloined his bill matter, calling himself "The Woman Who Knows." This happened after Scott had died. One of Errol's most popular routines in that period was "When Cleopatra Got the Needle" in which he burlesqued the legendary Egyptian queen.[22] His impersonation of Queen Victoria did not find favour with a staunch royalist in the audience of his show at Shea's Hippodrome, in Toronto, Canada, who took exception to his depiction, demanding an apology for what he perceived as a grave insult to the late monarch.[23] Errol also sent up contemporary personalities including Mae West. He introduced more overtly comedic elements into his act and perfected a drunken routine.

In 1938, his daughter Betty married Wilfred Wells, an analytical chemist, at Erdington, and gave up the stage.[24] The following year Bert practically retired from performing, but he emerged briefly during the war to play some nostalgic, morale-boosting shows for the services. In 1944 he was the star of a revue, *We Were in the Forces* at the Aston Hippodrome, returning to his old home town after a long absence.[25] He successfully toured the provinces with the show in which he appeared in several sketches and was billed as 'The Perfect Lady.' With the end of the war he retired once again. He died in the Royal Sussex Hospital, Brighton on 28 November, 1949 after an attack of asthma at the age of 66.[26] Despite his popularity overseas in his glory years, his death went largely unreported in the American and Australian press, and there were only a few mentions in the papers in Britain, showing perhaps the fickleness of fame and the low esteem in which female impersonation was held.

Curiously, he never recorded any of his songs which was a major oversight considering the fact that he sang a great many and had by all accounts a remarkable voice. His sheet music has some attractive and highly evocative cover designs which epitomise an era of impossible glamour and romance that is long gone.

Errol was a pioneer of female impersonation who deserves credit for the way he battled against the inherent hostility against what he did to establish himself as probably the most glamorous of the British practitioners of the art. He was perhaps an influence on Danny La Rue, particularly in terms of his ornate costumes, with the plumes of feathers headdresses and high heels. Errol's female persona afforded him an escape from ordinary life into a romantic make-believe. As a man he passed unnoticed, but when he applied the make-up, he became someone else, and displayed flashes of diva-like temperament. A visitor to his dressing room watched him transform himself and observed of the change; "He seems to assume something of a vivacious, almost feminine nature with the make-up, and the frocks, for when he is met later in masculine attire he is like another individual, wearing almost an air of reserve."[27]

See discography and list of credits on page 246.

The Entertainer at the Piano

THE ENTERTAINER AT THE PIANO began life on the concert platform and as a society entertainer. Several of the most successful enjoyed excellent careers on the music hall stage in the early years of the twentieth century.

The comic songs of Gilbert and Sullivan were the precursor to those of the piano entertainer. Many of the early songwriters were friends or rivals of the much-loved composers. Some of the key names in the development of the genre in the latter third of the nineteenth century were George Grossmith, Corney Grain and Orlando Parry. Richard Corney Grain (1844-95) was far removed from the music-halls and appeared exclusively at the German Reed Entertainments given in the Royal Gallery of Illustration at 14, Regent Street, which had once been the home of the architect John Nash. The German Reed Entertainments were named after composer and theatre manager Thomas German Reed (1817-88), who initiated the musical evenings in 1871, and which were continued by his son until 1895. The seating capacity at the Gallery was only five hundred, so those gatherings were intimate and attracted a select clientele who were keen to see the latest thing and also to be seen among the fashionable set. One of the mainstays of the entertainments was Richard Corney Grain, a lawyer by trade, who produced sketches, monologues and songs including "The Masher King of Piccadilly." Another was John Orlando Parry (1810-79) who had made his debut as a baritone as far back as 1830, and was by turns an artist and actor. By the 1840s he began composing comic songs that he gave in concert-rooms and, by 1860 in the German Reed Entertainments. Some of his song titles give an indication of his type of material, for instance; "Wanted: A Governess" and "Don't Be Too

Particular." The multi-talented George Grossmith (1847-1912), besides being an author and an actor, was a talented songwriter and comedian. As a comedian he essayed many roles in the plays of G & S, including the Major General in *The Pirates of Penzance* (1880). His most enduring work as a writer was as co-author with his brother Weedon of the classic *Diary of a Nobody*. He wrote eighteen comic operas and around 600 songs including "See Me Dance the Polka."

The German Reed Entertainments ended in 1895 but over the next few years there were many others who followed Grossmith and Grain in composing and performing clever and witty ballads. Most began as society entertainers and ultimately found success on the Music Hall stage including Hamilton Hill, Nelson Jackson, Harry Fragson, Mel B. Spurr, Leslie Harris, Barclay Gammon, Fanny Wentworth and J. G. Pellisier, to name but a few. Melanethon Burton Spurr (1846-1904) was born at Selby and practised law in Hull for eight years. However, he found his true vocation in writing and performing comic songs after seeing Corney Grain. Spurr got his big break when he was employed by Mr. Maskeline at the Egyptian Hall in an engagement which lasted eleven years. He toured the provinces and then made a trip to Australia for eleven months (1903-04). He died suddenly at the end of his tour at St. Kilda, Melbourne, at the age of 58. He had suffered from diabetes for the last decade of his life.

Barclay Gammon (1866-1915) spent much of his life working for a railway company, only appearing at concerts after hours and at weekends. He was persuaded to go professional and in 1903 was invited to play at the Palace theatre. This was the springboard to his greatest fame and effectively piqued the public interest in what had hitherto been confined to the concert hall. Like Spurr, Gammon also toured Australia successfully in 1909. He recorded a number of sides, but few have been collected on any compilation with the exception of "The Suffragette's Anthem." He died in 1915 aged 48. Physically similar to Gammon, Leslie Harris (1868-1923) was an excellent mimic and actor quite apart from his musical and humorous ability. From the early 1890s until his premature death in 1923, he was a tireless entertainer who travelled the globe and spent almost two years in Australia. Doyen of concert halls, assembly rooms and town halls, he appeared at theatres and pier shows, and on the vaudeville stage. Sadly, he never committed his songs to cylinder or shellac so there is no recording of his voice, thus he is almost entirely forgotten today. His works of satire included "Had the Old Noah's Ark Got Wrecked," "The

Hinglishman" and "Middle Class Society Tea." He co-wrote many songs with Mel B. Spurr such as "Five Little Flies," "The Woman That's Coming" and "It's the Usual Thing to Say." Harris often impersonated Grossmith and others including Albert Chevalier, whose songs he also rendered.

Harry Fragson (1869-1913) was especially remembered for "Hello, Hello, Who's Your Lady Friend?" He wrote many other comic songs including "The Other Department Please" but found perhaps his greatest fame in France, where he used his fluent ability to speak the language to impersonate famous figures of the French music hall. He had a lucrative career but suffered a terrible fate. He was unintentionally murdered by his

Harry Fragson *The Music Hall Shakespeare* (Music Hall Masters, 2003), a splendid compilation of some twenty-seven tracks by one of the outstanding piano entertainers. The CD has extensive sleeve notes and many rare photographs.

mentally-ill father in Paris, at the age of 43, and buried at le Pere-Lachaise cemetery. A number of compilations have been released. See Fragson *Ladies Beware* Windyridge CDR 71

Tom Clare (1876-1946) was a fine satirist whose songs were often topical. A standout was his "What Did You Do in the Great War, Daddy?" The title came from a famous propaganda poster of the time and the song took a pop at those who profited from the war or did practically nothing. He had a long career which began at the age of eight and he became a regular broadcaster who often recorded. See Windyridge CD *The Fine Old English Gentleman* CDR 30

Ernest Hastings (1879-1941) was a Mancunian who used his accent to effect in his songs, recitations and monologues. Sentimental and satirical by turn, he proved popular away from his usual metier of the concert hall and made a large number of recordings which gained him a good following. One of his earliest successes was "The Commissionaire" published when he was nineteen. Among his own compositions were "There Isn't Any Girl Like My Girl" and "Mother Always Sends the Very Thing." Several of his recitations were recorded by others, especially Stanley Holloway, who brought "And Yet I Don't Know" and "My Word, You Do Look Queer" to wide attention. On record Hastings sang both his own work and that of others, including many by the prolific songwriters Weston and Lee. "Nothing Over Sixpence in the Store" was based on the slogan that Woolworth's used to advertise their newly-opened shops in 1909. "Perverted Placards" and "The Song of the Ford Motor Car" are good examples of his art, and he also sang several amusing yet curiously sad numbers including "A Soldier's Reminiscences." His "Church Bells as We Hear Them" showed his musical inventiveness and gift for observation. By 1919 his popularity earned him a place on the bill of the Royal Command Performance. See *The Seaside Posters* CDR 72

The inter-war years witnessed the zenith of the clever satirical ballad, with the undisputed genius of the age Noel Coward leading the way. Among the best-known and loved artists on the variety stage were two duos, The Western Brothers and Mr. Flotsam & Mr. Jetsam. Kenneth (1899-1963) and George (1895-1969) Western specialised in witty and perceptive numbers rendered in a style of upper-class ennui while wearing monocles and immaculate evening dress. With songs like "The Old School Tie," "Play the Game, You Cads" and "We're Frightfully BBC" they satirised anything and everything, providing a priceless insight into the preoccupations and personalities of their era.

The work of the popular inter-war duo Flotsam and Jetsam was brought together on three superb CDs issued on the Vocalion label in 2008 with sleeve notes by Tony Barker.

Flotsam & Jetsam was the moniker of Bentley C. Hilliam (1890-1968) and Malcolm McEachern (1883-1945). Hilliam was a talented and prolific songwriter, McEachern an Australian with one of the deepest bass baritones ever. The contrast of Hilliam's light tenor and McEachern's resonant voice made their work immediately appealing. Among their best songs were "Little Betty Bouncer," "The Spooning of the Knife and Fork" and the telling "Only a Few of Us Left." Their work has been collected in three first class CD compilations on the Vocalion label.

The art form did not long survive the Second World War, by which time many of the big names had departed the scene. However, the flag was kept flying by the wonderful Flanders and Swann. Highly popular in the 1950s, Michael Flanders (1922-1975) and Donald Swann (1923-1994) recorded a series of EPs and LPs including *At the Drop of a Hat* recorded live, which captured their unique sound for all time. Scottish singer Ian Wallace (1919-2009) also helped to popularize their work. Flanders and Swann were remembered for their animal songs including "The Hippopotamus" and "The Gnu." Their songs were highly satirical and of-the-moment, for instance their play on the title of a Eugene O'Neill opus "The Gas Man Cometh." With such numbers as "Tried by the Centre Court" and "Some Madeira M' Dear" they mined a quintessentially British vein of humour that took the traditions of the Music-Hall and of all the piano entertainers who had gone before, but with their own unique approach. Their poignant "Slow Train" was a lament for the end of steam railways and the way of life it symbolised, written in response to the swingeing Beeching cuts which decimated the rail network in the early-1960s.

In some ways the ultimate parodist of the genre was an American mathematician, Tom Lehrer, whose recordings of the fifties became cult classics, in particular his "Poisoning Pigeons in the Park" and "The Elements" which set the periodic table to Gilbert and Sullivan's "Major General's Song," thus coming full circle back to where the piano entertainer came in.

There were so many clever entertainers, and in the following chapters I discuss at length two who were among the most popular of their time, Margaret Cooper and Norman Long. Cooper encapsulates much of the charm of the earlier era and Long of the satiric inter-war spirit. Both found success in the ever-changing world of the Music-Hall during the turbulent twentieth century and proved that piano entertainers deserved their place on the bill.

Margaret Cooper
(1877-1922)
The Diva of the Humorous Song

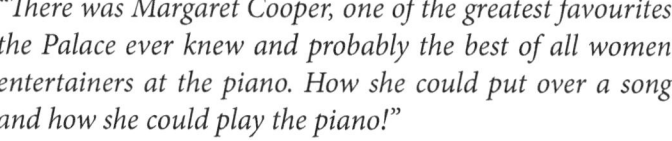

"There was Margaret Cooper, one of the greatest favourites the Palace ever knew and probably the best of all women entertainers at the piano. How she could put over a song and how she could play the piano!"

– W. Macqueen Pope *The Melodies Linger On*

(I) Meddlesome Matty

Margaret Cooper was the leading female practitioner of entertainment at the piano, which was up until then mostly a male preserve. Supremely elegant, she was the embodiment of refined English womanhood in the opening years of the twentieth century. Her classical musical training and hauteur style made her an unlikely star of the popular stage, but she succeeded, against the odds, in bringing the much-derided art of the light and witty sentimental ballad into the robust world of the music hall. In the process she became one of the highest paid women entertainers of her generation. Despite her patrician appearance she brought a playful spirit to her songs, delivered in a light soprano voice which had a decided vogue at that time. Perhaps her surrealism and elusive sense of self-parody at the keyboard calls to mind the great Marx Bros. stooge Margaret

Margaret Cooper was the leading lady entertainer at the piano of the early twentieth century. The epitome of poise and style, she was also something of a trendsetter in fashion.

Dumont, who in her guise as the music-loving Mrs. Claypool would surely have approved of her fellow Margaret. Like Dumont, la Cooper never seemed to quite get the joke—or did she?

Margaret Gernon Cooper was born 28 June, 1877 in Camberwell, the second child and only daughter of James Cooper and Isabella Catherine (nee Gernon). The Coopers were bakers by trade and the business had been run by James' mother for many years. Both James' parents John and Margaret Cooper (nee Duncan) were born in Scotland and married in Fife in 1836. Isabella Gernon came from a large family; her father Andrew was Irish and her mother Catherine (nee Robinson) came from Doncaster in Yorkshire. Andrew Gernon was a Superintendent of the Metropolitan Police. A member of the force for over forty years, he was in charge of Camberwell district until 1877 when he was appointed Superintendent at Whitehall. He died suddenly in 1885 aged 61.

Margaret described herself as a sickly child and her parents believed that music would be good for her health and that singing in particular would help her. Music was always an important part of her life from an early age, in which pursuit she was greatly encouraged by her parents; "My father was a fine singer," she recalled, "and my mother an accomplished musician."[1] One of her earliest memories was of bashing out pretend music-hall songs on a table, including "Champagne Charlie" and "How I Wish My Mother-in-Law were Far, Far Away." Her parents regularly took her to concerts including the promenades at Convent Garden and once, while Coutts' band played the patriotic airs of the nations, little Maggie stood on her chair and sang along, which caused much merriment among the crowd. Another of the "bright recollections of her childhood" was of hearing George Grossmith singing "He Was A Careful Man."[2] One night at the Theatre Royal, Drury Lane, she was so captivated by the show that she cried when they had to leave their box and had to be carried out. Wilful from the first, she was indulged by her parents who gave her the kind of leeway only a middle-class child of the Victorian era could have enjoyed. "Do you know," she once declared, "I can make anyone do just as I want, and do it immediately. I had this faculty as a child. I am never overlooked, and never was, and never will be!"[3] She went through a succession of governesses but showed marked ability on the piano which she played from the age of five. She was sent to a day school at Craven Hill, Paddington where she continually misbehaved but impressed on the piano. The old lady who ran the school nicknamed her "Meddlesome Matty." When Margaret was ten, she moved to a select music school at Westbourne Park, Bayswater. There she spent the next four years and did well academically, winning six prizes; but she lost two of those because of her "bad conduct."[4] The conductor Henry Wood, then in his early twenties, taught singing at this school and was reputed to have resigned because "out of the whole school the only singer worth teaching was little Margaret Cooper."[5] Around 1891 her parents sent her to study music at a school in the village of Quaregnon near Mons, Belgium. There she learned French, German, and more importantly, the piano and violin. She lived with a Protestant minister and his family and admitted that she "led them an awful dance." Nevertheless, they understood that she was talented and made allowances. She progressed rapidly in her studies under a good tutor, August Vastersavendts, who was also a composer. He taught her both piano and violin. She continued her study of the violin after she left, for twelve years in total. However, the piano was always her first and last love. It was everything to her and she practised constantly; "They used to have to drag me away from it," she reflected.

In July 1894 she returned to England and after the November half-term began her studies at the Royal Academy of Music. She was taught singing by Richard Cummings, and worked hard on it but admitted; "My voice was tiny then, I used to say it wouldn't fill an egg-cup!" She learnt sight-reading and harmony and studied elocution with Ian Robertson, the brother of actor-manager Forbes Robertson. Her hard work paid off and in 1896 she won three bronze medals for the piano, singing, and sight-singing. In 1897 she was appointed accompanist to all the medal examinations, which was an experience she relished. Among others, she accompanied the West Indian mezzo-soprano Alice Gomez. Margaret was an exacting singer to accompany, and few volunteered to do so because of her quick temper. In 1898, she won the silver medals. Her three certificates for graduation were awarded for singing, the piano and the violin and she was later made a licentiate of the academy. Later still she was given the ultimate accolade and made a Fellow of the Royal Academy of Music. She made her concert debut shortly after graduation in one of the chambers at the St. James's Hall. Despite her extensive studies and seemingly supreme self-possession, she admitted to being incredibly nervous for her first appearance in public. "That moment I shall never forget," she said, "I well remember being so frightfully nervous that, when I opened my mouth, I felt grave doubts whether I should be able to get out a note." For her debut she sang "When Fairyland was Young."[6] She even composed a number of songs at that time including "Romanca" around 1899, and a correspondent to *The Times* recalled her as one of the earliest singers of songs to the violin.[7]

Her first paid engagement was for singing two songs at a chapel in Ealing, for which she received half a guinea.[8] She found it hard to make a living solely as a pianist and became a music teacher. For about two years after leaving the academy she played in classical concerts and in oratorio with various choral societies, including those of Leeds, Selby and Derby.

Cooper insisted on playing exclusively Chappell pianos, and frequently advertised for the company.

She sang in *Elijah, The Messiah, Creation,* Sullivan's *The Light of the World,* Villiers-Stanford's *The Voyage of Mael Dune* and Elgar's *Caractacus*. Other concerts included municipal events and city dinners for Trades corporations, cricket club concerts, society functions and private entertainments. In those days her songs were mainly sentimental. One of the first pieces in which she made an impact on the concert stage was in Coleridge-Taylor's *Hiawatha*.[9] At times she was accompanied, and at other times accompanied others. From the beginning she preferred to accompany herself. From 1899 she gave organ recitals at several churches and at Bridlington played a full choral service. She also played the organ at St. Peter's Church, Garford Street, Limehouse. Her first Chappell Ballad Concert was in 1901, but her insistence on accompanying herself led to her non-appearance at that event for several years. However, she was determined not to sing at the platform while someone else accompanied her, which became a bone of contention; "It was difficult to persuade anyone—teachers or managers—to let me do it" she once commented, "But you see I got my way."[10]

She joined an amateur company in Barnstaple with which she played many leading roles in the works of Gilbert and Sullivan, including *Patience* and *The Gondoliers*. In 1904 she tried her hand at operetta in a short-lived production of Frank Lambert's *Lady Land,* at the Avenue theatre, in which she played the role of Susan. This proved a sobering experience, as she later recalled: "We rehearsed for the best part of six months, gave a capital performance, and got no pay after the first week! The venture was a failure. That cured my aspirations for operetta!"[11] She toured as Rosaline in Vere Smith's opera *The Dandy Duke* and was praised for her acting as much as her singing ability. She also appeared in Sterndale Bennett's *The May Queen*. In between times she followed the typical life of a society entertainer with the endless rounds of "at Homes" for sometimes demanding and irksome suburban hostesses. Adding to her experience, she also took part in Pierrot shows at Margate and other places. From the first she cut a stylish figure and an early review noted that even in a concert party she "looked chic in her pierrette costume."[12]

In the early days she often sang the songs of Edward German, who she counted as a friend. She began to be drawn to the light humorous ditties and one of her first successes in that vein was "The Paper Fan" from *The Chinese Honeymoon* which she sang for two years. Among others she was attracted to the work of Frederic Norton, including "The Elephant and the Portmanteau" and "The Camel and the Butterfly." At one time she seriously considered making a go of musical comedy and in 1905 signed a contract with Seymour Hicks to tour America in *The Catch of the Season*. However, ill-health forced her to withdraw from that venture. She was once offered a role in *Tom Jones* at the Lyceum but declined. Her true ambition was for grand opera, and in truth she longed to play the serious roles, especially that of Marguerite in Gounod's *Faust*. She never achieved that goal but she often played her own arrangement of "The Jewel Song" from the same opera at private and public gatherings. In 1906 she played in the Bernhardt Sunday concerts at the Palace Pier, Brighton, with the beloved Irish tenor John McCormack.

Portrait of Margaret by Claude Harris c1906.

(II) Nights at the Palace: From Concert Hall to Music Hall

> *"When I first walked on and saw that sea of faces, I felt as though I were on an Atlantic liner in a storm ... The moment, however, I was at the piano, my nervousness left me and I felt as cool and collected as I had ever felt in my life."*
>
> –Margaret Cooper *Myself and My Piano*

After establishing herself on the concert platform, Margaret was persuaded to try her songs on the Music Hall stage and found against all prevailing orthodoxy that she was surprisingly successful. From that moment her career was assured and she became a public figure—famous as much for her fashion sense and *sang froid* as her singing.

A charity concert in aid of the Charing Cross Hospital held at the Palace theatre proved the biggest turning point in her life. The manager

Sir Alfred Butt heard her entertain and offered her a six-year engagement at the theatre. Her engagement began there on 22 October, 1906, and was for two seasons a year lasting eight or nine weeks. At first, she was doubtful that it was possible to find success with her lightly humorous ballads on the halls, and was discouraged further by a manager who told her she would be hissed off the stage. However, her particular way of delivering her material found instant favour with Palace audiences, not just with the stalls but with the gods too. This catapulted her into the limelight and gave her security in her career; "I thought the world had little else to offer me," she admitted. She sometimes appeared on the same bill as the French singer Yvette Guilbert, to whom she was often compared in the early days, although in terms of personality they were Poles apart. There were other women who entertained at the piano in a similar manner including Fanny Wentworth, whose chief success was with "The Tin Gee-Gee." Butt strove to attract the best entertainers he could, and there was a distinct touch of class about the acts he gathered there. Alongside Malcolm Scott, Vesta Tilley and George Robey, there was Barclay Gammon, who remained a great favourite there until his death in 1915. Butt attracted such diverse entertainers as the Americans Marie Dressler and Will Rogers.

It was at the Palace where Margaret's extraordinary vogue made her the hit of season after season and darling of the social set. She soon became a decided favourite of royalty who gave her many signed photographs and she often entertained the royal family at private performances. At one country house gathering she gave a recital for honoured guests, which included King Edward and his family. The King congratulated her on her performance, then he and other members of the party adjourned to another room. However, the Prince of Wales (the future George V) stayed behind and listened enraptured for two solid hours as he sat on the piano stool by the piano while Margaret went right through the score of *The Merry Widow*.[1] She played for many of the crowned heads of Europe and King Alfonso of Spain was so captivated by her rendering of "Waltz Me Around Again" that he requested it no less than three times in a row.

From the first she had her own unique style; even her entrances and exits became the stuff of legend. Once she sat next to a man at a dinner in the Piccadilly Hotel who informed her that he only went to the Palace to see her face and watch her come on and off stage. As W. Macqueen Pope recounted;

Publicity photo of Margaret with her Chihuahua Mitz,
given to her as a birthday present in 1907.

"Beautifully dressed, she would sail onto the stage and acknowledge the welcoming applause with a short, sharp, spasmodic smile. There was no warmth in it, it was just a contraction of the muscles of the mouth. Then she would seat herself and take off her elbow-length gloves with great care, and then proceed to remove her numerous rings and bracelets which she placed one at a time and with considerable exactitude of touch on top of the piano.

It was a routine which the audience watched spell bound with apparent enjoyment. And then she would begin."[2]

She looked at the audience while she played, not at the keys, and acted out each song with facial expressions. It took her many hours of practice to appear so effortless at the piano, and she worked tirelessly on her songs, in some cases for six months, until she was entirely satisfied. She kept introducing new material and found different ways of presenting her perennial favourites such as "Hullo Tu Tu" and "Catch Me." She spoke of her approach to her performance: "I always look straight at my audience after I play an opening bar. In the silence of the hall I speak the name of the song. As I am doing that a wave seems to come over me, and I feel the spirit of the audience vibrating to my will."[3] From the first her repertoire included the novel and unusual, the dreamy and occasionally the sentimental and sad. She had a penchant for singing songs for children in the character of a child, such as "Heaps o' Lickens" and "Fairyland." These were among her most popular pieces. She also sang settings of Stevenson's *Child's Garden of Verses* and Tennyson's "Birds in the High Hall Garden." There was a rare child-like quality to her approach; she retained a perennial sense of wonder. She always had the ability of inhabiting her songs and drew on a natural acting talent. Whether by royal command at Windsor Castle or on the pier at Brighton she gave it her all. At a small seaside concert on a sleepy Sunday, a local correspondent observed; "To have heard this lady's rendering of "The Maiden with the Dreamy Eyes" was both an intellectual and an artistic treat."[4] She often favoured the songs of her fellow lady composers, such as Liza Lehmann and Guy d'Harelot. It was an extraordinary era for women writers who were in the ascendancy as never before, or arguably, since. As an example of their great popularity, the sheet music of Teresa del Riego's "Oh, Dry Those Tears" sold 60,000 copies in its first six weeks alone.[5] Cooper's *oeuvre* was typified by clever but inconsequential material such as Fred Weatherly's "My Little Friend":

> "I had a little friend, a kind of confidential kitten,
> You know the sort of mixture of a magpie and an elf;
> She told me every detail of the man whom she had smitten,
> Which was really rather funny as I knew the man myself.
> She ran through all the things that he had promised her by dozens;

And how *she'd* no intention to be left upon the shelf;
He was handsome, he was rich, and had some noble Irish cousins,
All of which I could have told her—for I'd married him myself:
But I let her go on gushing, how he lov'd her how he miss'd her,
And how when they were married they'd be really in the swim;
Then I kissed the little darling like a most devoted sister.
And I went home in a taxi, and had it out—with him!"[6]

Portrait of Margaret in the Opalette postcard series, dated 1909.

Her natural preference was for serious songs, and she usually began her turn with one, but she was wary of veering too often away from the light-hearted. However, when she did so, the effect was often mesmerising to an audience. One reviewer described the spell she weaved with such a song as H. G. Pelissier's "My Moon"; "The pathos and longing which surged through each tuneful note converted the singer as if by some occult power into a creature of the song, and while the soulful air of 'My Moon' fell on the ear, everything else was forgotten. It was as though some rapturous enchantment came stealing over the listeners."[7] She often sang the works of Pelissier, a fellow pianist-singer who never made it as a solo act and was seen almost exclusively in revues. He died at the age of only 39. Her own personal favourite of his was "I Want Somebody to Love Me".

"I've sought the world;
Where can I find?
Lover who's constant,
Never unkind.
Men don't remember vows made in May
When comes December, love flies away."

Among Pelissier's Follies company was Ethel Allandale, whose impersonation of Margaret was deemed "almost cruelly true to the original" as an excerpt from her burlesque clearly shows;

"Oh! Sing to us once again, Maggie!
　　　Again, again, again;
Don't mind if the song hasn't got any sense,
　　　But let's have a catchy refrain.
My disdainful expression the public may blight,
But they swarm round the box-office every night,
Crying sing to us once again, Maggie,
　　　Again, again, again."[8]

If imitation is the sincerest form of flattery then Margaret was flattered a lot. Some of them merely mocked her, others tried to emulate her and some just sang the songs she made famous. There was then great novelty in what she was trying to do and the fact that she was one of the few women doing it. By sheer force of personality, she proved that an art which was usually the preserve of the concert stage or drawing room could be successful in the music-hall.

She was a good friend of Vere Smith, and sang many of his songs. Smith was a talented composer and driving force behind The Grotesques concert party. He even persuaded Margaret to join him in his show. Sadly, Smith died suddenly of a heart attack at the age of only 26 and was mourned by a large circle of friends and fellow professionals. As much as her musical ability it was her appearance that often caught the imagination of the audience. The Women's correspondent of a Scottish newspaper encapsulated her visual appeal; "Miss Cooper is tall, beautifully formed, with a slim, graceful figure, and from the moment she appears her winsome beauty captivates the audience."[9] Even the American poet Ezra Pound was not immune to her appeal, although he was predictably snide about her art. After seeing her at a concert at the Aeolion Hall he

Cooper's charming memoir *Myself and My Piano* was published in 1909 and is extremely rare. Everything about it is evocative of her era, particularly the Art Nouveau cover design

wrote; "Miss Margaret Cooper ... has far more personal charm than the pictures on her ads. would lead us to expect; she has magnificent arms and a figure the Greeks would have envied. She brings the British sentimental ballad as near to art, perhaps, as this highly autochthonous product is capable of being hoisted."[10] Moreover, she had the esteem of her fellow musicians. One of her most cherished possessions was a signed photo presented to her by the Polish pianist-composer Natalia Janotha inscribed "To Margaret Cooper whose art cheers the world's heart."[11]

At the height of her popularity in 1909 she was persuaded to write a small memoir, *Myself and My Piano*. This was published by John Ouseley in their One Shilling series. A slim but engaging volume issued in paper covers it is now an extremely rare item. Only a few libraries hold this, but it is unavailable on the inter-library loan scheme. It is a charming book with a period cover in the Art Nouveau style depicting a caricature of Margaret at her beloved piano. There are some pictures of her as a girl and many anecdotes about her life, stage experience and the famous personalities she encountered. Throughout she displays a gift for observation and a light touch with a self-effacement that belies her rather aloof public persona. She dedicated the book to her father who had died in March of that year.

(III) Mrs. Humble-Crofts on Tour

> *"She is a delightful humourist, her humour being subtle, dainty, sparkling and always infectious, but never forced."*
>
> – *Port Pirie Recorder*, 22 May, 1912

On 22 June, 1910, Margaret surprised almost everyone by her sudden marriage to Arthur Maughan Humble-Crofts, youngest son of the Rector of Waldron, Sussex. According to reports not even her closest friends were in on the secret. Arthur was a schoolmaster; at 27, he was six years her junior. Like his brothers, he had been educated at Eastbourne College where he was a member of Gonville (1894-1901). He went on to Keble College, Oxford, and graduated B. A. in 1905. He first worked as a teacher in Fermoy, Co. Cork in Ireland, and later at Cottesmore School, Brighton.[1] It was while he was teaching in Brighton that they met, when Margaret visited the school to give a recital. Unbeknownst to most of their friends, they became engaged in 1907. She had never felt the slightest nerves while performing before royalty, but admitted to being in agony in her fiancé's small village. There were only a few guests at their Wednesday morning wedding, mostly immediate relatives. The service was conducted by his father while his mother played the organ. According to a contemporary report; "Miss Cooper motored down from London with her aunt and brother (Alexander), who gave her away, arriving at Waldron a short time before the hour fixed for the wedding. She was married in a travelling dress [of grey silk]. The service was non-choral and simple in the extreme." After the ceremony there was a small lunch in the Rectory then the happy couple sped off in the car to spend their honeymoon in some quiet spot in Kent.[2] Arthur became her secretary, manager and chief support; he wrote the lyrics to some of her best songs, including "Catch Me" and "Agatha Green." He also took care of the business side of everything for her so that she could concentrate solely on her art. "My husband and I are great chums," she once remarked. "The firm is, 'We, Us, and Company, Limited!' We Both work hard!"[3] Shortly afterwards the couple moved into their house at 103 Dartmouth Road, Willesden Green. They named the house "Framba" which was because Margaret was a Fellow of the Royal Academy of Music (F. R. A. M.), and Arthur was a B. A.

Margaret with Mitz, possibly in the garden of her house in Willesden Green which she named Framba.

With her husband, she wrote some of her most popular songs, including "You Always Have to Pay a Little More." He contributed the lyrics and she the music. Some of these capture the essence of her idiosyncratic spirit. A particular favourite was "Agatha Green" in which an adventurous seventeen-year-old girl goes for a spin in an aeroplane with her uncle never to return:

> "Agatha said, as she gazed overhead
> 'How ripping to visit the stars
> We're up a good height, she's going all right

I'd love to see something of Mars'
So faster they went in a rapid ascent
And nearly got lost in a cloud
They hurried through space at a terrible pace
While Agatha shouted out loud,

"Isn't it heavenly, Uncle, up in an aeroplane
The speed is terrific, now that's the Pacific
And there in the distance is Spain
Hip, hip, hip, let her rip, Uncle
We'll show them what we are worth
You shall make merry, on whiskey and Perrier
When we get back to the earth."

Unsurprisingly, these unusual ditties captivated contemporary audiences. She also sang songs made famous by other people, and one of her biggest hits was "Waltz Me Around Again, Willie" which was originally sung by George Grossmith and later became associated with Florrie Forde, doyen of the halls. Margaret admitted to getting tired of singing the same songs, especially "Hullo, Tu Tu" but always contrived to find some new way of presenting it.

In the same year as her marriage, Margaret took part in the historic Centenary Concert of the Symphony Orchestra at Bournemouth. This was a showcase for some of the foremost composers of the day, and many of the greats in the growing renaissance of English music and culture in the Edwardian era were assembled. A famous photograph of the event shows Sir Dan Godfrey, Sir Hubert Parry, Sir Edward Elgar, Sir Charles Stanford and Sir Edward German. Among such august personages, the name of Margaret Cooper was something of an anomaly to many, and when Parry saw it on the list he demanded of conductor and organiser Dan Godfrey "Why on earth have you included her?" Godfrey replied tactfully "To give more variety."[4] Godfrey had known Margaret since her early days as a young student at the Royal Academy of Music and had followed her career with interest. In his memoir, he expanded on his reasons for including her in the concert which was taken as representative of the best of the national music; "I wanted to make sure of a good attendance, for I knew that British music, even in 1910 was not a sure magnet, and that Margaret Cooper's well-merited popularity would guarantee a full house and welcome for our leading composers."[5] Margaret was an integral part of the national music scene of that time, a fact confirmed when she was among those singers heard in Antarctica. When Capt. Scott set off on his ill-fated mission to reach the South Pole in 1910, one of the important items that the party took along was a gramophone and a selection of records. On those lonely nights far away from home and loved ones, the songs of half a world away had a special resonance for the men gathered there. Among these was one by Margaret, "Love is Meant to Make Us Glad" which had been adapted from *Merrie England*. Thomas Griffith Taylor, one of the survivors of the expedition remembered that between all the symphonies and comedy records, "Margaret Cooper's "Tis folly to run away from love" is the only clear girl's voice."[6] On the centenary of the expedition in 2012, a 48-song compilation of the records the party listened to was released, including her song.

She had always wanted to travel and had a special desire to visit Japan. As early as 1907 she discussed plans to tour the United States, and in 1910 it was announced that she would open on 14 March, 1911 in New York for P. G. Williams. However, this tour never took place, although another lady pianist from the Palace Theatre, Willa Holt Wakefield, successfully played at a theatre on Fifth Avenue.[7] Messrs. J. and N. Tate had tried to persuade Margaret to visit Australia for some time, and she finally began an Australasian tour in February, 1912. This year-long tour encompassed Australia, New Zealand and South Africa. She was supported by a company of artists including H. Scott Leslie, a cultured comedian who sang character songs; Horace Witty, a baritone and Charles Lawrence, a pianist. On the farewell leg of the tour they were joined by the Italian-Australian mandolin virtuoso Oreste Manzoni.

In Australia, her main itinerary was centred on Melbourne, Adelaide and Sydney, then in New Zealand in Christchurch and Wellington. However, she visited numerous other settlements in both countries, including some out-of-the-way places such as Wallaroo, Corawa, Geelong, Bendigo and Wagga Wagga. She visited the Blue Mountains and was fascinated by the curious natural phenomena of Whakarewarewa where the presence of sulphur in large quantities turned everything a different colour. Admitting that this was her first real holiday in eight years, she developed a love of travel and relished the wide-open spaces. She described the Australians as wonderful people; "The people here are so independent, so broad-minded, and such good sportsmen."[8] The one thing she did not like about the country were the mosquitos which were a real menace.

She travelled well-prepared, with a repertoire of about 140 songs and extensive luggage including eighteen dress boxes. Apparently cool and collected she was the victim of nerves at times and was especially nervous on her first night in Melbourne. "I had heard about the Australians, and of how keenly developed their critical faculties are," she commented. "But they received me so warmly that I have come to regard them as old friends."[9] She enjoyed her time in the city and declared that the audiences there were light and easy. Initially she gave seven performances a week, but such was her success that that was extended to eight.[10] On the final night of her season she was presented with a boomerang by a lady who had attended twenty-three of her twenty-six concerts there.[11] In June, she moved on to Sydney, where she proved just as popular, although she did say the audiences were a little slower to see the joke than they had been at Melbourne. She tailored her material to suit her audience and had much success with the Aboriginal-inspired ditty "I'll Build You a Gunyah" by local comedian Jack Cannot. In several shows she augmented the song with limelight effects. With this number, critics averred that she "completely caught the public taste."[12] There were several imitators in the antipodes, many of whom sang her songs without permission, and she considered the music publishers too lax in regard to protecting copyright. Even so, it was generally agreed that she was a unique artiste who brought her own inimitable style to bear on everything she did. As she explained "I vocalise my songs; mostly adhere to the melody except here and there where it may be necessary to emphasise the sense of a word or to point the humour or pathos of a line." She revealed that on average she received about 500 songs a week, out of which she found only a few that were worthwhile.[13]

Several commentators noted that her photographs seldom did her justice and made her look rather solemn and dark-haired. One theatrical journal described her actual appearance; "The real Margaret, musician, reciter-singer and witch-in-general, is a lively blonde with a seraphic smile." She was a decided trend-setter and fashion icon for style-conscious females of the day, and it was said of her that she never wore the same dress twice for any performance. Young girls copied her hairstyles and fashion diarists often reported on her latest assemblage; "A foam-white gown substantial enough in its outer filmy drape to be part of a mountain mist, sparkled with the glitter of gold fringe. The tunic of this heavenly creation … had a floating tail of white foam."[14] On another occasion "Margaret wore an inspired gown whereon ghosts of silver butterflies on a pale pink silk background glimmered through a blue veil. A girdle of rose buds completed a dainty effect."[15] She loved to wear beautiful dresses and particularly delighted in buying hats. On stage, she was picked out in a spotlight to great effect. Always immaculately turned-out, it was a major annoyance to her on tour that many of her clothes suffered during packing and emerged full of creases. In Perth she bought an electric iron and spent a long time trying to make her gowns presentable.

She found the audiences in Adelaide were hard work and later described them as "stolid." By far her best experience was in Ballarat where the audiences were most responsive and caught on to her charms quickly. In July she travelled on to New Zealand. She made an excursion into the country at Rotorua where she found the Maoris friendly and, in her own words "embarrassingly demonstrative." She and Arthur were honoured to be invited to the funeral of a Maori chief. Her appearances in Dunedin and Ashburton at the end of the month were cancelled because by then she was suffering from laryngitis.[16] In September she returned to Australia, beginning at the YMCA Hall in Sydney. This "Farewell" leg of the tour was intended to finish by the beginning of December, but her ship to South Africa, on the SS Marathon, was delayed, so the season ended instead on Boxing Day at the St. George's Hall in Perth. In the south of that city she enjoyed seeing the zoo, as she did in most cities she visited. She loved animals and was especially taken with the exotic birds in Australasia. She wished she could take home a cockatoo but that was not possible.

Margaret's style involved a certain air of hauteur; she played her songs with, metaphorically speaking, a disdainful smile, whether intentional or otherwise. At times, both she and her husband came over as haughty and high-handed to the literal-minded among the audience. Margaret was sure of her talent and had supreme self-confidence in her ability to win over any audience. Sometimes, their comments were taken the wrong way and some sections of the Australian press took great exception to both of them, but especially Arthur, and never passed an opportunity to make fun of him or belittle him either at the time or afterwards. He was viewed as tall, languid, aloof and disdainful. The papers said he smoked endless cigarettes and used to sign her pictures. The press felt slighted by comments she made in an interview at the end of her tour. So much so that even over a decade later when she died, this ill-feeling had not been forgotten. Margaret's obituary writer in the journal *The Bulletin* wrote; "She did well here, but gave a lamentable display of Clapham Junction superiority before departing by telling an interviewer what she thought of the 'colonials'."[17] The interview in question, one of a great many she gave, appeared to sour her long-term reputation in the country, at least as far as some elements of the press were concerned. Considering how successful the tour had been overall, this was indeed unfortunate. Both she and Arthur worked hard during the eight or nine months they spent there and Margaret gave a vast number of shows in some remote places. She was incredibly accommodating to interviewers, but her forthrightness was not appreciated by the famously straight-talking Australians. It is important to see her comments in the context of the time in which she lived when social etiquette was decidedly rigid. She was a traditionalist. For instance, she expressed surprise at the level of freedom in Australia and particularly that girls as young as fifteen were allowed out alone at nights, and, in her view, there was too much equality. The real objection came with another observation about how to improve the stock "What is wanted, I think, is that Australia should get a good number of the better class of English families out here. Canada, you know, is absorbing quite a number of aristocratic families."[18] Unsurprisingly, the Australians took great offence at this, although she clearly had not meant to do so, and had at best misjudged her remarks. In the aggregate the tour was a success and there was talk of a return to the country but in the event this did not happen.

In January, 1913 she travelled on to South Africa, where she ruffled some diplomatic feathers, but savoured her time in the country as a whole. Her main itinerary took in Durban, Pietermaritzburg and Cape Town. She reflected on her experience; "You cannot imagine how quaint it is to go to one's work on a rickshaw, instead of a motor, and hear the Zulu boys pattering round with their bare feet, singing chants as they work night and day. They soon get to know an artist, and some of them very curiously caught up snatches of my songs." The locals were especially fascinated by her ditty "On the Banks of the Serpentine" which they evidently thought was all about snakes.[19] She was supremely "in the moment" during her songs, but could be put off her stride by anyone in the audience who was not entirely with her. She instinctively knew if someone was not on her side. Anyone making a noise or coming in late would incur her wrath and she was the mistress of the withering put-down, sometimes just using the piano itself. Once, during her entertainment at a civic banquet an audience member suddenly got up in the middle of one of her songs and, in her words "waddled across the

Margaret the fashion icon in 1909.

room to talk to a boon companion." She waited until he was halfway across and then stopped suddenly and told him to sit down, which he did, totally embarrassed. She often used the piano to convey her displeasure at the ignorant or thoughtless behaviour of late entrants. She expressed this with a low, deep chord, "well thumped-out." That always did the trick. She upset several latecomers at a grand concert at Cape Town, when she gave a satirical musical accompaniment to the arrival of several Government House bigwigs. She plonked a bass note as each in turn sat down, which caused the people in question acute embarrassment and led the press to get into high dudgeon.

(IV) Her Glory Days

> *"She comes on the stage like an invigorating breath of air from the regions of melody and mirth, and when she retires at the end of her performance it is as though the sun has gone down."*

In March, 1913 she returned to England after more than a year away, and in June she began her engagement at the Coliseum for Oswald Stoll. By then she had reached the top of her profession and was especially popular during the war years when she gave many shows for soldiers on leave. The end of the war brought personal tragedy for her.

Some of her personal idiosyncrasies were remarked upon, such as her defiance of superstition evinced by her insistence on having dressing room 13, even though most theatres did not have one, and bringing with her a green rug to cover the red carpet purely because green was considered an unlucky colour.[1] Paradoxically, she always wore a particular copper bangle on her wrist for luck. This may have stemmed from an incident on London Bridge when the horse driving the carriage in which she was travelling was scared by something and bolted out of control for several miles. Margaret was convinced her number was up, and declared to her aunt who was with her inside the buffeted carriage "It's all over; there's no more singing for Margaret Cooper."[2] She had a delicate metabolism and admitted to being highly strung. As a rule, she never drank tea or coffee, only cold water because of problems with her digestive system since childhood. Famous for her poise on stage, she was once described as "supremely fair, divinely tall, and smilingly self-possessed."[3] She was also reserved to the point of shyness and acutely over-sensitive. Once she visited the London Stock Exchange with her husband who went there to meet his brother who was a broker. At that time women were not allowed inside, so Margaret waited outside the entrance. She was soon recognized by the young bloods of the Exchange and a crowd gathered around her, much to her mounting horror. Meanwhile, Arthur and his brother had slipped past her into a hotel. As she described the incident;

"I stood there feeling more horribly self-conscious every moment. Just as I was feeling every eye in the neighbourhood was fixed on me, a band of men came out of the Exchange whistling 'Hullu, Tu Tu.' When they had finished that they all bowed gravely to me, and proceeded to whistle 'Let Us Waltz Around Together.' I felt like gathering up my skirts and making a run for it. I was hot all over, when my husband and his brother arrived upon the scene. And the brutes merely laughed at me and told me it was a fine compliment."[4]

Perhaps her diffidence and skittishness hid a well of deep emotional feeling. She had some inner resolve which helped her cope with setbacks. For instance, she was once barracked mercilessly by the gallery at a theatre in Glasgow and fled the stage in floods of tears. Undaunted, she returned to the city on many occasions and over the years became a great favourite there. For relaxation after a long year spent doing "at homes," charity concerts and stage work, she took off in the summer to her beloved Broadstairs, which remained her favourite place.

With the outbreak of war, Arthur joined the Royal Navy Volunteer Reserve, and in 1915 transferred to the Royal Navy Auxiliary Service, where he worked in the Admiralty Office. Margaret gave a number of concerts for the troops. Rather than sing songs about the war, she often kept to her escapist favourites. This tactic was appreciated by many of the Tommies, who grew rather tired of hearing the same songs. At a typical smoking concert, one of the soldiers wrote of her performance; "She kept us amused from eight until half-past ten, sang eight songs, concluding with 'Waltz Me Around Again, Willie' She seemed to enjoy herself as much as we did, and I bet she never had a more appreciative audience. There was 'some' row when she did her last song."[5] She did a great deal of charity work throughout her life, but especially so during the war when she made many private visits to hospitals. She once appeared in the short, sentimental play *A Lesson in Love* in which she played an elderly vicar's wife. Her beloved Mons was in the headlines, and the peaceful town she had known as a girl became ever afterwards a byword for wholesale slaughter. "Dear old Mons," she once reflected, "I shall go and see it again when the war ends. It was there I spent some of my happiest days studying languages and music. I often wonder what it looks like now."[6] Margaret's brother Alexander was an officer on board HMS Tyndareus during the war, and was one of those rescued when the ship foundered in 1916.[7]

She sometimes sang songs about the war and towards the end of the conflict had some success with "My Angel Jim (of the Flying Corps)" which must have been one of the first songs about the airmen who risked their lives daily over France in flimsy biplanes. In November, 1917 Arthur received his commission, and as Lieutenant he was sent to Tynemouth where he continued to serve in a seaplane unit until the end of the war. Tragically, Arthur died just a week after the Armistice in November, 1918 of pneumonia following influenza at the age of only 35.[8] All four brothers joined up, and one of them, Capt. Cyril Mitford Humble-Crofts, of the Royal Sussex Regt. was killed in action on June 30, 1916.[9] They are both commemorated on the War Memorial panel inside the church at Waldron, as well as on the Roll of Honour at Eastbourne College. Arthur's funeral was conducted by his father who had the melancholy task of reading the benediction at the side of his grave. Apart from family and friends there was a large contingent of Officers and NCOs from the R. A. F. Naval Exchange. Margaret laid a large floral cross on top of the coffin.

After Arthur's death, Margaret initially appeared less often on stage, but then gradually re-commenced her tours. She remained a regular at the Coliseum, as well as the Victoria Palace, the Hippodrome et al, and was frequently seen on the concert platform. She was always available for local concerts and charitable events and made several successful northern tours. In many ways, the post-war years saw her at the height of her fame and the top of her chosen profession. By then she was reputedly the highest paid female entertainer at the piano, and was variously dubbed "the Diva of the Humorous Song" and the "Greatest Lady Society Entertainer in the World." Her detractors considered her "the Apotheosis of Triviality" and denigrated her art as that of timid suburbia. To others she was almost like a force of nature who put everything into her art.

She continued to seek out new material and had a knack of uncovering those genuine oddities that suited her eccentric style so well. These included several by St. John Brougham such as "Eric, the Egg" and she displayed her skill with elocution in the tongue-twister "She Shot Her Sister in a Fish Sauce Shop."[10] She continued to champion the works of T. C. Sterndale Bennett in particular. In "Six What-Nots" he set various anonymous verses to solemn music, and the effect on an audience as delivered by Margaret was immediate even in such an inconsequential limerick as "The Cam":

"There was a young man of the Cam
Who went in for his final exam;
When he said, "Have I passed?"
They replied, "No, you're last,"
He turned on his heels and said—
"Gentlemen, you surprise me!"[11]

Herman Lohr, Scott-Gatty and Paul Rubens were among the other composers who she favoured, and many wrote songs especially for her. She was known to sing several numbers of Noel Coward, and in a letter to his mother he wrote of having successfully placed a ditty with Margaret entitled "Bertha from Balham."[12] Her songs consisted of inconsequential lyrics with not even one foot in the real world, but they had undoubted charm and appeal to her audience. No one else could do such justice to "My Bungalow in Bond Street" and "Yachting in Regent's Park." In an interview in 1921 she spoke about the prospect of visiting Canada and the United States, but in the event this did not happen.

Margaret died suddenly on 27 December, 1922 at her home, due to a heart attack. She was 45. Her condition was said to have been complicated by asthma, and it was also stated that she had suffered a nervous breakdown. She had been appearing at the Victoria Palace until only a few weeks before, and continued to fulfil engagements throughout November. She had been due to play at the Boxing Day concert in the Pump Room, Bath, but withdrew a week before on account of acute gastritis.[13] Only a short while before she had promised in a letter to give a concert for St. Peter's church at Whitsuntide in aid of the Scout hut fund. Rev. C. H. S. Matthews, the vicar of St. Peter's reflected in the parish magazine; "She was very ill when she wrote, and it was entirely characteristic of her, despite her pain and weakness, to make this generous promise."[14] The funeral service was held at the Golder's Green crematorium and conducted by Rev. West Taylor of Christ Church, Brondesbury. The violet-coloured coffin was almost hidden beneath a mountain of flowers. There were so many flowers that a special carriage was commissioned for them. Among the tributes were a vast array from her musical friends and colleagues, including her long-time publishers Chappell & Co. A bouquet of heather and Eucalyptus was sent from Henry J. Wood and his wife Muriel, which had an inscription that read: "To a great artiste whose wonderful talent and the pleasure she gave will always remain a living memory."[15] There were other floral tributes from Ellen Terry and Sir Oswald and Lady Stoll.

Margaret died intestate and left property worth over £5,000 which went to her brother Alexander. In March, 1923, all her furniture and effects were auctioned off at the house, including her piano.[16]

At the time of her death, Margaret was engaged to the actor and singer Harry Welchman, who was then appearing in *The Lady and the Rose*. Nine years her junior, Welchman was going through a divorce from his first wife, although Margaret had not been named as correspondent. She often went to watch him at the theatre and he also helped out during

In the pre-WWI era Cooper often favoured esoteric and idiosyncratic numbers such as "In the Dingle Dongle Dell" (Above). The song is the title track on the compilation CD of her oeuvre released by Windyridge.

her own performances in flying matinees such as those in the summer of 1922 at the Cinema, Broadstairs and the Winter Garden, Bournemouth. Welchman's divorce was due to be finalised in January, 1923. He and Margaret were set to be married in February.[17]

Margaret Cooper is little remembered today and the few recordings that survive put her firmly in the dim and distant past. Her premature death robbed the entertainment world of a unique talent who might well have gone on to better things. She would have been an ideal broadcaster for the nascent BBC, founded in the year of her death. As Archibald Haddon noted "In these days, on the wireless, this artiste would have been a planet amongst the stars. Her 'Waltz Me Around Again, Willie' would have enraptured a million listeners."[18] A radio career would also have ensured that she was better remembered than she is now. Although few of her songs have appeared over the years, she is well-served by a CD compilation issued by Windyridge, entitled *Dingle Dongle Dell*. These twenty-four songs may well comprise her entire recorded output and alongside those released by HMV also includes the early sides she made for Pathe in 1907. Curiously, she never recorded "Waltz Me Around Again, Willie" which was one of the most popular numbers in her repertoire.

Other women followed in her wake including her friend Olive Fox, wife of Clarkson Rose, to whom she had passed on some of the work that she was unable to accept. Margaret's niece Enid Cooper continued to sing her aunt's songs at small-scale entertainments. Still, there was never anyone else quite like Margaret. Joyce Grenfell was perhaps in some ways similar, but she was more of an actress-comedienne, and never accompanied herself on the piano. Cooper was a unique artist, entirely apt for her era. In her lifetime she was often taken to task for her diffidence, and even chided for not being French. She was standoffish and contradictory, but quintessentially English. Had she lived on into the post-war age she may have become an anachronism. For a while in the early twentieth century she practically defined the point at which low and high culture coalesced. By sheer force of personality, she achieved the seemingly impossible and made the concert hall ballad successful on the music hall stage. In the process she helped the development of popular entertainment itself into a more sophisticated and varied art form than it had hitherto been.

See discography and list of credits on page 248.

Norman Long
(1893-1951)
"A Smile, a Song and a Piano"

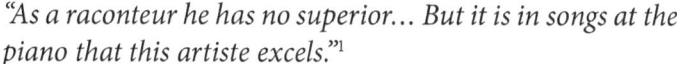

"As a raconteur he has no superior... But it is in songs at the piano that this artiste excels."[1]

(I) Concert Party

Norman Long was a pioneer of British radio and one of the first popular entertainers whose reputation was largely built up through his broadcasting and recording career. He had, however, risen in the usual way on stage and was popular on the halls, in concert parties and society entertainments alike. He was practically the last in the tradition of the entertainer at the piano. He flourished during the inter-war period, and his satirical, charming humour was apt for the age in which he lived. His observations, delivered in a disarming manner often gave telling insights into the complex social history of those turbulent years.

Norman Stuart Long was born in Deal on 26 March, 1893, the son of George Henry Long and Maud (nee Denne). In contrast to his evening-suited image, he came from a fairly humble background. His father was a boot maker descended from generations involved in the craft. Some of Norman's siblings helped out in the shop. His father was born in Walmer, Kent, of an old family of the county, but moved to Sydenham, south east London by around 1897. Norman's mother was one of eight children of David Denne, a grocer in Upper Deal who died young leaving a widow, Elizabeth, who later carried on the business and raised her family singlehandedly. As a teenager, Maud assisted in a local school and

Norman Long signed publicity still, c1926.

married George Henry Long at the parish church of St. Mary, Deal, in 1880.[2]

Norman was the youngest of four children and the only member of the family to show any musical ability. As a boy he studied the piano and violin, and sought to be a professional musician. Needing a steady income and, not feeling inclined to follow the family trade, he entered the prosaic world of Insurance instead where he became an agent. He spent five frustrating years in the office which did not pay that well, but all the while he began playing the piano at night and gaining experience at local concerts. He also organised a staff band among his co-workers. One of his earliest appearances locally, aged eighteen, was in April, 1911 at the Wesley Hall, Lower Sydenham, where his solos were considered one of the main highlights of the evening. Wherever he could he found work as an accompanist in concert parties, for dancers, at evening soirees, supper clubs or as entertainment during intervals in plays and films. A typical gig was that at the Stanley Hall, South Norwood, when he provided the music for the ballet dancer and teacher Gladys Groom in the fantasy *The Dryad*.[3] His repertoire in those years consisted mainly of classical works ranging from *Samson and Delilah* by Saint-Saens to *Norwegian Dances* by Grieg and *Humoresque* by Dvorak. He could have made his name as a serious musician; his real love was chamber and orchestral music, which he played and listened to in his spare time throughout his life.

In 1914 he joined Charles Heslop's "Brownies" concert party and made his professional debut that Easter at the Normanton Pavilion, Derby for £3 a week.[4] He enjoyed much success playing pier shows with that and other groups including "The Impromptus" run by Guy Stevens. Among the personnel of the latter group there was Eliot Makeham, billed as a comedian and stage manager. Makeham became a familiar screen character actor in the 1930s and 1940s and was especially memorable as the organist in the classic *A Canterbury Tale* (1944). *The Stage* observed of Long that he was "a pianist far above the average and accompanies the whole programme from memory."[5] In addition to his classical solos he also began to branch out into humorous ditties such as "When Mr. Kill Joy Comes to Town" which proved highly popular even then.[6] For a while he ran a small dance band with some success. Norman's father George did not live to see his son's burgeoning career. He died in 1914 at the age of 60, but his mother Maud lived on until 1931 when she was 75.

With the start of the war, Long initially served as a Private with the City of London Yeomanry. He continued to perform across the British Isles at intervals up until 1915. In a show at the Pavilion Gardens, Kingstown, Dublin, in September that year, a reviewer noted that he "showed his versatility in playing the violin and piano. As a violinist he possesses a beautiful touch, and played with artistic grace and finish."[7] He transferred to the Infantry and saw much service in France and Belgium. After that he joined the Royal Flying Corps, which he thought would be much more exciting. At the time of the Armistice in November 1918, he was just finishing his pilot's course. During his years in the services he had much success running regimental concert parties. He was a popular figure who was known for his eternally sunny disposition, and was given the nickname 'old teeth and trousers' which stuck.[8]

In 1919 Long was demobbed and resumed his professional career in earnest. He had already made his variety stage debut at the Lewisham Hippodrome, a splendid theatre with a distinctive dome and an impressive, ornate interior. It was one of the largest suburban theatres, with a seating capacity of 3,500.[9] He played all kinds of events such as rugby club and cricket dinners, school reunions, charity lunches, municipal entertainments, church hall functions and railway fundraisers.

It was while playing at the Connaught Rooms that he met the comedian Harry Hall who he credited with persuading him to abandon being an accompanist and try his luck instead with humorous songs. Hall gave him "The Ideal Homes" by the Music Hall artist Tom Clare. Long found this went down well and thereafter he decided to switch to comic songs and patter instead.[10] He appeared again in pier shows and began to attract attention as an artist in his own right with Herbert Burney's "The Zeniths" concert party. At the Rusholme Pavilions, Manchester, Long was praised not just for his talent on the piano but for his natural facility as a storyteller. A witness wrote; "Mr. Norman Long at the piano, is not only an accompanist and helper of others, but combines the humour strongly, his

The impressive Lewisham Hippodrome, opened in 1911 and designed by the great Frank Matcham, where Long made his theatrical debut.

stories receiving added weight in the admirable skilful handling."[11] By the dawn of the 1920s he widened his repertoire and was soon established as a class act. At a War Memorial Concert at the West Cliff Hall in Ramsgate, he was judged the main attraction on the bill. The local correspondent wrote of him; "Whether in "dude" or humorous songs, in variations of a popular melody, or with storyette, Mr. Long was delightful and upon his second appearance was compelled to give two encores."[12] He combined his natural facility with humour and his musical skill to great effect and his interpolations of popular songs furnished in different styles proved a popular part of his act. He would take an innocuous tune such as "I'm Forever Blowing Bubbles" and interpret it as a Chopin nocturne, a Debussy military march, a Liszt rhapsody or a futuristic fantasy. Following this he would give a topical song and tell stories in his own inimitable style. This variety within his act was part of the secret of his success and although modest by nature he was a fine musician in his own right. He became a fixture at the Savoy Hotel where he proved a decided hit with the Savoy Orpheans, and appeared as compere on several sides they recorded. In the summer seasons of 1921 and 1922 he was a regular at the Chalet in Skegness, run by George Burrows, for whom he had a high regard. It was while he was filling in for an indisposed Melville Gideon for a week, he appeared in a prestigious engagement at the Palace Theatre, London with "The Co-Optimists." It was then that he began to attract the attention of West End audiences and even scouts from the newly-established British Broadcasting Corporation.

(II) "All for Ten Shillings a Year"

The BBC was founded on 18 October, 1922, and broadcasting began on 14 November from Marconi House on The Strand. Ten days later, Long was the first comedian heard on the station and his opening number was "Down at Our Village in Zummersett."[1] In the days of "cat's whiskers" radio sets and granite microphones, the equipment was still fairly rudimentary not to say cumbersome and recording took a bit of getting used to. Things were informal at Marconi House, where the recording took place in a little room on the seventh floor. He recalled "My first experience of broadcasting was of a man standing over me with a little telephone receiver, and every time I moved my head anywhere this damn thing followed me." One had to be careful where one walked, as he further described the scene; "The room contained more yards of wire than I ever dreamed existed, gadgets fixed up on sugar boxes, microphones like hand telephones; but principally wire—wire everywhere!"² For this historic first he was paid precisely nothing. Nevertheless, it was all good publicity and he was soon invited back. He also received his first deluge of fan mail. "By December," he wrote wryly "I had become such 'value' that I was actually rewarded with a cheque 'for nominal expenses.' It was for one guinea." It might have been history in the making, but few had any conception of what impact the new medium would have on national life. He later recalled; "I may as well confess that I hadn't a glimmering of what radio was going to mean to the listening public or to me as an artist."³ He soon became a mainstay of the network in those early days, his clear tones, easy manner and light touch came over the ether well and he proved a natural broadcaster. When broadcasting began from Savoy Hill the following year in May, 1923, Long was also among the first artists heard there, and in addition was an early outside broadcaster. He became such a regular and popular figure that before long he earned the sobriquet "The Charlie Chaplin of the Wireless."⁴

The tone of the early BBC was set by the edict that announcers should always be attired in evening dress, despite the fact that they were unseen. There was a distinctly refined feeling to the output and red-nosed comics were not the order of the day. Bertram Fryer, the light entertainment programme controller in those days, had a distinct vision in mind of the kind of quality required for the new medium. His mission was to raise the bar for vaudeville; "The public only wants to listen to the very best artists and listen to the very best in comedy," he averred. It was by no means easy to reach the standard required, and although between 1500 and 2000 amateurs and professionals auditioned each year only one percent were ever successful. The programmes were carefully put together so that they reflected Variety in the true sense of the word, with singers, instrumentalists and dance bands prevalent, and only one comedian per show. There would be one show with a broad comedian and dance band along with other entertainers, and a different show with a more cultured audience in mind with several classical pieces, a French song and a more highbrow comic. A visiting American critic who caught Long's act observed that he "… looked like a golf caddy, but sang and entertained with material he had written himself in unique style."⁵

His broadcasting fame meant that he was in constant demand and invited to appear at smart West End cabaret shows. He provided the entertainment at the opening of several exclusive restaurants in London, including Whiteley's on Queen's Road and Oddenino's on Regent Street.[6] He was among the guests at the grand exhibition of the phonograph at Harrods in conjunction with HMV, along with other famous artists on the label including Jack Hylton. The week-long event displayed the leading technology of the electronic age and demonstrated the whole process from recording to manufacture of the disc.[7] He also played at such venues as the short-lived Lido club near Oxford Street, which was never able to shake off its shady reputation. After just a couple of years it was raided by the Flying Squad, and although nothing was found it closed soon afterwards.

"Rahnd the Houses" was a comic and sentimental Cockney character song of the kind Long brought to life so well.

In conjunction with his broadcasting career, Long began recording from the mid-1920s onwards. He bought several songs from his friend Clarkson Rose, and one of his first records was a version of his "The Drage Way" with its refrain "We always lay your lino on the floor." Furniture retailer Drage pioneered the Hire Purchase scheme to buy furniture on the never-never and sought to make debt seem almost respectable among the aspiring young middle class. The company insisted that customers didn't need references and that they would send the furniture discreetly so the neighbours wouldn't be suspicious. Such easy credit sounded too good to be true and probably was;

> "'See, I've only just got married, and I'm on the rocks and broke,'
> He said, 'Don't let that worry you, why money is a joke!
> We only run our business to oblige you sort of folk,
> And we always lay your lino on the floor.'

...

Then I said, 'The neighbours in our road are bound to know we're new,

> And when they see your van, they're sure to say a thing or two.'
> He said, 'They won't, we send the stuff in vans as plain as you,
> And we always lay your lino on the floor.'"

Rose recalled in his memoir; "I sold him a song for eight guineas, which, he told me, lifted him from comparative obscurity to an established position on the music-halls. Its reception was electrical." Some years later, Rose wanted to buy the song back to use on a Stoll tour and Long reluctantly agreed.[8] He recorded mostly for Columbia, as well as HMV, and there were also some sides for Regal as well as Decca.

In 1927 Long received one of the ultimate accolades when he appeared in the Royal Command Performance at the Victoria Palace theatre, alongside Billy Bennett, Lily Morris and many others. This was the first Command Performance to be broadcast. Long admitted "I was perhaps a trifle nervous when I first went on the stage, but as soon as I found the audience were on my side, and that their majesties could appreciate a joke, my nervousness disappeared."[9] Both the King and Queen laughed heartily at his jokes and the King was seen to make a note of his name. It was not

"You Mustn't Do It After Eight o' Clock" was typical of Long's satiric approach to the edicts of the nanny state, and a popular number during his summer season at Blackpool in 1929.

his first appearance before royalty; he had previously played for the Duke of York (the future George VI), as well as Prince Henry, Princess Mary, Viscount and Viscountess Lascelles and others.[10] In all he appeared at three Command Performances and also played for European royalty. But Long never lost the common touch and followed up his Royal appearance in 1928 with a summer season at Blackpool in Lawrence Wright's *On with the Show* revue. He said he had the time of his life there where he loved to spend most of his leisure hours on the nearby golf links. He was a bit of a golf fanatic and loved the sociability of the game, especially when the players could adjourn to the 19th hole.

The rise of broadcasting led to an inevitable clash between the long-established interests of the theatres and those of the nascent medium of radio. The first stirrings of discontent were voiced in 1923 when the Concert Artists' Association held a meeting to discuss the subject. When called on to address the meeting, Long managed to keep things light-hearted but made his views clear. In his remarks he said; "On the basis of payment suggested by Mr. Warren, if £2 2s. was a proper fee for entertaining fifteen men, then two Sunday League engagements should provide sufficient for a long holiday in the South of France (Laughter). He was not absolutely in favour of broadcasting, but he was not going to be bullied into doing one thing or the other."[11] He was true to his word. Nonetheless, the theatres were not about to back down in establishing their rights in the matter and a powerful combine, the General Theatre Corporation, exerted great influence in the late-1920s and early-1930s to fight their cause. The G. T. C. warned artists that if they should broadcast it would violate their contracts, thereby establishing a precedent. Hence, by agreeing to fulfil an engagement with the BBC in January, 1933, Long forfeited his chance to appear at the London Palladium, even though the dates were several days apart.[12] He expressed the hope that his future bookings would not be affected. "I am not adopting a defiant attitude towards General Theatres Corporation," he declared, "But I do not feel disposed to sever my association with the BBC which has lasted over ten years."[13] The issue divided opinion generally and led to a stand-off with the BBC, who held the broadcasting monopoly. The G. T. C. sent warnings to all the other leading artists and several, including Gracie Fields and Layton and Johnstone, came into line with the theatre combine. In the long term, this action did not interfere with Long's career greatly and he continued to appear on stages around the country for many years afterwards, often playing several engagements in a day. At the same time, he remained a valued employee of the BBC.

In 1933, as if to reassert themselves as independent artists greater than both theatres and broadcasters, sixty of the most famous vaudeville artists formed their own company called "Town Hall To-night Limited." The idea was to do one-night-stands and fit-up shows at town halls across the country, like the buskers of old. Most of the long-established names of the profession were involved including Nellie Wallace and Billy Merson, as well as more recent stars, Long among them.

In recognition of his recording and radio success, Long made several short films for Pathe in the Pathetone series, and also featured in a couple of feature films. The Pathetone shorts recorded for posterity the essence of his stage act and persona. His first feature was a musical revue produced by the Stoll company. *The New Hotel* (1932) was largely centred around a couple of acrobatic dancers but was essentially a platform for several cabaret acts. Of these, Long received much of the praise from critics for his turn. He appeared as himself in *Royal Cavalcade* (1935), sometimes known as *Regal Cavalcade,* a semi-documentary celebration of the Silver Jubilee of King George V. The film was a sweeping survey of the momentous years between 1910 and 1935. Actors played famous figures of history such as Robert Falcon Scott and Lloyd George. A key selling point of the film was the presence of such old music-hall favourites as George Robey, and Alice Lloyd.

(III) "We Can't Let You Broadcast That!" His Songs of Satire and Social Comment

Long composed the music for most of his songs, but generally speaking not the lyrics. He sometimes used the works of other notable writers. Apart from those of Clarkson Rose and Tom Clare previously mentioned, he also favoured composers such as Malcolm Ives and H. M. Burnaby. His choice of material reflected many of the preoccupations and concerns of the fraught inter-war years. His re-imagining of the 1812 Overture as the "1914 Overture" used some of the popular tunes of the First World War. His music was often inspired musically, such as his "Prelude in Asia Minor." Songs such as "Marrers" and "Them Days 'as Gorn" delivered in character encapsulated much of his unique appeal. His dry delivery was perfect for "It Wouldn't Have Done for the Duke, Sir," the tale of a nouveau riche employer as seen under the withering gaze of his butler. Occasionally, his material overlapped with other performers such as The Western Brothers ("It's All Too Terribly Thrilling") or even his friend Billy Bennett ("No Power on Earth"). Bennett and Long were good friends and enthusiastic members of the Vaudeville Golfing Society and other social organisations, including the Water Rats, relishing those after-hours concerts for fellow professionals only. Long also co-wrote songs with other friends including Ronald Frankau, with such ironic ditties as "I Wonder What Made Her Go." He sang a version of Frankau's classic "Going Down" about a department store lift, which was surely an early template for the signature tune to the popular sitcom *Are You Being*

Served? Long kept changing his material which was often topical, and sometimes included some totally unexpected things such as a burlesque of a Spanish senorita.[1] There was the familiar complaint since the Great War of declining standards, whether in the quality of building as in "Ideal Homes" or food as seen in "Why is the Bacon So Tough?" He often sang Cockney character songs which attacked bumptiousness including "The Council Schools Are Good Enough for Me"

> *"It's just a lot of tosh, this trying to talk all posh*
> *And a high falutin' accent down in Whitechapel don't wash."*

Another number was "The Barrers in the Walworth Road" where it was possible to get anything—with no questions asked;

> "You can buy a marble clock
> What'll land you in the dock
> On the barrers in the Walworth Road
> And if you're burgled one night late
> You can find your silver plate
> On the barrers in the Walworth Road."

The characters he portrayed dispensed a kind of down-to-earth wisdom and common sense. They were vaguely content with their lot, but sometimes sought to escape to better things, as typified by "Ten Pahnds Dahn" (1933) in which a resident in run-down Hackney is persuaded to attempt to buy a house in suburbia via an early version of the 'right to buy' scheme:

> *"I never really liked the 'ouse in 'ackney Road,*
> *It wasn't nearly worth the rent we always owed.*
> *But now I pay instalments till the 'ouse belongs to me,*
> *And I done a bit o' reckoning and as far as I can see*
> *It's going to be mine for keeps in 1983*
> *And I'm only paying ten pahnds dahn."*

He had a penchant for songs about home in which he often longed for settled but strangely elusive domesticity ("That Little Back Garden of Mine"). He sang affectionate tributes to bus conductors ("Nothing Else to do All Day") and dustmen ("Working for the Mayor and Corporation").

"Hidden Heroes" was a satirical salute to milkmen, postmen, policemen, doctors and taxi drivers. He showed a great affinity for the honest hard-working man struggling to find a bit of pleasure despite the efforts of the government of the day ("Is it British?"). There was a decided undercurrent of nostalgia running through his work, and a feeling of empathy with old comrades-in-arms from the war who had fallen on hard times, "Rahnd the Houses" being a good example of this, a charming, sentimental character song about a street musician playing outside a select West End restaurant. Beneath everything there was a sense of betrayal about the longed-for "Land fit for heroes" promised by the politicians after the war, and the creeping sense of doom that the same thing might happen again. Often, his comment on the economic situation in an age of austerity showed that nothing ever really changes:

> "Now they say the country stands in need of real economy,
> So sacrifices none of us should mind
> They'll tax my beer and baccy and my sugar and my tea
> And every other thing that they can find.
> The politicians know who's going to save them from the wreck
> I know what the result is going to be
> 'Cos I'm the silly mutt who always gets it in the neck
> And the bloke who'll save the country will be me."

In "Firty Fahsand Quid" he imagined what he might do if he won the Irish Sweepstake and realised it was the small everyday luxuries that meant most, but concluded that having so much money might cause more problems than it was worth:

> "I'll take the wife and family down to Margate by the sea
> Cockles, rock and winkles; shrimps and strawberries for tea
> A-sittin' in them deckchairs with your conscience clear and sound
> A-smilin' at the bloke and saying "Can you change a pound?"
> Instead of hopping out of 'em each time he comes around.
> Firty fahsand quid!"

Long was a favoured subject of cartoonists, such as Nerman in *The Tatler*. Signed postcard, c1932.

In "Toasts" he satirised the changing mores and new-found sense of independence of the flappers of the post-war generation. In a similar vein he provided an ironic comment on the "fast girls" of the Jazz age in "Otherwise She's Mother's Kind of Girl":

> "Can she to a nightclub be persuaded?
> Only if she knows it will be raided.
> Does she wear nice frocks?
> Oh yes—more or less, mostly less
> Otherwise she's mother's kind of girl."

He also sent up the 1920s predilection with a particularly Western form of Eastern exoticism in "Under the Bazunka Tree" and the tantalising dancer in De Sylva, Brown and Henderson's "Seven Veils":

*"She wriggled like a worm with Hives
And the King said, you can poison all my wives,
Off came another veil..."*

In many of his numbers, women were often viewed as figures of distant desire. There was sometimes a hint of melancholy in such songs as the lament of a bachelor who longs for marriage but feels he's missed the boat ("I'm Looking Now for Any Kind of Sweetheart"). Elsewhere he dealt with class fixations ("We Montmorencies") and the everyday nuisances of the age such as "Stiff Collars." Class-consciousness was prevalent at that time and he was scathing about pomposity and pretentiousness everywhere. In "The Willows" he satirised those who give themselves airs by calling their house a name rather than settle for a number like the hoi polloi:

"The Glorious Month of May" one of a number of songs Long co-wrote with Leonard Pounds.

"We've a nice little house in a nice little street,
And the name on the gate is The Willows;
We've a nice little maid in an apron so neat
At the Willows the Willows, the Willows.

On outward appearance our money is spent,
Folks think we're rich, but we haven't a cent;
But will-owe the tradesman and will-owe the rent
At the Willows, the Willows, the Willows."

He was especially trenchant on pettifogging officialdom in "You Mustn't Do It After Eight O' Clock" and gave a brilliant interpretation of the insufferable snobbery represented by The Western Brothers' "Aren't We All?"

"Aren't we rather wealthy, aren't we all select,
Absolutely healthy, cultured and correct;
Thoroughly expensive, blood precisely blue,
Clientele extensive—county too.
Oh, we're really most *delight*ful people
Aren't we all?

Living in the suburbs in a house of new design,
Busy talking platitudes, and pouring out the wine
Sitting with the blinds up every evening when we dine
Oh, we're really most *delight*ful people
Aren't we all?"

On radio, one of the most interesting programmes in which he played a prominent role was *Reminiscences of Piano Humour*, presented by Tom Clare and featuring many of the icons of the field including Nelson Jackson, Margaret Cooper and Barclay Gammon. Long was often compared to Gammon whom he resembled somewhat. Another programme in a similar vein was *Sing Me a Song of Social Significance*. In 1934 Long was appropriately enough asked to open a special variety show to celebrate the BBC entitled *The First Twelve Years*. Beginning in 1922, with himself, this charted the years up to 1934, ending with a hitherto unknown artist as the final act.[2] He was a regular on *Music Hall* for many years, as well as sister programmes *Vaudeville* and *Variety*. From 1935 to 1940 he was a key member of *Stanelli's Stag Party*, also known as *Stanelli's Bachelor Party*. This was a kind of musical crazy gang of the airwaves and comprised several entertainers such as Jim Emery, Tommy Russell and Ernest Marconi, who were each week joined by guests such as The Two Leslies (Leslie Sarony and Leslie Holmes). Irish-born Stanelli was a talented violinist who had studied at the Royal Academy of Music but made a career on the variety stage as an entertainer, either solo or in a double-act. He and Long were the nucleus of the group whose infectious buoyant spirits proved popular and they toured the halls for three years, playing to packed houses. One of his duets with Stanelli was "All for Ten Shillings a Year" a satiric song about what great value the BBC licence fee represented. When broadcasting, Long said he preferred smaller audiences of forty to sixty rather than big gatherings of five hundred, which he thought tended to make a performer play to the crowd at the expense of good microphone technique.[3] He was such a well-liked personality and delivered his songs so disarmingly with a smile that he was able to satire his employer the BBC pointedly at times on record and still be feted by them, as with "London and Daventry Calling" and, more pertinently, "Luxembourg Calling." This latter was an apt comment on the monopoly enjoyed by the corporation and specifically its denigration of the main competition by blocking the signals from Luxembourg. One of his songs that landed him in trouble and received posthumous fame was "We Can't Let You Broadcast That!" This was a cleverly-worded stab at the censor and the BBC's avowed policy of public service broadcasting, which led it to avoid giving offence at all costs. It was a witty dig at the 1930s equivalent of political correctness. Needless to say, it did not go down well with his employers who felt so offended they banned the record. Banning anything always leads to more interest as time has proved, and the song has appeared on several compilations over the years including the 75-track compilation *This Record is Not to Be Broadcast*. John Peel brought it to widespread attention on his radio show. Long's song may seem mild enough but showed that his satire, however disarmingly delivered, hit the mark.

> "I said, 'Here's a nice song called Violets,'
> They said, 'Oh that's much too blue,'
> I said, 'Is Robin Adair okay?'
> They said, 'Robin Adair? My hat!
> Just think of the bald-headed men you'll upset!
> We can't let you broadcast that!'
>
> ..

> So I looked my list of songs up,
> The position was getting grave,
> I said, 'Here's a nautical song, A Life on the Ocean Wave,'
> They said, 'Life on the Ocean Wave,
> With all these cruises on the mat?
> Why, you're advertising the steamship lines,
> We can't let you broadcast that!'"

Such a song seems prescient given current debates, and prefigured Stan Freberg's equally incisive "Elderly Man River" by over twenty years. Another inspiration for satire was television. After some experimental broadcasts in the early 1930s, BBC Television made its debut in November, 1936 from studios in Alexandra Palace. The earliest programmes were seen by the few people who had television sets, estimated at around 500. Sets were expensive but the number grew as the novelty caught on. Shortly after, Long introduced "When Your Television Set Comes Home" a witty song about the new medium before anyone knew quite what to expect:

> "There'll be fashion shows on Mondays,
> Girls in frocks and girls in undies
> When your television set comes home.
> By mannequins so gorgeous
> Your emotions will be stirred
> You can wink at them all through the show
> And never get the bird."

Long recorded prolifically and there are several excellent compilations of his songs available, including a comprehensive 2-CD release by the Australian company Crystal Stream Audio. Please refer to the detailed discography.

(IV) Keep Smiling

> "It seems but yesterday when Norman was on the pier at Blackpool for the season, giving visitors a taste of the breezy joie de vivre so akin to the bracing air outside the pavilion, which wrapped the promenaders in its life-giving folds."[1]

The intimacy of small venues was suited to his style, but he got over the footlights remarkably well in big auditoriums and was a hugely popular star in variety theatres. For many years he topped the bill at the Victoria Palace and other halls. He possessed undoubted warmth as an artist, and this, together with his infectious humour and unassuming nature made him a decided favourite. At the Penge Empire on Whit Monday in 1932 he stopped the bill with his act. A local reviewer declared "Curtain after curtain he took and appeared in front of the tabs innumerable times, before he finally had to make a speech and introduce the next act."[2] He often played several engagements in a day, and on Jubilee Night, 1935, he played the first house at the Theatre Royal in Chatham, caught a special plane to Brighton, where he recorded his Jubilee broadcast for the BBC, then hopped on the plane back to Chatham where he appeared at the second house.[3] He continued to appear in concert parties and Pierrot shows throughout his career such as "The Paramount Pierrots" alongside Ernest Butcher and Charles Hayes. Butcher was at one time the husband of actress and singer Muriel George, with whom he had a successful act singing folk songs. In 1935 Long joined veteran Clarkson Rose's *Twinkle* show which, despite being an old-fashioned kind of spectacle in the age of revue, was surprisingly well-received. Long was proud to be elected chairman of the Concert Artists' Association with whom he enjoyed many a convivial evening at the annual dinners held at the Park Lane Hotel. "I can recommend the concert party to any youngster who wants to find fame in later life," he once remarked. "The happiest days of my life were spent as a pianist in concert parties. When I retire, I intend to form my own party."[4] As a familiar radio personality of the 1930s he appeared several times on highly collectable cigarette cards. He was often caricatured by cartoonists and

Long was a naturally cheerful soul both on and off stage. Signed publicity photo, c1935.

was a favourite subject of impressionists by such entertainers as Stanley Holloway.

In July, 1937 he made a brief tour of Canada and the United States, travelling with his sister Maud, although it is not certain if he did any shows there. In Canada they were the guests of Al and Bob Harvey's parents. Al and Bob were singers with Stanelli's Stag Party.[5] He returned with several new jokes and songs. Over the years Norman appeared in some advertisements for such items with relevance to his profession as Philco radios and Boyd's Pianos as well as Cherry Blossom shoe polish no doubt recalling his days in the services.

In 1939 he took a turn entertaining at the first ever Butlin's holiday camp at Ingoldmells near Skegness, along with a young Mantovani and His Tipica Orchestra.[6] In December, 1940, due to the Blitz on London, Norman and his sister Maud left Sydenham and took a bungalow at Mablethorpe, on the Lincolnshire coast. While there he appeared locally at numerous charity functions, his first being a Home Guard dance. Throughout the war he continued to entertain across the stages of the country and on radio he was a regular of the forces' programmes such as *Naafi Presents the Ensa Half Hour, Workers' Playtime, I Break for Music, To Meet the Army* and *Navy Mixture*. Some of his appearances on *Workers' Playtime* were issued on a compilation album recently, including his song "Let's Have a Damned Good Grouse." In *The Happidrome* he appeared alongside such big radio stars as Tommy Handley, and also the old stalwarts Harry Champion and Nellie Wallace. *Stanelli's Bachelor Party* was revived with Leslie "Hutch" Hutchinson as a guest, and Long also featured in the New Years' Eve broadcast *Ring Out the Old*. In addition, his records were regularly heard on the listeners' request show *Morning Star*. On 2 November, 1940, he was playing at a theatre in Bristol on the first night of a heavy bombing raid and witnessed much of the devastation. He was distinctly impressed by the spirit of the people of the city who showed great pluck and fortitude; "It was wonderful," he said.[7] He always kept changing his material to suit the times and some of his popular war songs and monologues included "Shikelgruber," "Where Does Poor Pa Go in the Blackout?" "When We Win the War" and "In Our Village ARP." He did countless shows during the war entertaining the troops and patients in hospital, often gratuitously. He was equally happy to do shows in out-of-the-way Lincolnshire villages as favours for his many friends in the county, as elsewhere in the country. His niece was a Land Army girl for four years. On radio, Norman was profiled in the series *King Pins*

With the end of the war in 1945, Long was semi-retired from the business and went to run the Bolt Head Hotel in Salcombe, Devon, until his death in 1951. The hotel is the large building almost in the centre of the picture.

of Comedy in which he was interviewed by Wilfred Pickles, and also contributed to a programme of theatre reminiscences, *The Ghost Walks on Fridays*. In 1942, Long celebrated twenty years as a broadcaster when he presented a show about the development of variety broadcasting, appropriately entitled *There's a Long, Long Trail*.

At the end of the war in Europe in May 1945, Norman and Maud, not forgetting their beloved dog Billy, left Mablethorpe and moved to Devon where Norman became a hotelier. He bought the Bolt Head Hotel in Salcombe, which re-opened for visitors on 23 June. It was a comfortable place that had modern electric fires in all rooms. It was described in contemporary advertisements as "the hotel with the friendly, intimate atmosphere above the sea." On occasion he could be persuaded to give a few numbers at the piano. He lived at Tarifa Lodge in Salcombe and was frequently in demand locally for charity functions and galas. Several charities were close to his heart including the Variety Artistes Foundation and the Not Forgotten Association of disabled ex-Servicemen. He was semi-retired from the stage but maintained his broadcasting career. His last official theatrical performance had been at the Palace Theatre, Plymouth, in February, 1945, but he occasionally did the round of theatres after the war. His links to Salcombe went back several years and an evacuee to the town remembered that Long regularly visited his father's shop;

> "He entertained the American sailors in Cliff House, a large communal building overlooking the harbour and used for local events such as dances and town meetings. Of course, when Norman did his repertoire in front of the yanks it was a little more risqué … He often came striding into our shop with a walking stick and swagger, rather like a sergeant major. He and dad would ponder, and put right, the state of the country and the war. I suspect Norman was a bit of a Bolshie too. Or perhaps he just longed for the sound of a Cockney voice."[8]

In *Who's Who* Norman listed his interests as golf, motoring, horse-riding and boxing. One of his favourite pastimes was playing darts, and he made certain there was a dartboard in his hotel. Another of his interests was cine-photography. He was also a Freemason with the Thornton Heath Lodge.[9] In the post-war years he was still heard on the radio in such programmes as the perennials *Music Hall* and *Monday Night at Eight*. On the light-hearted quiz *Whatever Next* in 1948, recorded in nearby Bideford, he was the mystery guest. He appeared on several episodes of the panel show *Can You Beat It?* in 1950, the last of which was broadcast in the autumn. He was taken ill quite suddenly not long after Christmas that year suffering from Broncho-pneumonia. He was admitted to the Mount Stuart nursing home in Torquay on a Saturday but rapidly declined and died there on the following Wednesday, 10 January, 1951, aged 57. His death was mourned by his many friends in the business and his fans. There were many co-professionals at his funeral at Efford Cemetery in Plymouth.[10] A memorial service was held at St. Martin-in-the-Fields in February. Long was recalled with great affection and generous tribute was paid to him. The correspondent of *The Stage* wrote that friends "will miss his genial personality, his infectious smile and a man who had the best interests of the profession at heart."[11] There were many of his fellow performers present including Arthur Askey, and colleagues from the BBC. It was a simple but moving service. Ted Ray read the lesson and the B. B. C. singers sang Bunyan's "Valiant for Truth." Long's friend and colleague Stuart Hibbert recalled: "When I first met him, I was immediately struck by his friendliness, genial personality, charming smile, and that flash of light in the eye that told of a sharp mind. He was always the same, no sign of age or change came to him. His single-mindedness and sincerity were outstanding; it was certain he was a happy man; he revelled in his work, giving pleasure through it."[12]

In his will, Long left over £20,000 gross (£11,000 net), mostly to his sister Maud, and to several charities including the V. A. F, which was always close to his heart.[13] The copyright to his songs was passed to his sister. The Bolt Head Hotel along with all fixtures and fittings was sold at auction the following September.[14] He was heard once more on radio in *These Radio Times,* broadcast in the year of his death. This was an

Several first-rate CD compilations of Long's songs are available, including *My Little Austin Seven* from Windyridge.

affectionate salute to the world of music-hall which was rapidly passing from the public consciousness.

Talented but modest, if not shy, Long was greatly liked in the profession and out of it. One of his friends from his days at Skegness in the early 1920s reflected on his unaffected personality; "I should say he does not know the meaning of the word "side." Success has not, as it does so many, spoilt him."[15] He never took himself seriously and delighted in telling stories against himself. He was one of the last of the line of witty entertainers at the piano. Tastes, as ever, changed, and the art that flourished in the first third of the twentieth century, dwindled in the second third and practically vanished after that. There were some later comedians who mined similar territory to Long, including Flanders and Swann, who were perhaps closest to him in spirit. They wrote songs about gasmen, tennis and a poignant paean to the end of steam railways which one could easily imagine would have appealed to Long. There was a streak of skilful musicality and whimsy in later artists such as the Danish pianist Victor Borge and the multi-talented Gerard Hoffnung, although his instrument of choice was the tuba. A similar playful musical talent is seen in a modern comedian, Bill Bailey. Long was recalled with fondness by many later artists, including the great blind jazz pianist, George Shearing. In an interview with Brian Johnston on *Test Match Special* Shearing revealed that he used to imitate Long's monologues in his show.[16] Recently, South London singer Alexandra Carter has performed some of Long's songs at such events as the Sydenham Arts Festival at a church near to his old house.

Norman Long represented the best of the tradition of the true entertainer, who seeks not to belittle or berate his audience but merely to entertain them. His charming songs were ideal for their time—refined, nostalgic with deceptively gentle but often sharp satirical humour underscored by an elusive trepidation for the future. He was of the generation who remembered the world before 1914, who came of age in the conflict and never forgot their experience of "the war to end all wars." They lived to see the futility of that statement when they witnessed yet another war. Weary but undaunted, the country battled through and the breezy, ever-optimistic world that Long epitomised cajoled everyone to keep smiling in a land that needed cheering up more than ever.

See discography and list of credits on page 260.

Epilogue

WHEN MARIE LLOYD died in 1924, T. S. Eliot lamented that music hall had died with her. Almost forty years later the same was said after the death of Max Miller. However, as an idea, reports of its death were probably premature, because when Ken Dodd died over half a century later, the press said largely the same thing. What survived those years was not Music Hall in a pre-1914 sense, but its spirit, which was essentially the spirit of the people expressed through the most popular artists of the time.

The tangible aspects of music hall have all but vanished. The vast majority of theatres in which the artistes I profiled performed are long gone. If they could return to earth today, they would hardly recognize a single thing about their country. The loss of variety theatres has had a detrimental effect on the landscape and on entertainment. They were often beautiful ornate buildings with a style all their own. Now we value the few that remain as architectural gems. It is not just the theatres that have been torn down, but in many ways the entire fabric of the society they knew has been decimated by the destructive forces of the last hundred years. Today many provincial towns have few if any theatres, and in many cases, we are left with shadows and ghosts in soulless urban jungles that offer no window into an alternative world. Much of the past is obliterated, either deliberately or otherwise. It is as though they never existed.

The foreboding expressed by T. S. Eliot after the death of Marie Lloyd would effectively appear to have been fulfilled. His fear was that electronic entertainment would one day entirely replace the real thing and that people would forget how it feels to enjoy the moment, forget how to sing along with the chorus and consequently die of boredom.

For all that, the spirit of the halls lived on; not just in *The Good Old Days* which ran on the BBC from 1953 to 1983, but in many of the biggest post-war comedians. Technically-speaking they were variety

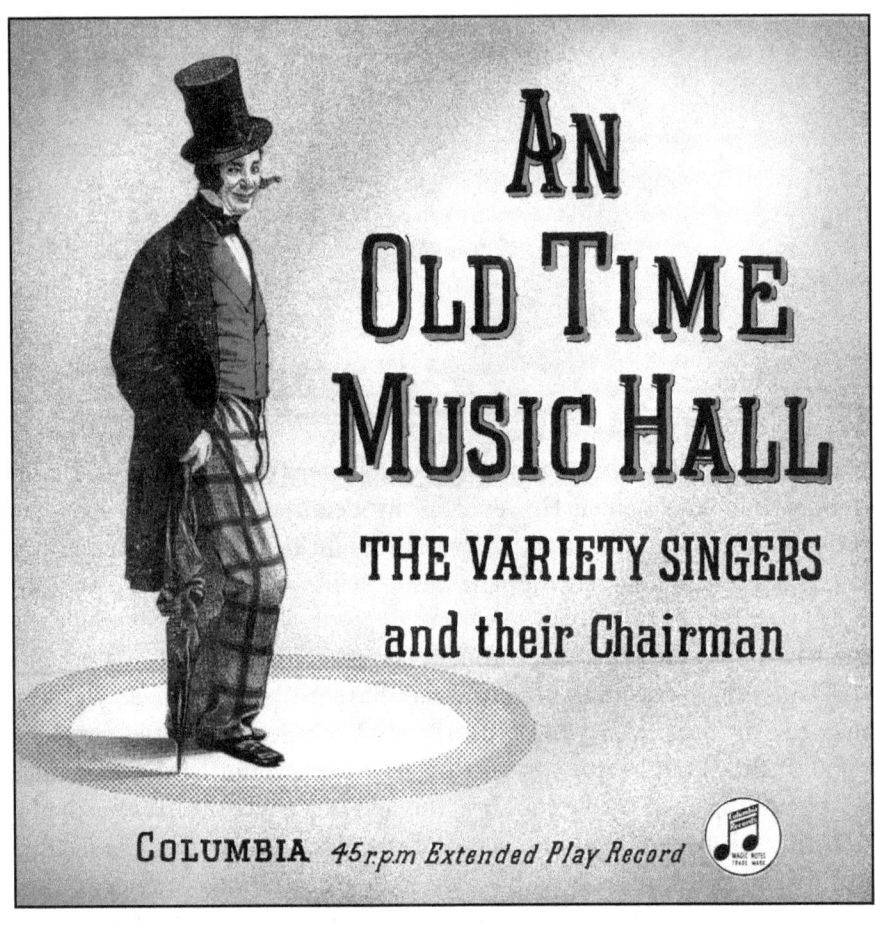

An *Old Time Music Hall* by The Variety Singers Columbia EMI 7" EP c1955, with sleeve notes by W. Macqueen Pope, who wrote evocatively about music hall and theatre in a series of highly collectable books.

artists, but they had about them the essence of a previous age. That generation was truly loved and arguably never replaced in the heart of the public. It is telling that Morecambe and Wise are still shown every year on television over forty years since their heyday. I well recall one of their exchanges:

> Ernie Wise: You make us sound like a cheap music-hall act.

> Eric Morecambe: But we *are* a cheap music-hall act!

They learnt their craft in time-honoured fashion in those same variety theatres and successfully brought their "cheap music hall act" to television to the delight of millions, just as Charlie Chaplin had done to cinema years before. The same spirit lived on in music. It was recalled in the psychedelic era and even in such diverse groups as Madness and The Monochrome Set.

It is sometimes tempting to view the past through rose-tinted spectacles, but I hope I have shown the day-to-day difficulties and practicalities of life that even the highest paid performers had to endure. It was so much harder for those who struggled along and barely made a living but somehow kept going, sustained by the hope that one day they would hit the big time. Undoubtedly music hall was a demanding profession, as the short lives of some of its greatest stars bear testimony. As we have seen a number died either on stage or as a result of performing. It was hard for a number of reasons; it was physically demanding, emotionally draining and required an artist to be funny at all times, and to keep being funny, if not funnier, on each occasion. Live theatre required energy and stamina. For some, it was not the ideal profession to suit their temperament. Dan Leno was arguably the most popular comedian of his generation, but the constant strain on his nerves proved too much for him and his mind gave way. They were wholehearted performers who did not just turn up and take the money. *Au contraire*, they put their heart and soul into what they did and gave their all, whether they were playing a grand gala for the crowned heads of Europe or a sparsely-attended matinee for crippled children.

It is beyond the scope of this book to cover all the many and varied artistes who brought their skill to the halls over a hundred years ago. The ventriloquists, magicians, conjurors, mind-readers, hypnotists, escape-artists, jugglers, tumblers, balancing-acts, contortionists, clowns, musicians, sword-swallowers, fire-eaters, knife-throwers, marksmen, trick-cyclists, animal acts and sundry others. Nevertheless, I hope my idiosyncratic if not eccentric saunter through the lives of some less discussed stars creates renewed interest in their seemingly lost world. Perhaps in addition it might reunite people with the wellsprings of their culture and help understand better the roots of entertainment. After reading my book if even one person feels the urge to listen to the old songs and can appreciate anew the craft and long years of striving that every artist underwent, then my endeavour will have been worthwhile.

Appendix

Nellie Wallace

Films

A Lady's First Lesson on a Bicycle (1902) Dir.: James Williamson. Cast: Nellie Wallace (The Lady), John Cobbold (The Instructor) Williamson Kinematograph Co. (Short)
Eve's Film Review 22: The Stars at Home Miss Nellie Wallace (1921) Pathe short
The Golden Pippin Girl (1920) aka *Why Men Leave Home* Dir.: A. C. Hunter. Cast: Nellie Wallace, Ray Forrest, Irene Tripod. Alliance Film Corporation
Acrobatic Novelty (1924) British Pathe short clip (without sound) featuring an acrobatic scene from *Whirl of the World* with Billy Merson and Nellie Wallace.
The Wishbone (1933) Dir.: Arthur Maude. Cast: Nellie Wallace (Mrs. Beasley), Davy Burnaby, A. Bromley Davenport, Jane Wood. Sound City.
Radio Parade of 1935 (1934) Dir.: Arthur B. Woods. Cast: Will Hay, Helen Chandler, Clifford Mollison, Billy Bennett, Lily Morris, Nellie Wallace (Charlady). British International Pictures. Nellie sings "What's the Use?" and "I'm Not What I Used Ter Be" (with Lily Morris)
Variety (1935) Dir.: Adrian Brunel. Scr.: Adrian Brunel, Oswald

Mitchell. Cast: George Carney, Billie Houston, Renee Houston, Barrie Livesey, Cassie Livesey, Roger Livesey, Nellie Wallace et al. John Argyle Productions.

Boys Will Be Girls (1937) Dir.: Gilbert Pratt. Cast: Leslie Fuller, Nellie Wallace (Bertha Luff), Greta Gynt, Constance Godridge. Joe Rock Productions. Nellie sings "Lo, Hear the Gentle Lark"

Cavalcade of the Stars (1938) Dir.: Geoffrey Benstead. Short.

Any Records Chums? (1942) With Syd Walker, Nellie Wallace, Stanley Holloway, Sandy Powell. British Movietone News (Short newsreel)

Alice Makes a Record (1945) With Ann Stephens, Nellie Wallace, Jeanne de Casalis, Tommy Trinder. Pathe newsreel item showing recording of *Through the Looking Glass* in aid of the Great Ormond Street Hospital for Children.

Discography

Through the Looking Glass Starring Ann Stephens, Jeanne de Casalis, Tommy Trinder, Nellie Wallace (Red Queen), Tommy Handley, Charles Williams HMV C3459 2 x 12" c1946

Golden Voices of Variety "The Blasted Oak" and "Three Times a Day" Ace of Clubs ACL 1077 LP 1961

Music Hall to Variety: Vol. 3 Second House "Under the Bed" World Records WRC SH150 LP c1977

Veterans of Variety "Bang! Bang! Bang!" & "Let's Have a Tiddley at the Milk Bar" World Records Retrospect Series SH 357 LP 1980

Nellie Wallace & Maidie Scott—Mother's Advice "Meet Me (The Sniff Song)" / "Three Cheers for the Red, White and Blue" / "Half Past Nine" / "Geranium" / "Under the Bed" / "Tally Ho" / "Cuckoo" / "Mother's Pie Crust" / "The Blasted Oak" / "Three Times a Day" / "Let's Have a Tiddley at the Milk Bar" / "Bang! Bang! Bang!" Windyridge CDR16

Nellie Wallace & G. H. Elliott: Two Old Troupers Cylidisc 512 CD 2003 (Includes all twelve recordings as above.)

Other Songs & Sheet Music

"Bonnie Dundee" at Dundee, April, 1893[1]

"Down by the River Side" (Paul Barnes) Charles Sheard & Co., 1900

"I Was Born on a Friday" (Fred Murray, George Everard) Francis, Day & Hunter, 1903

"Isn't it a Cruel World?" (J. W. Tate, F. C. Harris) Francis, Day & Hunter, 1903
"Where are You Going to My Pretty Maid?" (J. P. Harrington, W. H. Liddy) Francis, Day & Hunter, 1905
"I Wish I was Young Again" Colonial, New York, 1907[2]
"I Lost Georgie in Trafalgar Square" (H. Castling, C. Collins) Francis, Day & Hunter, 1907
"Mingle Your Eyebrows with Mine" Colonial, New York, 1907
"Come, Birdie, Come" (C. A. White) at Shea's Music Hall, New York, December, 1908[3]
"My Directoire Dress" January, 1909[4]
"By the Light of the Silvery Moon" American Music-Hall, New York, November, 1909[5]
"Daisy Bell" South Africa, c1909[6]
"Oh! The Hobble!"
"Who'll Buy Me?" at Edinburgh, January, 1918[7]
"Next Sunday Morning is My Wedding Day"
"Finesse" from *Sky High* (1925)
"He's a Dear Old Man" (H. M. Burnaby, Alec McGill) 1926
"I Do Like a Basin Full of Hot Pot" (F. Shuff, arr. H. J. Stafford) Chappell & Co., Ltd., London, 1928
"Queenie the Carnival Queen" (R. Rutherford, H. Arpthorp) 1934
"A Boy's Best Friend is His Mother" (H. Miller, J. P. Skelly) at the Royal Command Performance, 1 November 1948 (Her final song on her final appearance)

LILY MORRIS

FILMS

Elstree Calling (1930) Dir.: Alfred Hitchcock, Jack Hulbert, Andre Charlot, Paul Murray. Scr.: Adrian Brunel, Walter C. Mycroft, Val Valentine. Cast: Donald Calthrop, Cicely Courtneidge, Will Fyffe, Gordon Harker, Tommy Handley, Anna May Wong, Lily Morris (Herself) British International Pictures. Lily sings "Why am I Always the Bridesmaid?" and "Only a Working Man"

Pathetone Weekly—Lily Morris singing "The Old Apple Tree" (1931) Pathe

Pathetone Weekly—Lily Morris singing "Don't Have Any More, Mrs. Moore" (1932) Pathe

Radio Parade of 1935 (1934) Dir.: Arthur B. Woods. Scr.: James Bunting, Jack Davis, Jr., Paul Perez, from an original idea by Reginald Purdell & John Watt. Cast: Will Hay, Helen Chandler, Clifford Mollison, Dave Burnaby, Alfred Drayton, Billy Bennett, Lily Morris (Herself) et al. British International Pictures. Lily sings "What's the Use?" solo, and "I'm Not What I Used Ter Be" with Nellie Wallace.

Those Were the Days (1934) Dir.: Thomas Bentley. Scr.: Jack Jordan, Frank Launder, Frank Miller, Fred Thompson, based on *The Magistrate* by Arthur Wing Pinero. Cast: Will Hay, Iris Hoey, Angela Baddeley, John Mills, H. F. Maltby, Lily Morris (Herself) et al. British International Pictures. Lily sings "My Old Man (Said Follow the Van)"

Variety (1935) Dir.: Adrian Brunel. Scr.: Adrian Brunel, Oswald Mitchell. Cast: George Carney, Roger Livesey, Lily Morris (Herself) et al. John Argyle Productions.

I Thank You (1941) Dir.: Marcel Varnel. Cast: Arthur Askey, Richard Murdoch, Lily Morris (as Lady Randall), Moore Marriott, Graham Moffatt, Issy Bonn et al. Scr.: Marriott Edgar, Val Guest, from a story by Howard Irving Young. Gainsborough Pictures. Lily and Chorus sing "Waiting at the Church."

DISCOGRAPHY

"A—Be My Boy" (with Grock) / "Everybody Loves Their Little Old Home" 10" Pathe 1128 1919

"Why Don't He Come Home?" (Collins) / "Wee White Heather" 10" Pathe 1242

"Thuthie" / "At the Church Door I'm Waiting" 10" Pathe 1165 1919

"I Had A Little Drop with Martha" / "None of Your Soldier's Tricks with Me" 10" Pathe 1269 1920

"You'd Be Surprised" (I. Berlin) 12" Pathe 5460 1920[1]

"Who's Coming to the Tartan Ball?" / "Cupid Plays the Dickens with Us All" 12" Pathe 5603 n. d. c1922

"Don't Leave Me" (C. Collins, F. W. Leigh) 10" Pathe Actuelle 10595 October 1923

"Don't Have Any More, Missus Moore" / "Why Am I Always the

Bridesmaid?" 10" Edison Bell Winner 4479 September 1926
"What are You Going to Do About Selina?" / "Only A Working Man" 10" Regal G 8813 February 1927
"The Old Apple Tree" / "Don't Have Any More, Mrs. Moore" 10" Regal G 8897 March 1927
"Which of the Three?" / "Why Am I Always the Bridesmaid?" 10" Regal G 8987 September 1927
"We All Said 'No'" / "What's to Be Done?" 10" Regal G 9031 December 1927
"All Hers" / "Photo on the Wall" Regal (Unissued) August 1928
"Don't Have Any More, Mrs. Moore" / "Truly Rural" 12" Columbia 9597 November, 1928
"Truly Rural" / "Mr. Scott" 10" Regal 9248 November, 1928
"Say Goodbye" / "Tiddley-Hi" 10" Regal 9272 November, 1928
"Since Mother's Been a Lady" / "That's Where the Soldiers Go" 10" Regal G 9405 May, 1929
"Because He Loves Me" / "That's Where the Soldiers Go" 10" Columbia DX 22 June, 1929
"The Wives of Commercial Travellers" / "Charlie" 10" Regal MR 480 January, 1932
"None of That Now" 10" Parlophone R 4425 1-sided disc
Don't Have Any More, Missus Moore CYLIDISC CD 504 c2001 "What Are You Going to Do About Selina?" / "Only A Working Man" / "The Old Apple Tree" / "Don't Have Any More, Missus Moore" (Regal version) / "We All Said 'No!'" / "What's To Be Done?" / "Which of the Three?" / "Why Am I Always the Bridesmaid?" / "Truly Rural" (Regal version) / "Say Goodbye" / "Mrs. Scott" / "Tiddley Hi" / "Since Our Mother's Been A Lady" / "That's Where the Soldiers Go" (Regal version) / "The Wives of Commercial Travellers" / "Charlie" / "Don't Have Any More, Missus Moore" (Columbia version) / "Truly Rural" / "Because He Loves Me" / "That's Where the Soldiers Go" (Columbia version) / "The Old Apple Tree" (Live) / "Don't Have Any More, Mrs. Moore" (Live at Collins' Music Hall, 1950)
Why Am I Always the Bridesmaid? Windyridge VAR CDR 18 "Why Am I Always the Bridesmaid?" / "A—Be My Boy" (with Grock) / "Everybody Loves Their Little Old Home" / "Thuthie" / "At the Church Door I'm Waiting" / "I Had A Little Drop With Martha" / "None of Your Soldier's Tricks With Me" / "Don't Have Any

More, Missus Moore" / "Why Am I Always the Bridesmaid?" / "What Are You Going to Do About Selina?" / "Only A Working Man" / "The Old Apple Tree" / "Which of the Three?" / "We All Said 'No!'" / "What's to Be Done" / "Say Goodbye" / "Mrs. Scott" / "Tiddley Hi" / "Since Our Mother's Been a Lady" / "Because He Loves Me" / "That's Where the Soldiers Go" / "The Wives of Commercial Travellers" / "Charlie" / "Truly Rural" / "Don't Have Any More, Mrs. Moore"

SEE ALSO

Dora Bryan "Because He Loves Me" *Dora* Fontana SFL 13114 1964

SONGS & SHEET MUSIC

"When I'm a Little Older" (Maurice Crosby) at the South London Palace, June, 1894
"Lardi-doody-day" (Joseph Tabrar) Francis, Day & Hunter, 1894
"Two Little Girls in Blue" (Charles Graham) Walham Green Hall, February, 1895
"The Red, White and Blue" The Royal, 1895
"The Little Quakeress" (O. Barri) Cambridge, May, 1895
"Only a Soldier Boy" West London Theatre, June, 1895
"Hoop-La" (W. R. Gordon) Canterbury Music Hall, August, 1895
"Sister Sally, Oh!" The Middlesex, August, 1895
"Naughty Boy" Sadler's Wells, September, 1895
"Look the Other Way" Hammersmith Varieties, March, 1896
"Just the Same as Dolly Does" (Joseph Tabrar) Francis, Day & Hunter, June, 1896
"Only a Lad" The Standard, September, 1896
"A Fairy Up-to-Date" in *Dick Whittington* Leeds, 1896-97
"Ro-me-o and Juliet" (Joseph Tabrar) Francis, Day & Hunter, May, 1897
"Little Wosie Posie" (Joseph Tabrar) Francis, Day & Hunter, at Marylebone, August, 1897
"A Poor Soldier's Daughter in England" Drury Lane, November, 1897
"I'm A Poor Little Beggar in England" (Joseph Tabrar) Francis, Day & Hunter, 1897
"If I Hadn't Been Born at All" 1898
"Trousers" 1898

"Will You Walk into My Parlour?" at the Royal, London, September, 1898[1]
Song from "Moulin Rouge" at the Grand, Clapham, October, 1898[2]
"Major Puffem of the Guard" November, 1898
"Gay Paree" (R. Morton, E, Jonhgmans) August, 1899
"The Ship That Belongs to a Lady" (Edgar Bateman, Felix McGlennon) Francis, Day & Hunter, in *Robinson Crusoe*, The Royal, 1899
"I'll Marry You, John" Royal Standard, March 1900
"Since I Have Had A Row of Houses" Collins's, April, 1900
"I Wasn't Born with a Silver Spoon in My Mouth" July, 1900
"Daddy, I'm Going to Bye Bye!" (Maurice Crosby, C. Collins) Francis, Day & Hunter, 1902
"Goodbye, Dolly Gray" (Paul Barnes, Will Cobb) in *Puss in Boots*, 1901-02
"I'll Buy You a Mangle, Polly" (Joseph Tabrar) Francis, Day & Hunter, April, 1902
"She Didn't Like To" at the Empire, Stratford, August, 1902
"Fly Away, Pretty Bird" (Maurice Crosby, Charles Collins, Henry E. Pether) Francis, Day & Hunter, 1903
"The Way to Court a Lady" Hackney Empire, November, 1903
"I'm Coming Home to You, Love" (Herbert Darnley) Francis, Day & Hunter, in *Mother Hubbard,* Princess's Glasgow, 1903-04
"The Good Old Summer Time" (George Evans, Ren Shields) in *Mother Hubbard*, 1903-04
"Wipe Your Feet Before You Go In" (C. Collins, Barnes) Francis, Day & Hunter, 1904
"She's No Lady Some Folks Say" Holloway Empire, July, 1905
"There Goes My Soldier Boy" (Augustus F. Savage, F. W. Leigh) Francis, Day & Hunter, The New Cross Empire, July, 1905
"I Want to Be a Soldier" (Alfred J. Lawrance) Francis, Day & Hunter, 1905
"The Old Bull and Bush" at the Zoo-Hippodrome, Glasgow, 1905
"Hear the Pipers Calling, Jennie Mine" (Scott Bennett) November, 1905
"Riding on the Top of the Car" (F. W. Leigh, P. V. Bryan, H. Von Tilzer) Francis, Day & Hunter, in *Mother Goose* at Bristol, 1905-06
"Japanese Love Song" in *Mother Goose,* 1905-06
"Zuyder Zee" (Bennett Scott, H. J. Mills) in *Mother Goose,* 1905-06
"Waltz Me Around Again, Willie" (Will D. Cobb, Ren Shields) 1906
"Doggie in the Yard" Duet with Miss H. Smithson in *Aladdin* 1906-07[3]
"Put Me Amongst the Girls" (Charles R. Whittle) in *Jack and Jill,* 1907-

08
"She's A Lassie from Lancashire" (C. W. Murphy, Dan Lipton, John Neat) 1907
"Meet Me, Jenny, When the Sun Goes Down" (H. Castling, F. Godfrey) B. Feldman & Co., 1907
"There's A Girl in Berlin" (F. Godfrey, J. C. Moore) National Music Publishing Co., London, 1909
"Molly O'Morgan (With Her Little Organ)" (Will Letters, Fred Godfrey) 1909
"Lena Schmitz" (J. M. Reilly, H. W. Petrie) 1909
"I Do Like to Be Beside the Seaside" (John A. Glover-Kind) in *Mother Goose*, 1909-10
"If I Should Plant a Tiny Seed of Love" (Ballard MacDonald, J. W. Tate) T. B. Harms, Francis, Day & Hunter, 1909 Sung by Lily in *Humpty Dumpty*
"Can't You See I Want You to Be My Girl" (Frank Leo) Francis, Day & Hunter, 1909
"Ship Ahoy" (Bennett Scott, H, J, Mills, Fred Godfrey) Henrees Music Co, 1910
"Fall in and Follow Me" (Bennett Scott, A. J. Mills) 1910
"I Wonder if You Miss Me Sometimes, I Wonder if You Care" (A. J. Mills & Bennett Scott) Star Music Publishing Company Ltd, London, 1910
"Here Comes the Chocolate Major" (Charles R. Whittle) 1910
"Kiss Me, My Honey, Kiss Me" (Irving Berlin, Ted Snyder) B. Feldman & Co., 1910
"Why Did You Come Knocking at My Door?" The Empress, Brixton, 1913
"Sammy, Come Over Here" (A. J. Mills, Bennett Scott) Star Music Publishing Co., 1913
"Keep Walking All the Time" May, 1914
"May All Your Troubles Be Little Ones" June, 1914
"Sandy Boy" 1914
"Scotland, That's the Place" 1914
"Where Did You Get That Girl?" 1914
"Who Does the Lady Belong To?" (C. Collins) Francis, Day & Hunter, circa 1915
"Private Cassidy, VC" 1915
"Somebody Knows, Somebody Cares" 1915

"We Must All Fall In" (A. J. Mills, B. Scott) Star Music Publishing Co., 1915
"She Said She Didn't Like To" 1915
"Who Does the Lady Belong To?" (C. Collins) Francis, Day & Hunter, 1915
"If You Have Any Trouble at All" 1915
"My Soldier Laddie" (Luther A. Clark, S. E. Tudor) 1915
"Keep the Home Fires Burning" (Ivor Novello) January, 1916
"On These Dark Nights" (A. J. Mills, B. Scott) Star Music Publishing Co., 1916
"Take Me Back to Dear Old Blighty" (A. J, Mills, F. Godfrey, B. Scott) 1916
"I'm Better Off in My Little Dug-Out" (Charles Collins) Francis, Day & Hunter, 1917
"Keep a Little Bit of Something in the Larder" 1917
"The Tank That Broke the Ranks Out in Picardy" (H. Castling, H. Carlton) 1917[4]
"Why Am I Always the Bridesmaid?" (Charles Collins, F. Leigh) Francis, Day & Hunter, 1917
"Till We Meet Again" (R. B. Egan, R. A. Whiting) B. Feldman & Co., 1918
"Take My Arm and Take Me Home" (F. W. Leigh, C. Collins) Francis, Day & Hunter, 1918
"At the Church Door I've Been Waiting" Finsbury Park Empire, 1919
"Mademoiselle from Armentieres" South London Palace, August, 1919
"None of Your Nineteen-Fourteen Tricks with Me" (T. McGhee, H. Rule), Francis, Day & Hunter, 1919
"The Hunting Rag" 1920
"I'm Forever Blowing Bubbles" 1920
"There's the Wee White Heather Growing" (F. W. Leigh, C. Collins) Francis, Day & Hunter, 1920
"Jeremiah" (Tom Maguire) Palace Theatre, Plymouth, November, 1920[5]
"Leave Me with A Smile" (C. Koehler, E. Burtnett) B. Feldman & Co., 1921
"Oh, What a Difference the Navy's Made to Me" (Ralph Stanley, Leslie Alleyn) B. Feldman & Co, 1921
"There You Are, Then" (L. Silberman) 1921
"He Didn't Believe Me (When I Said That I Was Married)" (Herbert Rule, F. Holt) Finsbury Park Empire, April, 1921[6]

"Oh, Maria!" April, 1921
"See You Later" (L. Silberman, H. Rule, W. H. Wallis) L. Silberman 1921
"Coal Black Mammy" (Laddie Cliff) Glasgow, 1921-22[7]
"You'll Always Meet a Son of Bonnie Scotland" (F. Wood) Herman Darewski, 1921
"Cock-a-Doodle-Do" December, 1921
"When I Get Back Home" December, 1921
"He Meets Me Every Evening" October, 1922
"Shufflin' Along" (Nat D. Ayer) Feldman & Co., sung in *Jack and the Beanstalk* at the Empire Theatre, Sheffield, 1922-23[8]
"Hi, Hi, Ho" (Herbert Rule, F. Holt) Feldman & Co., from *Jack and the Beanstalk* 1922-23
"Honeymoon Bay" (Martin Fried) Feldman & Co., from *Jack and the Beanstalk* 1922-23
"Cute Little Love Nest" (T. Leason, H. T. Hanbury) Feldman & Co., Duet with Violet Kersey in *Jack and the Beanstalk* at Sheffield, 1922-23
"Charlie" (Leslie Sarony) Circa 1923
"I'm Getting Married Tomorrow Morning" 1923
"Mrs. Scott" (T. McGhee, Walsh)
"Passionetta" (Mort Dixon, Ernest Breuer) B. Feldman & Co., 1923
"Say Goodbye" (Marcus)
"Tiddley-Hi" (Wallace, Bedford)
"What Are You Going to Do About Selina?" (H. Castling, Magee)
"Something to Look Forward To" Finsbury Park Empire, October, 1924[9]
"I'm Going to Be an Old Man's Darling" October, 1924
"All Hot and Bothered" (Douglas Marshall, Cecil Macklin) Cary & Co., October, 1924
"It's All Sugar" (Herbert Rule, W. H. Wallace) Lawrence Wright Music Co., 1924[10]
"Say it While Dancing" B. Feldman & Co., with Eve Lynn in *Aladdin*, Wood Green Empire, 1923-24
"Ain't Love Grand?" B. Feldman & Co., in *Aladdin*, Wood Green Empire, 1923-24
"Joe is Here" in *Aladdin*, 1923-24
"If I Had the Lamp of Aladdin" (E. Hedges) in *Aladdin*, 1923-24
"Minnetonka" (Gus Kahn, Percy Wenrich) B. Feldman & Co, in *Aladdin*, 1923-24
"I Looked Inside the Shop" (Worton David) Worton David, Ltd., 1924[11]
"Teddy Bear Blues" (J. H. Jackson) c1924

"Pretty Pierrette" (M. Darewski) c1924
"Turned Up" (H. Castling, H. Rule) B. Feldman & Co., 1924
"Fell Out" (P. Edgar, T. Sullivan, J. P. Long) Francis, Day & Hunter, 1925
"I Know He Goes Straight Home to His Wife" at the Palace, New York, July, 1925[12]
"You Won't Be with Us Tomorrow Night" at the Palace, New York, July, 1925
"I Must Take Something Home with Me" the Palace, New York, July, 1925
"Why Did You Have Your Hair Bobbed, Mary?" (Ted Waite) J. Albert & Son, Sydney, 1925
"He Wouldn't Believe I Was Married" Tivoli, Sydney, 29 December, 1925
"He Wanted Me" Shepherd's Bush Empire, June, 1926
"Too Many Tots (Make You Totter) (Walter Hayden, Jay Francis) Central Music Publishing Co., 1926[13]
"Don't Have Any More, Missus Moore" (H. Castling, J. Walsh) B. Feldman & Co., 1926
"Since Father's Joined the Mustard Club" (Edgar Bateman, Maurice Scott) The Maurice Scott Music Co., 1926[14]
"I Don't Want to Get Old" The Alhambra, November, 1926
"There Ain't No Flies on Auntie" (W. Van Der Decken) Chappell & Co., 1926[15]
"I Only Got Married This Morning" Exeter Hippodrome, January, 1927
"Missus Dunn" Rexborough Music Publishing Co., 1927[16]
"Never Mind the Way Home" (D. Sonenscher, S. Finberg) Leo Jackson & Co., December, 1927[17]
"We All Said 'No!'" (H. Castling) Francis, Day & Hunter, 1927
"Don't Do That to the Poor Puss Cat" (L. Sarony, F. Eyton) Edward B. Marks & Co., New York/ Keith Prowse & Co., 1928
"Truly Rural" (R. Marcus) B. Feldman & Co., 1928
"Are Ideal Husbands Wanted?" Pantomime, 1928-29[18]
"I'm Not Worrying Now" The Metropolitan, May, 1929[19]
"There's His Picture Hanging on the Wall" 1929
"The More the Merrier!" (F. Wood, C. Harrington) 1929
"'Arriet" September, 1929
"That's Where the Soldiers Go" (T. McGhee, J. Walsh) 1929
"Old Mother Gunn" The Palladium, December, 1929
"Oh, You Ought to See Jemima Now" at the Hackney Empire, November, 1929[20]

"I'm As Old as I Look" The Metropolitan, February, 1930
"I Got Married Early This Morning" Holborn Empire, 1930[21]
"Let it Go, Reilly" Holborn Empire, October, 1930[22]
"The Night I Lost My Lot in the Lottery" 1931[23]
"He's a Nice, Kind, Clean Old Man" Empress, Brixton, November, 1932
"How Does a Fly Keep Its Weight Down" (Harry Castling) 1932[24]
"Oh, Charlie, Do Be Careful" The Metropolitan, February, 1933
"Bessie Buttons" (Bert H. Delmar) April, 1933
"Josephine" Victoria Palace, April, 1934
"Keep the Party Clean" Shepherd's Bush Empire, July, 1934
"Ready for Love Once More" Shepherd's Bush Empire, July, 1934
Comedyland—Grand Selection of Popular Comedy Song Successes B. Feldman & Co., 1934, Various artist songs including "Don't Have Any More, Mrs. Moore" and "Turned Up" by Lily Morris
"My Old Tin Pail" 1935
"At the Christening" Grand Theatre, Croydon, October, 1935
"Early Every Morning" Grand Theatre, Croydon, October, 1935
"Muffle Up Those Merry Wedding Bells" October, 1935 on the BBC broadcast *The Variety of Music*.[25]
"'Appy with 'Arry" at the Metropolitan, March, 1939

Billy Bennett

Discography

"Nell" / "Family Secrets" 10" Columbia 4004 August, 1926 (Speed 80rpm)
"The Green Tie on the Little Yellow Dog" / "Devil-May-Not-Care" 10" Columbia 4005 1926
"I'll Be Thinking of You" / "The Miser" 10" Columbia 4006 June, 1926 (Speed 80rpm)
"No Power on Earth" / "The Charge of the Tight Brigade" 10" Regal 9159 December, 1926
"No Power on Earth" / "The Charge of the Tight Brigade" 12" Columbia 9025 July, 1927
"My Mother Doesn't Know I'm On the Stage" / "The Club Raid" 10" Columbia 5719 August, 1927
"The Real Guy" / "Domestic Blisters" 12" Columbia 9105 1927

"Napoleon" / "She's Mine" 10" Regal 9021 January, 1928
"Napoleon" / "She's Mine" 12" Columbia 9237 1928
"Ogul Mogul" / "The Tightest Man I Know" 12" Columbia 9296 March, 1928
"Mottoes" / "The Memory Man" 12" Columbia 9454 May, 1927
"Buckshee" / "The Idol's Tongue" 12" Columbia 9469 c1928
"Ogul Mogul" / "The Tightest Man I Know" 10" Regal 9087 May, 1928
"Detective" / "If Winter Comes" 10" Columbia DX 8 circa 1929
"Mandalay" / "The Coffee Stall Keeper" 12" Columbia DX 28 December, 1929
"She Was Poor, But She Was Honest" / "Don't Send My Boy to Prison" 10" Columbia DB 164 May, 1930
"Christmas Day in the Cook House" / "Please Let Me Sleep on Your Doorstep" 10" Columbia DB 658 1930
"Daddy" / "The MP" 10" Regal 1930
"Daddy" / "The MP" 10" Columbia 5649 1930
"The Fisherman" / "From My Window in Vanity Fair" 12" Columbia 9671 circa 1930
"The Call of the Yukon" / "The League of Nations" 10" Imperial Broadcast 4010 January, 1934
"The Foreign Legion" / "The Bookmaker's Daughter" 10" Regal Zonophone MR 1724 March, 1934
"She Was Happier When She Was Poor" / "The Only Girl I Ever Loved" 10" Regal Zonophone 1935

REISSUE COMPILATIONS

Almost a Gentleman. "Nell" / "My Mother Doesn't Know I'm On the Stage" / "Mandalay" / "I'll Be Thinking of You" / "Ogul Mogul—A Kanakanese Love Lyric" / "No Power On Earth" / "She Was Poor, But She Was Honest" / "Family Secrets" / "Please Let Me Sleep On Your Doorstep Tonight" / "Christmas Day in the Cookhouse" / "The Club Raid" / "She's Mine" / "Mottoes" / "The Green Tie On the Little Yellow Dog" Topic Records LP 12T387 1978

Almost A Gentleman. Track listing as above, plus five extra tracks: "She Was Happier When She Was Poor" / "The Only Girl I Ever Loved" / "The Miser" / "Don't Send My Boy to Prison" / "The Charge of the Tight Brigade" Reissue CD TSCD780 1997.

The Art of the Monologue Various Artists, including Marriott Edgar, Stanley Holloway, Nelson Jackson, Billy Bennett "The Memory Man" Alfred Lester "Gardening" and Norman Long "A Tale of Other Times" Pearl CD 1999

Billy Bennett's Burlesque Budget: Surreal Songs and Monologues "Don't Send My Boy to Prison" / "Devil-May-Not-Care" / "No Power on Earth" / "The Charge of the Tight Brigade" / "She's Mine" / "Napoleon" / "Ogul Mogul" / "The Tightest Man I Know" / "Buckshee" / "The Memory Man" / "The Idol's Tongue" / "From My Window in Vanity Square" / "The Fisherman" / "Daddy" / "The M. P." / "If Winter Comes" / "The Detective" / "The Bookmaker's Daughter" / "The Foreign Legion" / "She Was Poor, But She Was Honest" Cylidisc 519 CD (2005)

The Real Guy. "Nell" / "Family Secrets" / "The Green Tie On the Little Yellow Dog" / "Devil-May-Not-Care" / "The Miser" / "The Real Guy" / "Domestic Blisters" / "No Power On Earth" / "Ogul Mogul—A Kanakanese Love Lyric" / "The Tightest Man I Know" / "Mottoes" / "My Mother Doesn't Know I'm On the Stage" / "The Club Raid" / "The M. P." / "Mandalay" / "The Coffee Stall Keeper" / "The Call of the Yukon" / "The League of Nations" / "The Foreign Legion" / "The Bookmaker's Daughter" / "She Was Poor, But She Was Honest" / "Don't Send My Boy to Prison" Windyridge VAR 33 CD circa 2010

See also

Linda Thompson Presents My Mother Doesn't Know I'm on the Stage Colin Firth "My Mother Doesn't Know I'm on the Stage" Omnivore Records OVCD-296 U. S. 2018

Filmography

Camera Interviews: Billy Bennett Almost a Gentleman (1927) Silent British Pathe short. Scenes of Bennett having fish supper, playing darts and golf. *Himself.*

London's Famous Clubs & Cabarets No. 9: The Cosmo Club (1927) Silent British Pathe short featuring scenes at the Cosmo Club including Bennett dancing. *Himself.*

Almost a Gentleman. (1928). 9-minute short sound comedy. Dir.: De Forest Phonofilm. With Billy Bennett. *Himself.*
Billy Bennett at Home. (1929) Silent Pathe Pictorial short. *Himself.*
Carnival—The Famous Three Arts Club Ball, London. (1929) Silent Pathe short showing scenes of Three Arts Club including Bennett joking with Sydney Chaplin and others.
Unnatural History. (1930) British Pathe short. *Himself (Lecturer).*
Pathe Magazine 25. (1930). British Pathe short. Bennett does cod acts including a lightning sketch, card trick and parody ventriloquist act. *Himself.*
Radio Parade of 1935. (1934). Dir.: Arthur B. Woods. British International Pictures. Cast: Will Hay, Helen Chandler, Clifford Mollison, Billy Bennett, Lily Morris, Nellie Wallace, Clapham & Dwyer et al. *Commissionaire.*
Soft Lights and Sweet Music. (1936). Dir.: Herbert Smith. British Lion Film Corporation. Cast: Ambrose & His Orchestra, Evelyn Dall, Western Brothers, Harry Tate, Billy Bennett, Elizabeth Welch, Wilson, Keppel & Betty et al. *Himself.*
Calling All Stars. (1937). Dir.: Herbert Smith. British Lion Film Corporation. Cast: Ambrose & His Orch., Evelyn Dall, Carroll Gibbons, Sam Brown, Larry Adler, Billy Bennett, The Nicholas Bros., Arthur Askey et al. *Himself.*
Almost a Gentleman. (1938). Dir.: Oswald Mitchell. Sidney Morgan Productions. Cast: Billy Bennett, Kathleen Harrison, Mervyn Johns, Gibb McLaughlin, Marcelle Rogez. *Bill Barker.*
Young Man's Fancy. (1939). Dir.: Robert Stevenson. Ealing Studios. Cast: Griffith Jones, Anna Lee, Seymour Hicks, Billy Bennett, Edward Rigby, Francis L. Sullivan, Martita Hunt. *Capt. Boumphray.*
This in Our Times (1950). Pathe documentary about Liverpool featuring short clips of local comedians including Bennett, Tommy Handley, Arthur Askey, Robb Wilton and Ted Ray.
Time to Remember: 1929 (c1950s) Pathe historical documentary narrated by Michael Redgrave featuring short scene of Bennett in character being thrown out of a pub.

Songs, Recitations & Sheet Music

"They Built Piccadilly for Me" (J. W. Rickaby) 1915

"Just as the Sun Went Down"—A pathetic incident of war time (L. Udall, Nellie Gannon, H. Wright) Originally published by Charles Sheard & Co., c1898, sung by Bennett April, 1915[1]
"Old Man Adam" from the revue *As You Were* 1920[2]
"Buck-Shee" (Val Parnell, Billy Bennett, Jack Sennoi) The Fred Allandale Music Publishing Co., London, 1920
"Save Your Heart for Me" (Billy Bennett, Peter Bernard, Claude Ivy) The Fred Allandale Music Publishing Co., 1920
"Don't Call Me Bay" (B. Bennett) 1921
"I Owe You Some Money, Don't I?" (B. Bennett) May 1922
"Dapper Dan" at the Victoria Palace, July, 1923[3]
"The Cheese It Stands Alone" at the Palladium, December, 1923[4]
"The Principal Boy's Lament" at the Victoria Palace, February, 1924[5]
"In the Rain" at Ilford Hippodrome, March, 1924[6]
"Beau Brummell" 1924
"Mine, All Mine" (Parody) at the Islington Empire, October, 1924[7]
"Pack Up Your Troubles" with chorus in *Ullo* 1925
"Mooching Round the Cook-house Door" (B. Bennett) 1925
"I Wish You Were Jealous of Me" October, 1926 [8]
"Barracky Bert the Soldier" (Fred E. Cliffe, Harry Gifford) Cecil Lennox Ltd., c1927
"The Bam-Bam Bammy Shore" (Recitation) at Victoria Palace, March, 1927[9]
"The Hungkum-Chungkum Isles" 1927
"The Wide, Open Spaces" The Alhambra, October, 1927[10]
"Napoleon's Farewell" with Margaret Yarde in *Will o the Whispers* 1928[11]
"Is Variety Dead?" from *Will o the Whispers* 1928
"The Balcony Girl" as Romeo in *Coo-ee*
"Daddie, Good Night" 1928
"Stay Out of the North" (B. Bennett) 1929
"The Fireman's Wedding" (Recitation) Holborn Empire, January, 1929[12]
"The Great White North" (Recitation) 1930
"Whiskers" (Percival Langley) (Monologue) 1931
"Hollywood, Hollywood, City of Sin" at the Palladium, September, 1931[13]
"Dr. Goosegrease" (B. Bennett) 1936
"Aunt Fanny's Album" (Recitation) (B. Bennett) 1936
"The Old Soldier's Tie"—A Musical Monologue (W. R. Bennett) W. Paxton & Co, London, circa 1939 (Covered by Stanley Holloway)

"I Loved and Lost" from *Black and Blue* 1939

Billy Bennett's Budget of Burlesque Monologues
Book I
"Nell" / "The Tightest Man I Know" / "Cecil, the Copper" / "The Postman" / "Black and White Cargo" / "The Foreign Legion"
Book II (1929) Written by T. W. Connor
"The Fire at the North Pole" / "The Gambler" / "The Sergeant's Overcoat" / "The Wedding—That Wasn't"
(1940) "Mandalay" / "The Sailor" / "The Broadcaster" / "The Bookmaker's Daughter" / "The Infernal Triangle" / "Father, Come Home"
Book III
"The Bugle Calls" / "The Travellers" / "The Scotch Express—From Ireland" / "The Prodigal Son"
"A Soldier's Soliloquy" / "Doctor Goosegrease" / "Sobstuff Sister" / "A Tale of the Rockies" / "The Street of a Thousand Lanterns" / "Trumpeter" / "The Danpoor Express"
Book IV (1930)
"The Poor Hard-Working Man" / "One of the Rank and Vile" / "The Sailor Comes Home—With the Washing" / "Do As You'd Be Done By"
Book V
"Limehouse Liz" / "Cucumbers Race!" / "One Over the Eight" / Shamms O'Brien—Oy! Oy!"
(1937) "The Lighthouse Keeper" / "The Shooting of Dan McGrew" / "Hometown" / "The Eskimos" / "The Drummer Boy" / "Greeneye" / "Nursery Rhyme Nonsense"
Book VI
"Christmas Day in the Cook House" / "Napoleon" / "The Wide-Open Spaces" / "This Medal" / "The Huntsman" / "The Member of Parliament"

CHARLIE HIGGINS

DISCOGRAPHY

"With Me Gloves in Me Hand" (Fred Shuff) / "In the Waxworks Late Last Night" Broadcast 659 1931

"The Girls of the Old Brigade" / "Sh...There's a Ghost in the House" Broadcast c1931

"The Day I Went to Wembley for the Cup Tie" / "Maggie and Me and the Baby" Broadcast c1931

"Running Up and Down Our Street" / "Down in the Field Where the Buttercups Grow" (William Hargreaves) Broadcast c1931

"I'm a Daddy at 63" / "Charlie in Spain" Broadcast 764 9" Dec 1931

"Down in the Old Churchyard" / "When I Was Twenty-One" Broadcast 799

"Charlie Goes Shopping on Saturday Night" / "Bumpity-Bump Again" Broadcast May 1932

"Round at Her Mother's on Sundays" / "That's What Women are For" Broadcast Aug 1932

"With Me Bagful of Nuts and Some Sweets in Me Mouth" / "When I Was Twenty-One" Broadcast 836 1932

"When the Jolly Good Times are Booming Later On" / "Charlie at the Christening" Broadcast 885 Oct 1932

"Jolly Old Uncle Joe" / "Mrs. McGrath & Mrs. O'Rafferty" Broadcast 908 9"

"Charlie Makes Whoopee" Part I / Part II (Assisted by Bert Bray) Broadcast 936 9"

"In the Waxworks Late at Night" / Part II Broadcast 959 9"

"Charlie's Breach of Promise Case" / Part II (Assisted by Bert Bray) Broadcast 962 9"

"Where the Violets are Blue-oo" / "Mother's Walking Round in Father's Trousers" Rex 8012 10" 1933

"I'm a Daddy at 63" / "Down in the Fields Where the Buttercups Grow" Rex 8065 10"

"With Me Gloves in Me 'And" / "She's Leading Me Up the Garden" (W. Hargreaves) Rex 8157 10" c1934

Compilations

All Poshed Up Windyridge WINDY VAR 34 (2008) "With Me Gloves in Me 'And" / "In the Waxworks Late at Night" / "Maggie and Me and the Baby" / "The Day I Went to Wembley for the Cup-Tie" / "The Girls of the Old Brigade" / "Sh! There's a Ghost in the House" / "Running Up and Down Our Street" / "Down in the Fields Where the Buttercups Grow" / "Charlie in Spain" / "Down in the Old Churchyard" / "Charlie's Saxophone" / "Charlie Goes

Shopping on Saturday Night" / "Bumpity Bump Again" / "Round at Her Mother's On Sunday" / "That's Why Women Were Born" / "Charlie at the Christening" / "When the Jolly Good Times Are Booming Later On" / "Jolly Old Uncle Joe" / "Mrs. McGrath and Mrs. O'Rafferty" / "When I Was Twenty-One" / "With Me Bag Full of Nuts and Some Sweets in Me Mouth" / "Mother's Walking Round in Father's Trousers" / "Where the Violets are Blue-oo and the Roses are Red" / "I'm a Daddy at 63" / "Navvies' Jazz" / "All Poshed Up"

Various Artists Compilations

Listen to the Banned. "All Poshed Up with Me Daisies in Me 'and" AJA 5030 1984
Vintage British Comedy Vol. 1. "Down in the Fields Where the Buttercups Grow" Fast Forward Music FFCD011 2004
Vintage British Comedy Vol. 2. "Daddy at 63" Fast Forward Music FFCD012 2004
Vintage British Comedy Vol. 3. "Charlie's Saxophone" Fast Forward Music FFCD013 2004
The Best of British Comedy. "Down in the Fields Where the Buttercups Grow" Go Entertain GO3CD7229 2013

Other releases

Bob Arnold & The Yetties *Mornin' All* Argo LP ZFB 83 1972 Includes a version of "Where the Violets are Blue"

Other Songs and Sheet Music

As Charlie Higginson
"K-K-K-Katy" (Geoffrey O'Hara) Sung by Higgins (as C. R. Higginson) with The King's Jesters, Victoria Palace, London, 1919

As St. Juste and Higgins
"Ev'ry Day You're Away Means a Teardrop" (George McCarthy) The Lawrence Wright Music Co., 1920[1]
"They'll Never Know Me in Old Dahomey" (G. McCarthy, Andrew Allen) The Lawrence Wright Music Co., 1920

"That Kentucky Home of Mine" (G. McCarthy) The Lawrence Wright Music Co., 1920
"Where the Cross-Eyed Claras Grow" (A. Allen, Wynn Stanley, Lawrence Wright) The Lawrence Wright Music Co., 1920
"Every Time He Kissed Her She Would Start to Sing" (A. Allen, L. Wright) Lawrence Wright Music Co., 1920
"My House is Haunted (By the Ghost of a Beautiful Girl)" (Wynn Stanley, Andrew Allen) The Lawrence Wright Music Co., 1920.
"You Never Gave Me Love" (C. R. St. Juste, Will Wise) Charles Austin Music Co., 1921
"Sneezing Song" (P. Jackman, L. B. Tisdale) at the Hippodrome, Belfast, November, 1922[2]
"Hiawatha's Melody of Love" (Alfred Bryan, Artie Mehliner, George W. Meyer) 1923
"How the Dickens are You Doing?" The Palladium, 21 August, 1923[3]
"K-K-K-Kiss Me Again" (A. Allen) The Lawrence Wright Music Co., 1923 (Originally sung in the revue *The Dumbells*)
"Cow-Heel Joe" (Wynn Stanley, Andrew Allen) The Lawrence Wright Music Co., August 1923
"Wembley" at the Stratford Empire, 8 July, 1924[4]
"A N'Egg and Some N'Ham and a N'onion" (C. R. St. Juste) The Lawrence Wright Music Co., 1925

As Charlie Higgins
"The Navvies Jazz" from *Out of Work* (1926-27)
"Ma! Look at Charlie" (E. Hedges) 1927[5]
"Mr. Waterhouse's House" (Ted Waite) from the revue *The Show World* (1928)
"Is Everybody Happy Now?" finale of *The Show World* with chorus
"The Porter's Blues" from *The Show World* (1928)[6]
"When I See an Oyster Walk Upstairs" (Ted Waite) 1928[7]
"Ol' Man River" (Parody using the tune of) The Metropolitan, April, 1929[8]
"The Top Hat My Grandfather Left Me in His Will" the Palladium, January, 1930[9]
"Why Build a Wall Around a Graveyard?" (Leslie Sarony) 1933
"I'm Going Back to Himazaz" (Fred Austin) c1934[10]
"I Tawt I Taw a Puddy Tat" (A. Livingston, Billy May, W. Foster) with Iris Sadler in *Dick Whittington* at the Shepherd's Bush Empire, 1950-51[11]

"The Thing" (Trad: The Lincolnshire Poacher) with cast, in *Dick Whittington,* Shepherd's Bush Empire, 1950-51.

Alfred Lester

Discography

"My Motter" (A. Wimperis, H. Talbot) / "The Property Man" (Melvin, Wood) Columbia 544 12" 1915
"Beautiful, Beautiful Bed" (C. W. Murphy, D. Lipton) HMV One-sided 12" 1915
"Higgins the Quack" (with Frank Leo) HMV 09280 1915
"Higgins on the River" (F. Leo) / "Higgins the Quack" (F. Leo) HMV C495 1915
"The Restaurant Episode" / "The Hair-Dresser" (Rome) (Assisted by Miss Buena Bent) HMV C496 12" 1915
"The Scene-Shifter's Lament" / "The Village Fire Brigade" HMV C497 12" 1915
"Beautiful, Beautiful Bed" (Murphy, Lipton) / Hennequin "Alphonse" HMV C498 12" 1915
"Longshoreman Bill" (Rome) with Miss Buena Bent & Co., & Orchestra Columbia 595 1916
"Dear Old Shepherd's Bush" / "Lady of a Thousand Charms" (Ayer) with Violet Loraine Columbia D1339 1916
"Another Little Drink Wouldn't Do Us Any Harm" with George Robey, Violet Lorraine, from *The Bing Boys are Here* Columbia L1034 1917
"The Conscientious Objector's Lament" (Rice) / "Hurrah for the Rolling Sea" (Finck) from *Round the Map* HMV C811 1917
"Is It Fair?" / "The Popular Poplar Sweetstuff Shop" (Popperty Pop) (J. P. Harrington, H. Darewski) from *The Shop Girl* Columbia F1053 1920
"Crimes" / "Lily of the Valley" Columbia 1920
"Ours is a Nice House, Ours Is" / "Germs" Columbia 887 1923
"Why Did I Marry My Wife?" (Stanley, Allen) / "Yes! We Have No Bananas" (Silver, Cohn) HMV B1683 1923
"I Do Like to Sing in the Bath" (Sterndale-Bennett) / "I Love Me" (Mahoney) from *Rats* HMV C1114 1923

"Gardening" / "Dandelions and Daffodils" (Demerell, Hargreaves, Baff) from *The Punch Bowl* HMV C1170 1924
"Fowls" / "Insuring His Life" (Rome) HMV C1177 1925
"Lolita" (Strachey) / "Stop Me if You've Heard It" (Blaney) HMV C1203 1925

Various Artists Compilations

Oh, What a Lovely War "A Conscientious Objector" World Records SH 130 LP c1970
Revue 1919-1929 "Germs" Parlophone LP PMC 7150 1972
The Bing Boys are Here: Original Cast Recordings of 1916 Pavilion Records Flapper Past CD 9716 1990
The Glory of the Music Hall Vol. 3 "Ours is a Nice 'Ouse Ours Is" & "Germs" Pearl GEMM CD 9477 1991
Round the Town: Following Grandfather's Footsteps Various Artists Bear Family 4 x CD Compilation featuring Alfred Lester "I Do Like to Sing in the Bath" and "Yes! We Have No Bananas" 2000
The Scene-Shifter's Lament "The Scene-Shifter's Lament" / "Ours is a Nice 'ouse, Ours Is" / "Hurrah for the Rolling Sea" / "The Conscientious Objector" / "Germs" / "I Do Like to Sing in the Bath" / "Gardening" / "Dandelions and Daffodils" / "Why Did I Marry My Wife?" / "I Love Me" / "The Restaurant Episode" (with Miss Buena Bent) / "The Hairdresser" / "Higgins the Quack" (with Frank Leo) / "Longshoreman Bill" (with Buena Bent) / "Crimes" / "Lily of the Valley" / "The Property Man" / "My Motter" / "Dear Old Shepherd's Bush" / Yes! We Have No Bananas" Windyridge CDR49 2010

Films

The Garden Beautiful Lester as doddery garden doctor, checking pulse of plants, etc. Pathe short. 1924
Britain Mourns: Mr. Alfred Lester Great Comedian Pathe short. 1925

Sheet Music and Published Sketches
"My Motter" (A. Wimperis, H. Talbot) Chappell & Co., 1909
"Germs" (B. Hapgood Burton, R. Atwell, Silvio Hein) Chappell & Co., 1915

"Another Little Drink" (C. Grey, N. D. Ayer) B. Feldman & Co., 1916
"Good Bye-Ee" (R. P. Weston, B. Lee) Francis, Day & Hunter, 1917
"The Property Man: The Stage-Hand's Lament" (H. E. Melvin, A. Wood)
"Ours is A Nice 'Ouse Ours Is" (H. Rule, F. Holt) 1921
"The Scene-Shifter's Lament" (A. Lester) Samuel French, Ltd., 1921
"A Restaurant Episode" (A. Lester) Samuel French, Ltd., 1921
"The Night Porter" (Harry Wall) Samuel French, Ltd., 1922
"The Village Fire Brigade" (Frank Collins) Samuel French, Ltd., c1925

Tom Foy

Discography

Original Releases
"Yorkshire Lad in Lundun" Pt. 1 & 2 10" Winner 2105 1910
"My Girl's Promised to Marry Me" (Godwin) / "Courting" (Foy) 10" Zonophone 578 1911
"Much Obliged to Me" (with piano) (Bateman) / "In Trouble Again" (Foy) 10" Zonophone 593 1911
"Coronation" / "Scouting" (Foy) 10" Zonophone 620 1911
"Donkey and Me" / "The Fool of the Family" (Foy) 10" Zonophone 636 1911
"Lizzie" (Foy) / "Mary Ellen" (Stevens, Ridgway) 10" Zonophone 666 1911
"A Little Shepherd" / 10" Zonophone 678 1911
"I'm Not One That Wants to Say Owt" / "If We Live to Be Ninety-Nine" 10" Zonophone 726 1911
"Amateur Dramatics" / "I've Been to China" (Foy) 10" Zonophone 764 1911
"I'm Excited" / "Aye Ah am Upset" (Foy) 10" Zonophone 883 1912
"My Bunker Bump" / "What's t'time?" 10" Zonophone 963 1912
"A Yorkshireman in London Pt. 1 & 2" Zonophone 1010 1912
"A Yorkshireman in London Pt. 3 & 4" Zonophone 1098 1912
"I've Been to a Wedding" / "Nearly Wedded" Zonophone 1118 1913
"Nineteen Bright Pounds" / "I've Had Some Money Left Me" 10" Zonophone 1191 1913
"Live and Learn" / "First Time That I Came Up to London" 10" Zonophone 1233 1913

"I've Been to America" / "My Aunt Martha Ann" 10" Zonophone 1308 1914
"Whales & Wales & Weals" / "Our Straits Canal" 10" Zonophone 1519 1915
"My Farewell to Sarby Brig" 10" Zonophone 1678 1916
"More Trouble" Pt. 1 & 2 10" Zonophone 1694 1916
"Ah've Had t'Nose Pulled" / "Getting My Temper Up" 10" Zonophone 1751 1916
"Ah'm Disguised" / "All Through t'Black Horse" 10" Zonophone 1816 1916

Compilations

On the Halls "The Fool of the Family" World Records SHB 43 2 x LP 1977

Donkey and Me "My Girl's Promised to Marry Me" / "Much Obliged to Me" / "Courting" / "Donkey and Me" / "The Fool of the Family" / "Scouting" / "If We Live to Be Ninety-Nine" / "Amateur Theatricals" / "My Bunker Bump" / "Nearly Wedded" / "Nineteen Bright Pounds" / "I've Had Some Money Left Me" / "Live and Learn" / "First Time That I Come Up to London" / "I've Been to America" / "My Aunt Martha Ann" / "Whales and Wales and Weals" / "Our Straits Canals" / "Ah'm Disguised" / "My Farewell to Sarby Brig" / "Ah've Had t'nose Pulled" / "All Through t'Black Horse" / "Getting My Temper Up" Windyridge CDR59 2014

Other Songs & Sheet Music

"Polly Perkins" duet with Ouida Macdermott in *Dick Whittington*
"I Wonder if They'd Let Me in if I Went" (F. V. St. Clair) August, 1904[1]
"I Reckon He'll Be Much Obliged to Me" (Edgar Bateman, Maurice Scott) Francis, Day & Hunter, 1904.

Vivian Foster

Discography

The Vicar of Mirth. Windyridge VAR9 "The Parson and the Sewing Party I & II" / "The Parson Addresses His Flock I & II" / "The Parson and the Collection I & II" / "The Parson Talks About

Marriage I & II" / "The Parson's Christmas Address I & II" / "The Parson in Defence of Parson I & II" / "The Parson and the Christmas Party I & II" / "The Parson and the Charleston I & II" / "The Parson Pleads for Happiness I & II" / "The Parson and Tales of Laughman I & II" / Alternative Takes—"The Parson and the Sewing Party" / "The Parson Talks About Marriage"

Songs & Monologues

"Up Went O'Connor (on His Wedding Day)" (Lester Bodine, George Maywood) at a concert in Brighton, November, 1903[1]
"We Should Like Very Much to Know" in double act with a Mr. Blackburn at Burgess Hill, Sussex, November, 1903[2]
"What Happened to Me" (Monologue) (Foster) at Brighton, December, 1903
"Love's Garden" (Edward Kent) at Brighton, 1903[3]
"How to Compose" with the Merry Mascots Company at Hayward's Heath, February, 1905[4]
"You Never Know!" (Paul Mill, J. Edward Fraser) at Rayleigh, April, 1907[5]
"Men and Women" (Burlesque lecture/monologue) in Derby, August, 1907[6]
"The Dear Vicar" (Foster) performed by Dennis Wilson, September, 1941

Films

Pathe Magazine 22 The Vicar of Mirth (1929) Pathe short.
Gaumont Sound Mirror (1931) Gaumont short.
This Week of Grace (1933) Dir.: Maurice Elvey. Cast: Gracie Fields, Henry Kendall, John Stuart, Frank Pettingell, Minnie Rayner, Douglas Wakefield, Vivian Foster (Vicar), Marjorie Brooks. Twickenham Studios.
See Also:
Findler, Gerald (Compiler) *Humour from Pulpit and Pew* with a Foreword by Vivian Foster (Heath Cranston, Ltd., London, 1934)

Bert Errol

Films

Ringing the Changes "A Peep at Bert Errol." Bert Errol does quick changes at the London Coliseum. Pathe (1922)
Equity Musical Revue No. 8. British Lion Film Corporation. Short (1935)[1]
Following in Father's Footsteps No. 2. Ralph Coram, Bill Coram, Betty Errol, Ena Grossmith. Betty Errol dances to piano accompaniment. Pathe (1935)

Songs and Sheet Music

"The Jewel Song" from Gounod's *Faust*
"Two Little Maids" (Duet with Dolly Summers) November, 1906[1]
"Il Bacio" (Luigi Arditi) from at least 1910
"Little Princess, Look Up!" (F. Fenn, P. M. Faraday) 1910
"Racing" 1910[2]
"Spring Is Coming" at the Vaudeville Club, November, 1910[3]
"When I Lost You" (Irving Berlin) Waterson, Berlin & Snyder Co., 1912
"My Hero" (O. Straus, S. Strange) from *The Chocolate Soldier* 1913
"Mysterious Kiss" (W. C. Duncan, F. de Gresac, W. F. Peters) Francis, Day & Hunter, 1913
"Beautiful Roses" (Earl Carroll, Anatol Friedland) Leo Feist, New York, 1913
"I'm On My Way to Mandalay" (A. L. Bryan, Fred Fisher) Leo Feist, New York, 1913
"When Love Creeps into Your Heart" (A. J. Mills, Bennett Scott) Star Music Publishing Co., 1913[4]
"Isle D'Amour" (C. Grooms, L. Edwards) Leo Feist, 1913
"Tony Traviata" (Earl Carroll, Arthur Behim) Shapiro, Bernstein & Co., New York, 1914
"He's a Rag Picker (Irving Berlin) Waterson-Berlin-Snyder Co., New York, 1914
"Sweet Kentucky Lady (Dry Your Eyes)" (W. Jerome, L. A. Hirsch, adapted from a theme by Stephen Foster) M. Witmark & Sons, London, 1914
"Lucille Love" (A. Rawlings) F. Howard, London, 1914

"Wonderful Rose of Love" (A. J. Mills, B. Scott) Star Music Co., London, 1914[5]
"Blue Eyes" Lawrence Wright Music Publishing Co., 1915
"You Gave Me Love" (A. J. Mills, B. Scott) 1916
"Oh! For a Night in Bohemia" c1918 in "The Gaieties" Concert Party[6]
"Something Oriental" Herman Darewski & Co., 1919[7]
"Moontime on the Mississippi" (E. Lynton) Lawrence Wright Music Publishing Co., 1919
"Kentucky, I'm Coming Home" (E. Lynton) Lawrence Wright Music Publishing Co., 1919[8]
"The Kingdom Within Your Eyes" (Worton David, Horatio Nicholls) Lawrence Wright Music Publishing Co., 1919[9]
"My Sahara Rose" (Grant Clark, Walter Donaldson) Herman Darewski Publishing Co., London, 1920
"La Veeda"—Castilian Foxtrot (Nat Vincent, John Alden) Jerome H. Remick & Co., New York & Detroit, 1920
"The Bells of St. Mary's" (A. Emmett Adams, D, Furber) at the Palace Theater, New York, May, 1920[10]
"Venetian Moon" (G. Kahn, P. Goldberg) Frank Magini, 1920
"Honolulu Eyes" (Howard Johnson, Violinsky) Leo Feist, New York, 1920
"Remember the Rose" (S. D. Mitchell, S. B. Simons) B. Feldman & Co., 1921
"Just Like a Rainbow" (M. Earl, T. Fiorito) B. Feldman & Co., 1921
"Himalaya" (H. Jordan, M. Herbert) 1921[11]
"Second-Hand Rose" (J. F. Hanley) 1922[12]
"Widows are Wonderful" The Alhambra, July, 1923[13]
"A Smile Will Go a Long Way" (B. Davis, H. Akst) B. Feldman & Co., 1923
"Look Up and See the Rainbow" (A. Sullivan) Chappell & Co., 1924
"(Kentucky's Way of Saying) Good Morning" (Gus Kahn, E. Van Alstyne) Jerome K. Remick & Co., 1925
"Let it Rain" at Douglas, Isle of Man, Summer, 1925[14]
"I Know That Someone Loves Me" (J. A. Tunbridge, E. Valentine) Summer, 1925[15]
"No, Pagliacci" from *Pagliacci* at the Palace, Chicago, October, 1925[16]
"Bam Bam Bamy Shore" (Mort Dixon, Ray Henderson) Jerome H. Remick & Co., 1925
"Sweet Georgia Brown" (B. Bernie, Maceo Pinkard, Kenneth Casey) Jerome H. Remick & Co., 1926

"Put Your Arms Where They Belong (and They Belong to Me) (L. Davis, H. Santley, H. Ackman) Irving Berlin, Inc., New York, 1926
"Gimme a Little Kiss, Will Ya Huh?" (R. Turk, J. Smith, M. Pinkard) Irving Berlin, Inc., New York, 1926
"I'm Going to Follow the Rainbow" 1926[17]
"I'm Tellin' the Birds—Tellin' the Bees How I Love You" (C. Friend, L. Brown) Irving Berlin, Inc., New York, 1926
"Rosy Cheeks" (S. Simons, R. A. Whiting) Irving Berlin, Inc., New York, 1927
"Dancing Tambourine" (W. C. Polla) Chappell & Co., 1927
"Marieta" (B. Scott) at the Palladium, September, 1927[18]
"Leave Me with a Smile" (C. Koehler, E. Burtnett) B. Feldman & Co., 1928
"At Twilight" (Maceo Pinkard) May, 1930[19]
"I Love You, I Hate You" Feldman & Co., 1930[20]
"Dancing with Tears in My Eyes" (Al Dubin, Joe Burke) 1930[21]
"When Cleopatra Got the Needle" (Fred Godfrey) November, 1931[22]
"Good Queen Bess" at West Pier Theatre, Brighton, December, 1934[23]
"A Fine Old English Lady" In Pantomime, 1935-36[24]

Margaret Cooper

Memoir

Margaret Cooper *Myself and My Piano* (John Ouseley, London, 1909) 8vo 84pp, 11 plates, 1 colour. Extremely rare: listed in four libraries: British Library, National Library of Scotland, Oxford University, Cambridge University.

Discography

Dingle Dongle Dell Windyridge CDR 60
"Under the Um-ber-el-la" / "Little Princess, Look-Up" / "In the Maytime" / "Cheero" / "Ma Dusky Maid" / "Love is Meant to Make Us Glad" / "Dingle Dongle Dell" / "Hullu Tu Tu" / "Heaps o' Lickens" / "Agatha Green" / "Catch Me" / "Let Us Waltz Around Together" / "Plumstones" / "Come to Town, Miss Brown" / "Dreamland" / "What's it Got to Do With You?" /

"Visitors" / "Inquisitive Ann" / "I Don't Seem to Want You When You're with Me" / "Bonjour Marie" / "Come Down to Brighton" / "The Foxtrot Hop" / "Mother's Darling"

Scott's Music Box: Music from Terra Nova: The British Antarctic Expedition (1910-1913) 48 Tracks including Margaret Cooper "Love is Meant to Make Us Glad" EMI Gold Double-cd & mp3 download 2012. G644 9492

ORIGINAL RELEASES

"Under the Um-ber-ella" / "Little Princess Look-Up" 10" Pathe 268 1907
"In the Maytime" / "Cheero" 10" Pathe 269 1907
"Ma Dusky Maid" 1-sided 10" HMV GC 3811 1909
"Love is Meant to Make Us Glad" 1-sided 10" HMV GC 3820 1909
"Dingle Dongle Dell" 1-sided 10" HMV GC 3831 1909
"Hullo Tu Tu" 1-sided 12" HMV 03164 1909
"Peter" (C. Scott-Gatty) 1-sided 12" HMV 01238 1910
"Heaps o' Lickens" 1-sided 10" HMV GC 3867 1910
"Catch Me!" 1-sided 12" HMV 03209 1911
"Agatha Green" 12" HMV 03228 1911
"Dreamland" 12" HMV 03264 1911
"Plumstones" 1-sided 12" HMV 03267 1911
"Let Us Waltz Around Together" 10" HMV 03270 1911
"What's It Got to Do with You?" HMV 03280 1911
"Come to Town, Miss Brown" 1-sided 10" HMV 03281 1911
"Bonjour Marie" 10" HMV 2-3134 1915
"Visitors" 10" HMV 2-7071 1915
"Inquisitive Ann" 10" HMV 2-7073 1915
"I Don't Seem to Want You When You're with Me" (Rubens) 10" HMV 03396 1915
"Come Down to Brighton" 10" HMV 03432 1915
"The Fox Trot Hop" 10" HMV 03452 1915
"The Green Hills o' Somerset" (Fred E. Weatherley, Eric Coates) 1918
"Dreamland" (Garstin) / "Hullo Tu Tu" (C. Scott-Gatty) 12" HMV D203 c1919
"Lonely" (Foulde) / "I Don't Seem to Want You When You're with Me" 12" HMV D204 c1919
"Peter" / "Mother's Darling" 12" HMV D205 c1919

"Inquisitive Ann" (T, C. Sterndale Bennett) / "Ma Dusky Maid" (Vere Smith) 10" HMV EA 37 c1920

Sheet Music and Additional Songs

"Nobody Knows" (C. Chaminade) 1896[1]
"The Jewel Song" from *Faust* (C. Gounod) c1897
"Life" 1897
"All Souls' Day" (E. Lassen, Mrs. M. Lawson) 1897
"When Twilight Dews" (MacCann) 1897
"When Fairyland Was Young" (Rev. Stopford A. Brooke, Arthur Somervell) Public debut at St. James's Hall, c1897
"Life's Little Cares" (M. V. White) 1898
"Come, Let's Be Merry" (E. German) Boosey & Hawkes, 1898
"A Bunch of Violets" (Guy d'Hardelot) Chappell & Co., 1898
"A Lesson with a Fan" (Guy d'Hardelot) 1898[2]
"Noon" (M. V. White) 1898
"An Den Mond" (Franz Schubert) c1899
"La Violette" (Scarlatti) 1899
"Sweet Lavender" (J. Muir, E. Cooke) 1899
"May Morning" (John Milton, Mary Travers) 1899
"Dolly and the Coach" (F. C. Smale, G. H. Stone) Boosey & Co., c1899
"Remembrance" and "Spring" (Garnet W. Cox) 1899
"Lusinghe piu care" Recitative and Aria from the opera *Alessandro* (Handel) 1899
"A Pastoral" (H. Lane Wilson) 1899
"Au Clair de Lune" c1899
"Songs My Mother Taught Me" (A. Dvorak) 1899
"Cavatina" from the opera *Les Hugenots* (G. Meyerbeer) 1899
"Nobil Signor" (G. Meyerbeer) 1899
"Romance" (M. Cooper) 1899
"Love's Garden" (Edward Kent) Reynolds & Co., 1899
"An Anthem of Love" (Florence Aylward) Chappell & Co., 1899
"Love in Arcady" 1899
"Only Memories" (Frank Moir) Metzler & Co., 1899
"Orpheus with His Lute" from *Henry VIII* (E. German) 1899
"Hay-time" (Ebenezer Jackson) 1899
"Goodbye" 1899

"She is Far from the Land" (Thomas Moore, F. Lambert) Chappell & Co., c1899
"Nymphes et Sylvains"—Val e Chantee (A. Ocampo, H. Bemberg, A. Larkcom) c1899
"Smile of April" (Maurice Depret, C. Bingham) Hachette e Cie, Paris, 1899
"The Spring Has Come" (Maude Valerie White) Chappell & Co., 1899
"Little Orphant Annie" (J. W. Riley, Alicia A. Needham) Boosey & Co., 1899
"The Beggar's Song" (R. Leveridge, arr. H. L. Wilson) Boosey & Co., 1899
"Who'll Buy My Lavender?" (E. German, C. Battersby) Boosey & Hawkes, 1899
"A Birthday—My Heart is Like a Singing Bird" (F. H. Cowen) Joseph Williams, 1900
"The Red Sarafan" (Varlamoff, F. Whishaw) 1900
"Love, the Peddlar" (C. Battersby) c1900
"Beloved, it is Morn" (F. Aylward, E. Hickey) c1900
"A Royal Rose" (Florian Pascal) 1900
Two Little Irish Songs—"To My First Love" and "You'd Better Ask Me" (H. Lohr) Chappell & Co., 1900
"Aime-Moi" (H. Bemberg) 1900
"L'ete" (C. Chaminade) 1900
Two Songs "Last Year" and "The Fifes of June" (M. V. White, W. E. Henley) Chappell & Co., 1900
"When Jack and I Were Children" (Herman Lohr, Fred E. Weatherly) Chappell & Co., 1900
"Tis Not Fine Feathers Make Fine Birds" (J. E. Carpener, J. N. Sporle) Joseph Williams, 1900
"Sea Lullaby" (Edward German, Harold Boulton) Chappell & Co., 1900
"The Path Ordained" (Vastoa, Charles P. Cooper) Chappell & Co., 1900
"Outcry" (A. O'Shaughnessy, F. H. Cowen) Joseph Williams, 1900
"The Guardian Angel" (E. Nesbit, L. Lehmann) E. Ascherberg & Co., c1900
"The Maiden with the Dreamy Eyes" (J. W. Johnson, B. Cole) Stern & Co., 1901
"Bric-a-Brac" (E. & H. Farjeon) Boosey & Co., 1901
"Dolly's Doctor" (Helmund) 1901
"An Old Romance" (Guy de'Hardelot) 1901

"The Story of the Cruise" (Franco Leoni) 1901
"Fairies" (Liza Lehmann) 1901
"Mustard and Cress" (L. Lehmann) 1901
"The Ould Plaid Shawl" (Battison Haynes, F, H, Fahy) 1901
"When Twilight Comes In" (Anton Strelezki) 1901
"Little Blue Cornflower" (Winifred Carnac) 1901
"Madcap Marjorie" (W. Carnac) Chappell, 1901
"My Dolly" (W. Cornelius, W. Earnshawe) c1901
"Little Lady Wide-Awake" (E. Fleming, E. Demain Grange) Joseph Williams, 1899. Sung 1902
"Birds in the High Hall Garden" (A. Somervell, A. Tennyson) Boosey & Co., 1898/1902
"Let the Bright Seraphim" (G. F. Handel) St. Peter's Church, Garford Street, Limehouse, 1902
"Lead, Kindly Light" (G. Aitken) St. Peter's Church, Garford Street, Limehouse, 1902
"Bloom On, My Roses" from *The Rose Maiden* (R. E. Francillon, F. H. Cowen) 1902
"The Elephant and the Portmanteau" (Frederic Norton) Chappell & Co., 1902
"The Camel and the Butterfly" (F. Norton) Chappell & Co., 1902
"The Owl and the Rook" (F. Norton) Chappell & Co., 1902
"Oh Peaceful England" from *Merrie England* (E. German, B. Hood) Chappell & Co., 1902
"Try to Forget" (E. Teschemacher, N. Johnson) Chappell & Co., 1902
"The Cuckoo" from "More Daisies" (Songs of Childhood) (Liza Lehmann, W. B. Rands) Boosey & Co., 1902
"Farewell Ye Limpid Springs" from *Jephtha* (G. F. Handel) 1902
"In Sympathy" (Franco Leoni, H. Blinn) Chappell & Co., 1902
"God's Eternity" (N. Johnson, K. Rhodes) Chappell & Co., 1902
"Love's Benediction" (F. Aylward) Chappell & Co., 1902
"Our Sunny Days" (Olga Rudd, Frances Wynne) Metzler & Co., 1902
"The Paper Fan" from *The Chinese Honeymoon* c1902
"Melisande in the Wood" (Ethel Clifford, Alma Goetz) Chappell & Co., 1902
"Till the Dawn" (H. Graham, P. A. Rubens) Metzler & Co., 1903
"Come Along with Me" from the musical play *The Orchid* (L. Monckton, A. Ross) Chappell & Co., 1903
"A Protest" (Noel Johnson, K. Rhodes) Chappell & Co., 1903

"Summer's in the World" (N. Johnson, H. Lonsdale) Chappell & Co., 1903
"Petie Boy" (F. W. Norton) c1903
"A Daffodil Song" (E. Teschemacher, W. P. Weekes) Turner & Philips, 1903
"Love's Afternoon" (H. Lonsdale, A. H. Hyatt) Chappell & Co., 1903
"In the Dingle Dongle Dell" from the opera *The Norsemen* (C. Beecher Kummer) J. Albert & Son, 1904
"My Little Chimney Sweep"—Song from the musical play *The Orchid* (Percy Greenbank, Lionel Monckton) Chappell & Co., Ltd., 1904
"A Naughty Word" (F. Norton) 1904
"A Fancy" c1904
"Heigh-Ho" (P. Barnes) 1904
"Evermore" (Here Below) "Ici Bas" (Cora Fabbri, Frank Lambert) Chappell & Co., 1904
"The Apple Tree" from the comic opera *Veronique* (A. Messager, P. Greenbank) Boosey & Co., 1904
"Four Child Songs" "A Good Child" "The Lamplighter" "Where Go the Boats?" "Foreign Children" (R. Quilter, R. L. Stevenson) Chappell 1904
"A Rustic Maid" (W. Rubens) 1905
"Come Along with Me" (A. Ross, L. Monckton) from *The Orchid* Chappell & Co., 1905
"Never Mind the Weather" (T. Heffernan, Liza Lehmann) Hopwood & Crew, 1905
"My Sweet Bird of Paradise" (H. E. Pether) Francis, Day & Hunter, 1905
"I Don't Seem to Want You When You're with Me" (Paul A. Rubens, M. Cooper) Chappell & Co, Ltd, 1905
"The Rose" and "The River and the Sea" (Noel Johnson) Chappell c1905
"Once Upon a Time" (P. A. Rubens, H. P. Humphry) Chappell & Co., 1905
"I Would Like to Be a Grand Lady" and selections from the musical play *The Little Michus* (A. Messager, P. Greenbank) 1905
"Little Crimson Rose" (D. Eardley-Wilmot, Vere Smith) Chappell & Co, Sung by Margaret in *The Dandy Duke* 1906
"A Little Bit Shy" (Noel Johnson) Chappell & Co., 1906
"Dear Little Boy Next Door" (A. du Soir, J. Airlie Dix) Francis, Day & Hunter, 1906
"The Better Land" (F. H. Cowen) 1906

"I Mean to Marry a Man" (Howard Talbot) Chappell & Co., 1906
"Sonnie" (J. F. Barron, J. Airlie Dix) Boosey & Co., 1906
"I Want Somebody to Love Me" (H. G. Pelissier, A. Davenport) J. Williams, 1906
"Jest Her Way" (G. B. J. Aitken, E. Sylvester) c1906
"Experience" (Ivan Caryll, Adrian Ross) Chappell & Co., 1906
"Sweep! Sweep!" (Jacques Tarre) 1906
"The English Rose" (Edward German, Felton Rapley, Basil Hood) c1906
"In Fair Arcadia" (M. C. & D. Forster, M. Cooper) Cary, London & Shubert, New York, 1906
"Waltz Me Around Again, Willie" (Will D. Cobb, Ren Shields) 1906
"Fairyland" (D. Eardley-Wilmot, Vere Smith) Chappell & Co, 1906
"Won't You Come Off to the Zoo?" (Cyril M. Hall) Lublin & Co., London, circa 1907
"They Pretend They Really Couldn't but We All Know That They Do" (Arthur Trevelyan) Francis, Day & Hunter, London, circa 1907
"Life's Lucky Bag" (Harold Simpson, Douglas M. Leighton) Lublin & Co., circa 1907
"My Sunday Best" (Talbot Owen, Rupert Vine) Lublin & Co., 1907
"The Home of Sunny Hours" (C. Bingham, R. Eden) Elkin & Co., 1907
"Margery Green" (F. Barron, A. Beresford) J. B. Cramer & Co., 1907
"Master and Man" (Fred Weatherly, R. Coningsby Clarke) Chappell & Co., 1907
"A Dainty Pair of Shoes" (A. du Soir, J. Airlie Dix) Francis, Day & Hunter, 1907
"Johnny! Me and You!"—The Street Arabs—Musical Monologue (Corney Grain) Price & Reynolds, London, 1907
"The Pessimistic Crow" (Roland Henry, Percy Vere) Keith, Prowse & Co., Ltd., London, circa 1908
"Dear Little Jammy Face" (Kennedy Russell) Lublin & Co, London, circa 1908
"In Butterfly Time" (J. Anthony McDonald, Spencer Dyke) The John Church Co., Wigmore Street, London, 1908
"Cupid & Co." (P. A. Rubens, A. Wimperis) Chappell & Co., 1908
"Mother's Maxims" (Arthur Davenport, H. G. Pelissier) Joseph Williams Ltd, 1908
"A Delicate Question" (Beresford Rode, Percy Vere) Chappell & Co., 1908
"Ypsilanti" (Arthur Davenport, H. G. Pelissier) Joseph Williams, 1908

"What Rot" (Horace Mills) W. & G. Baird Ltd., Belfast, 1908
"Vivandiere" (E, Newton) 1908
"Janie" (C. Scott-Gatty) Chappell & Co., 1908
"Ma Dusky Maid" (Vere Smith) Chappell & Co., 1908
"Lancers" (M. Cooper, Arr: H. M. Higgs) Chappell & Co., 1909
"Hullo Tu-Tu" (C. & M. Scott-Gatty) Chappell & Co, 1909
"My Moon" (Arthur Davenport, H. G. Pelissier) Joseph Williams Ltd, London, 1909
"You'll Get Heaps o' Lickins'" (F. L. Stanton, Robert Coningsby Clarke) Chappell & Co, 1909
"Moonstruck" or "Moon, Moon, Mischief-Making Moon" from the musical play *Our Miss Gibbs* (Lionel Monckton) Chappell & Co., 1909
"The Little Black Dog" (Vere Smith) Enoch & Sons, 1909[3]
"When I Dream of You" (H. Simpson, E. Newton) London, 1909
"Fairy Dreams" (Vere Smith) c1909
"Do You Think You Could Love Me?" (C. Bingham, H. M. Goldstein) c1909
"My Love Awaits Me There" (F. C. Leister, Florence Cooper) 1909
Four Songs of Childhood "Tell Me Goosey Gander," "White Bread and Brown Bread," "Robin Red-Breast" and "Which is the Way to London Town?" (R. E. Mack, T. C. Sterndale Bennett) Chappell & Co., 1909
"Oh! Mister Bunny" (Frederic W. Norton, W. Graham Robertson) Chappell & Co., 1909
"Heaven for Two" (M. Cooper) c1910 Date unknown[4]
"A Little Heart" (Cecil Trent) 1910
"She Stoops to Conquer" (Joseph L. Roeckel, Fred E. Weatherly) 1910
"Peter" (C. & M. Scott-Gatty) Chappell & Co, 1910
"Shadow March" ("All around the house is the jet-black night") Songs from *Children's Pictures* adapted from *A Child's Garden of Verses* (Teresa Del Riego, R. L. Stevenson) Chappell & Co., 1910
"Catch Me!" (M. Cooper, A. M. Humble-Crofts) Chappell & Co, circa 1910
"When I'm Grown Up" (D. Eardley-Wilmot, George Aitken) Chappell & Co, 1910
"Visitors" (H. H. Whitney, Waddington Cooke) c1910
"Sunshade Sue" (H. M. Tennent) Chappell & Co., 1910
"Suzan's Sabots"

"Hello! Martha" (Vere Smith) c1910
"Morning Mood" and "Anitra's Dance" from the opera *Peer Gynt* (Eduard Greig) c1910
"My Dusty Man"
"Rabbit Town" c1910
"The Little Dancing Girl" c1910
"Maudie's Party" c1910
"Coon" (T. C. Sterndale Bennett) Chappell & Co., 1910
"Rain" (T. C. Sterndale Bennett) Chappell & Co., 1910
"Bobby Dear" (C. Scott-Gatty) Chappell & Co., 1910
"Come to Town, Miss Brown" (T. C. Sterndale Bennett) Chappell & Co., 1910
"Dusky Sue" (H. Lane Wilson) Chappell & Co., 1910
"The Faithful Lover" (David Emmell) Chappell & Co., 1910
"Mister Nightingale" (Bernard Rolt) Chappell & Co., 1910
"Cherchez la Femme" (Eric Baring) 1910
"My Bungalow in Bond Street" (T. C. Sterndale Bennett, G. Arthurs) Keith, Prowse & Co, 1910
"The Witch in the Glass" (S. Piatt, Maude Bruce) Dedicated to Margaret Cooper; Weeks & Co., 1910
"Philosophy" (David Emmell) The B. F. Wood Music Co, 1911
"Agatha Green" (M. Cooper, A. M. Humble-Crofts) Chappell & Co, 1911
"Plumstones" (Hartford Worlock) Chappell & Co, 1911
"You Always Have to Pay a Little More" (M. Cooper, A. M. Humble-Crofts) Chappell & Co., 1911
"Yachting in Regent's Park" (George Arthurs, T. C. Sterndale Bennett) Keith, Prowse & Co, 1911
"The Beautiful Planet of Mars" (H. M. Tennent) Chappell & Co., 1911
"Trixie's Taxi" (Harold E. Scott, 'Percy Petrol') Chappell & Co., 1911
"Let Us Waltz Around Together" (R. Penso) Chappell & Co., 1911
"Love's Coronation" (Florence Aylward) Church & Co., 1911
"Are You Coming Out?" 1911
"After You Had Gone" 1911
"I Feel So Silly When the Moon Comes Out" 1911
"The Beat of a Passionate Heart" (Montague F. Phillips, G. Hubi-Newcombe) Chappell & Co., 1911
"A Modest Little Maiden" c1911
"My Little Friend" (Bernard Rolt) Chappell & Co., 1911
"Dreamland" (Harold Garsten, Lancelot C. Shadwell) Chappell & Co., 1912

"Roller-Skating Katie" (H. M. Tennent) Chappell & Co., 1912
"Dream Girl" (H. M. Tennent, R. S. Hooper) Chappell & Co., 1912
"I'll Build a Gunyah for You" (Jack Cannot, Victor Prince) Allan & Co, Pty, Ltd, Melbourne, 1912
"If Nobody Ever Marries Me" Adelaide 1912[5]
"Wonderful Garden of Dreams" (Dorothy Forster) Chappell & Co., 1912
"Love is Meant to Make Us Glad" (E. German) Chappell & Co., c1912
"A Baby's Reflections" (H. W, Chuter)[6]
"Turn Dem Eyes Away" (Hugh E. Wright, Philip Braham) Chappell & Co, London & Melbourne, 1912
"A Tiny Touch" (P. A. Rubens) Chappell & Co, 1912
"I Love the Moon" (P. A. Rubens) Chappell & Co., 1912
"Hush Me to Dreams" (Kennedy Russell) Gould & Co., Oxford Street, London, 1912
"Scent of the Clover" (Ernest Newton) Gould & Co., London, 1912
"Perfectly Polite" 1912
"The Breezy, Briny Sea" (H. M. Tennent) 1912
"Tender Thoughts" (J. Thomson, H. W. Chuter) Collard Moultrie, 1912
"O, Lovely Dream" (J. Thomson, H. W. Chuter) Collard Moultrie, 1912
"I Love You" 1913
"Dreams" 1913
"On the Banks of the Serpentine" (T. C. Sterndale Bennett, B. Lee) 1913
"Little Mary Fawcett" (J. & F. Witty) Chappell & Co, 1913
"The Summertime Moon" (Leslie Elliott) Chappell & Co., 1913
"The Country of Dreams" (J. & F. Witty) Cary & Co., 1913
"What's It Got to Do with You?" (R. S, Hooper, H. M. Tennant) Cary & Co, circa 1913
"Gathering Nuts in May" (H. Simpson, Gatty Sellars) Francis, Day & Hunter, 1914
"Coquette" (Fedden Tindall, Harold Garstin) Chappell & Co, London & Melbourne, c1914
"Twilight Hours" (David Worton, Bert Lee, Harry Fragson) Frank Howard Ltd., London, 1914
"Waltz Me, Dearie" (G. Paul) Chappell & Co., 1914
"A Fat Little Fella with His Mammy's Eyes" (Sheridan Gordon) c1914
"Always Hitch Your Wagon to a Star" 1914
"Bonjour! Marie" (Max Brunell, C. Vernon Francis) Cary & Co., 1914
"More Hero Than Saint"—A stirring little Trafalgar song (A. K. Blackall) Priestley & Sons, London, 1914

"Inquisitive Ann" (T. C. Sterndale Bennett, H. Simpson, M. Cooper, F, W. Schmidt) Walsh, Holmes & Co, London, 1915
"The Colours" (M. Cooper, A. M. Humble-Crofts) J. B. Cramer & Co, 1915
"Ellen" (B. Rolt) Chappell & Co., 1915
"I'm Going to Be a Soldier" 1915
"Lots of Things" (H. Simpson, A. K. Stewart) Walsh, Holmes & Co., 1915
"Old Chap" (Ada Leonora Harris, Martin Rosse) J. Albert & Son, Sydney; Francis & Day, London, 1915
"My Mother Says Angels" (Claude Arundale) J. B. Cromer & Co., Ltd., 1915
"Lucky Dog" (Claude Arundale) J. B. Cramer & Co., Ltd., 1915
"Just One More" (Fred G. Bowles, George L'Estrange) J. B. Cramer & Co., Ltd, 1915
"This Hour with You" (M. Cooper. F. Kensey Peile) Chappell & Co.,1916
"Liza Brown" (Marjorie E. Harrison, Freda Wilmot) Chappell & Co., 1916
"The Houseboat" from the song cycle *The Silvery Thames* (J. P. Harrington, Frederic Mullen) Osborne & Co., London, 1916
"Bertie and Belinda" (Robert Green) Newman & Co., London, 1916
"Six What Nots" (Anon., T. C. Sterndale Bennett) 1916
"The Youthful Guest" 1916
"I'll Dream of You" (Charles & Sydney Berkeley) The Lawrence Wright Co., 1916
"The Sugar Baby" (H. M. & G. A. Vernon, G. Arthurs) B. Feldman & Co., 1917
"Touchin' Fings"—Musical Monologue (Leonard Cooke, Henry E. Pether) Francis, Day & Hunter Ltd., London, 1917
"You Can't Love as I Do" (P. Rubens) 1917
"Goodbye, Dixie! (I'm Off to France)" (P. Bernard, A. M. Swanstone) 1917
"Mother's Darling" (Frank Dunlop, Howard Carr) Herman Darewski Music Publishing Co., 1917
"Too Too Was A Dainty Doll" (Maudesley Dudley, Lawrence Wright) Chappell & Co., Ltd., 1917
"Bertha from Balham" (Noel Coward) c1917[7]
"It's Just Lovely Being with You" (G. Paul) Chappell & Co., 1917
"Only Got One Heart" (Pedro de Zulueta) Chappell & Co., 1918
"Only Seven" (Lillian Grey, M. Cooper) Chappell & Co, 1918
"The Fish Sauce Shop" (F. St. John Brougham) Chappell & Co, 1918

"My Angel Jim (of the Flying Corps)" (Stanley West, F. A. Armstrong) Chappell & Co., circa 1918
"Away in Athlone" (H. Lohr, E. Lockton) Chappell & Co., 1918
"Mr. Orchestra" (F. St. John Brougham) Chappell & Co., 1918
"Eric, the Egg" (F. St. John Brougham) Chappell & Co., 1919
"Uncle John" (Stanley West, F. A. Armstrong) J. B. Cramer & Co., London, circa 1919
"The Mummy Hobble" (James Heard, F. St. John Brougham) Chappell & Co., London, 1919
"Jumpers" (F. R. Burrow, Herman Lohr) Chappell & Co., London, 1919
"Just Remember" (F. Daly, Herman Lohr) Chappell & Co., 1919
"His Little Teddy Bear" (Sivori Levey) Chappell & Co, 1919
"Daddy & Babsy" (Sivori Levey) Chappell & Co., 1919
"He Met Her on the Stairs" (Sivori Levey) Chappell & Co., 1919
"Last Year, Sweetheart, Last Year" (H. Lohr) 1919
"Just a Little One" (Clifford Seyler, T. C. Sterndale Bennett) J. B. Cramer & Co., 1920
"The Soozletoo" (Hugh E. Wright, T. C. Sterndale Bennett) Chappell & Co., circa 1920
"When All the Children Pray" (J. C. Holliday, H. J. Brandon) Chappell & Co., 1920
"Little Yaller Dog" (James M. Gallatly) Herman Darewski, Charing Cross Road, London, 1920[8]
"The Portals of the Forest" (D. Eardley-Wilmot, Herman Lohr) Chappell & Co., 1920
"Li'l' Cannibal Coon" (Charles Hayes, T. C. Sterndale Bennett) Chappell & Co., 1921
"The Chumptown Carnival" (K. Parker, W. Prinz, M. Cooper) Chappell & Co., 1921
"Flapper Songs" including "Johnny Parker" / "Uncle" / "Algernon Rolf" / "Cousin Maudie" / "Aunt Lucilla" (Comfort Parry, Herman Lohr) Chappell & Co., 1921
"Little Corner of Your Heart" (Mary Orton, Herman Lohr) September, 1921 Regent, Brighton
"Honey, Dat's All" (L. B. Curtis) 1922
"Love Up-to-Date" (Charles Hayes, T. C. Sterndale Bennett) Chappell & Co., 1922.

Norman Long

Discography

The Savoy Orpheans "It Ain't Gonna Rain No Mo'—Fantasie" Pts I & II N. Long as compere (Recorded at the Savoy Hotel, London) 10" HMV B 1994 April, 1925

"The Drage Way" (Clarkson Rose) / "Homes" (R. P. Weston, Bert Lee, N. Long) 10" HMV B 2257 December, 1925

"Prophecies" / "I'm Blasé" (Taylor) 12" HMV C1235 c1926

"London and Daventry Calling, Part I & II" (N. Long) The Savoy Orpheans 10" HMV C1251 1926

"Toasts" (Clarkson Rose) / "Down in Our Village in Zummerzet" (Clarkson Rose) 10" HMV B 2296 June, 1926

"The Good Little Boy and Bad Little Boy" (Lee, Weston) / "Under the Bazunka Tree" (Lee) 10" HMV B 2454 March, 1927

"I Think of You" (K. G. Weston) / "Is it British?" (K. G. Weston) 10" HMV B 2580 March, 1927

"My Little Austin Seven" (H. M. Burnaby, N. Long) / "Monday Morning" 10" Columbia 5112 May, 1928

"Sing Ho! For the Days of Drinking" (Rose, T. C. Sterndale-Bennett) / "Down on the Beach at Bangaloo" (N. Long) 10" Columbia 5159 May, 1928

"Why is the Bacon So Tough?" (Arkell, Prentice) / "Never Have a Bath with Your Wrist Watch On" (Squiers, Goodall) 10" Columbia 5162 1929

"That's Why I Love Her" / "You Mustn't Do It After Eight O'Clock" (A. McGill) 10" Columbia 5324 January, 1929

"Overture 1929" (Founded on the Turkish National Anthem; Carlton, arr. Long) / "What Did the Village Blacksmith Say?" 10" Columbia 5299 April, 1929

"Otherwise She's Mother's Kind of Girl" (Squiers, G. Barker) / "A Tale of Other Times" (N. Long, L. Pounds) 10" Columbia 5447 April, 1929

"Aren't We All? (H. M. Burnaby, N. Long) / "That Little Back Garden of Mine" (Eyton, N. Long) 10" Columbia 5478 April, 1929

"Ideal Homes" (Clarkson Rose) / "Hidden Heroes" (Clarkson Rose) 10" Columbia 5494 1929

"I Do Hate Lying in Bed" (N. Long) 10" Columbia 5666 circa 1929

"I Ain't Never Been Kissed" (Leslie, Gilbert) / "A Hundred Years from Now" (Silvers, Baker, McBoyle, Carlton) from *On with the Show* 10" Regal G 9312 June 1929

"Our Dog" / "Rule Britannia—A Travesty" 10" Columbia DB 10 May, 1929

"What Would Mr Gladstone Say to That?" (Rutherford, Wilcock) / "That Rests Entirely with Me" (Vernon) / 10" Columbia DB 185 January, 1930

"The Barrers in the Walworth Road" (Leslie Sarony) / "Because No Power on Earth Can Pull it Down" (Rutherford, Wilcock) 10" Columbia DB 292 c1930

"The Single Man and the Married Man" (Weston, Lee) / "She Does it All for Me" (K. & G. Western) 10" Columbia DB 344 c1930

"Dear Old Fashioned Thing" (Harrington, Hobson) / "Seven Veils" (DeSilva, Brown, Henderson) 10" Columbia DB 383 c1930

"In the Morning" (with unnamed lady) / "The Willows" (Long) 10" Columbia DB 576 c1930

"National Economy" (Parr, Long) / "I'm Waiting Now for Any Kind of Sweetheart" (L. Pounds, Long) 10" Columbia DB 676

"Grandma's Days and Nowadays" (Clarkson Rose) / "The Bushes at the Bottom of the Garden" (Clarkson Rose) 10" Columbia DB 738

Columbia On Parade: Christmas. Various artists: Spoken introduction by Long. 12" Columbia DX 299 December, 1931.

"I Wonder What Made Her Go" (N. Long, R. Frankau) / "Going Down" (R. Frankau)
10" Columbia DO 722 (Issued in Australia) August, 1932

"It's Really Too Terribly Thrilling" / "Dick Turpin's Ride to York" 10" Columbia DB 825 1932[1]

"Stillness of the Night" (Cecil Harrington) 10" Columbia 978

Columbia On Parade; Crazy Pantomime. "Cinderella" Various artists including Binnie Hale, Stanley Holloway, Flanagan & Allen, Harry Tate, Norman Long et al. 12" Columbia DX 410 December, 1932

"The Council Schools are Good Enough for Me" (Morris, Ives) / "When I Get My Rag Out" (F. Dunlop, N. Long) 10" Columbia DO 1315

"(Phantasy On) Side by Side" 1 & 2 (Woods, arr. Long) Columbia 10" WA 7372 c1932

"We Can't Let You Broadcast That" (H. M. Burnaby, N. Long) / "'Oles" (H. M. Burnaby, N. Long) 10" Columbia DB 1216 1933

"Luxembourg Calling, Part I & II" (N. Long) 10" Columbia DO 1815 1935

"When My Lady Walked in Her Garden Green" (L. Pounds, N. Long) / "In the Parlour When the Company's Gone" (K. & G. Western) 10" Columbia DB 317

"Firty Fahsand Quid" / "Stillness of the Night" 10" Columbia FB 1164 1935

"Dear Old-Fashioned Thing" (Harrington, Hobson) / "Seven Veils" (De Sylva, Brown, Henderson) 10" Columbia FB 1183 Also DB 383 1935

"We Ought to Have a Basin Full of That" / "Them Days is Gorn" 10" Columbia FB 1191 1935

"Anything Can Happen Nowadays" / "Wot For?" 10" Columbia FB 1245 c1935

"On the Day Chelsea Went and Won the Cup" (L. Pounds, N. Long) / "Ten Pahnds Dahn" (H. Parr, N. Long) 10" Columbia FB 1263 1935

"I Had to Go and Draw Another Pound Out" / "Isle of Hootcha Kootcha" 10" Columbia FB 1295 1936

Stanelli's Stag Party Pt I & II Stanelli with Norman Long, Trevor Watkins, Al and Bob Harvey, Mario de Pietro, Jack Wynne "We're Nobody's Husbands Now" / Stanelli & Long "All for Ten Shillings a Year" Columbia FB 1309 February, 1936

"Nothin' Else to Do All Day" / "We Montmorencies!" 10" Columbia FB 1315 1936

"For the Glory of Old England" / "Scrahnging" 10" Columbia FB 1349 1936

"I've Brought You Some Narcissus, Cis" (Marris, Ives) / "Marrers" (H. M. Burnaby, N. Long) 10" Columbia FB 1511 1936

"To Wish You A Happy Christmas" / "Don't 'Old with It" (H. M. Burnaby, N. Long) 10" Columbia FB 1658 1937

"It Wouldn't Have Done for the Duke, Sir" (Kennington, Wass) / "Rahnd the Houses" 10" Columbia FB 2094

"Working for the Mayor and Corporation" (H. M. Burnaby, N. Long) / "Where Does Poor Pa Go in the Blackout?" 10" Decca F 7298 c1940

"Nice Kind Sergeant Major" / "In Our Village ARP" Decca F 7461 1940

Reissue Compilations

Entertainer at the Piano Greenhorn Records 007 2003 Transcription CD "The Day that Chelsea Went and Won the Cup" / "We Can't Let You Broadcast That" / "Ten Pahnds Dahn" / "Oles" / "Come and Join the No Shirt Party" / "Otherwise She's Mother's Kind of Girl" / "S-M-Y-T-H-E" / "A Tale of Other Times" / "My Little Austin Seven" / "I Had to Go and Draw Another Pound Out" / "Monday Morning" / "The Isle of Hootcha Kootcha" / "I'm Waiting Now for Any Kind of Sweetheart" / "Never Have a Bath With Your Wrist-Watch On" / "National Economy" / "Why is the Bacon So Tough?" / "Buy British" / "I Do Hate Lying in Bed" / "Resolutions for 1932" / "The Imports of England" / "The Barrers in the Walworth Road" / "Grandma's Days and Nowadays" / "Because No Power on Earth Can Pull It Down" / "The Bushes at the Bottom of the Garden" / "What Would Mr. Gladstone Say to That?"

My Little Austin Seven Windyridge VAR 21 2006 "The Drage Way" / "Homes" / "Toasts" / "Down in our Village in Zummerzet" / "The Good Little Boy and the Bad Little Boy" / "Under the Bazunka Tree" / "I think of you" / "Is it British?" / "Sing Ho! For the days of drinking" / "On the beach at Bangaloo" / "My little Austin Seven" / "Monday Morning" / "Why is the bacon so tough" / "Never have a bath with your wrist-watch on" / "That's why I love her" / "What did the Village Blacksmith say?" / "You mustn't do it after 8 o'clock" / "That Little Back Garden of Mine" / "Ideal Homes"/ "Aren't We All?" / "Otherwise she's mother's kind of girl" / "Our Dog" / "A Tale of other times" / "Hidden Heroes" / "Rule Britannia - A Travesty"

A Smile, A Song and a Piano Crystal Stream Audio IDCD 121 2004 (Australia) "My Little Austin Seven" / "Monday Morning" / "Overture "1929" / "That Little Back Garden of Mine" / "Ideal Homes" / "Aren't We All" / "Our Dog" / "Hidden Heroes" / "Rule Britannia, A Travesty" / "That Rests Entirely with Me" / "What Would Mr. Gladstone Say to That?" / "Because No Power on Earth Can Pull it Down" / "The Barrers in the Walworth Road" / "Dear Old Fashioned Thing" / "Seven Veils" / "The Isle of Hootcha Kootcha" / "In the Morning" / "Grandma's Days and Nowadays" / "The Bushes at the Bottom of the Garden" / "The

Five Year Plan" / "They Can't Make a Vule Out of Oi!" / "On the Day That Chelsea Went and Won the Cup" / "Ten Pahnds Dahn" / "The Council Schools are Good Enough for Me" / "When I Get My Rag Out"

Volume Two: We Can't Let You Broadcast That Crystal Stream Audio IDCD 135 2005 (Australia) "The Drage Way" / "Homes" / "Toasts" / "Down in Our Village in Zummerzet" / "The Good Little Boy and the Bad Little Boy" / "Under the Bazunka Tree" / "We Can't Let You Broadcast That" "'Oles" / "Marrers" / "I've Brought You Some Narcissus, Cis" / "We Ought to Have a Basin Full of That" / "Luxembourg Calling" / "We Montmorencies" / "Nothin' Else to Do All Day" / "To Wish You a Happy Christmas" / "Don't 'Old with it" / "Round the 'Ouses" / "It Wouldn't Have Done for the Duke, Sir" / "Working for the Mayor and Corporation" / "Where Does Poor Pa Go in the Black-Out?" / "Nice Kind Sergeant-Major" / "In Our Village A.R.P." See: www.crysteam.com.au

VARIOUS ARTISTS COMPILATIONS

The Great Radio Comedians "Tar" and "I'll Never Love a Barmaid Any More" BBC Records REC 151 M 1973

Harry Tate's Motoring and Other Comedy Classics. "It Wouldn't Have Done for the Duke, Sir" and "We Can't Let You Broadcast That" Columbia EMI (Australia) 33OSX 7715 n. d. c1974

Radio Days. "Commercial—Scrimplethorp's Talcum" / "Commercial—Schnotzelheimer's Suspenders" / "All for Ten Shillings a Year" (with Stanelli) / "We Can't Let You Broadcast That!" Conifer Records MHCD 163 1989 (Notes by Geoff Milne)

Cabaret's Golden Age Vol. II. "Come and Join the No-Shirt Party" Flapper PAST CD 9737 1991

Radio Fun: Happy Days "Seven Veils" Conifer Records CDHD 208 1993

Ma, I Miss Your Apple Pie: Great Comedy of the War Years. "Where Does Poor Pa Go in the Blackout?" Conifer CD CDHD303 1994

Songs That Won the War. "In Our Village ARP" MCA Spoken Word GAG DMC 003 Cassette x 2 1995.

75 Years of the BBC. With Stanelli "All for Ten Shillings a Year" BBC Records ZBBC 2038CD 2 x CD 1997

British Music Hall 1927-41 "We Montmorencies" / "Nothing Else to Do All Day" Crystal Stream Audio IDCD38 1999

Dance Band Rarities "You Are My Heart's Delight" Dance Band Days CD 3 n. d. c1999

The Best of British Vol. 2 1928-40 "(Phantasy On) Side by Side" Crystal Stream Audio IDCD66 2001

The Best of British Vol. 3 1930-49 "Going Down" Crystal Stream Audio IDCD75 2002

Double Acts. Sketch with Stanelli "All for Ten Shillings a Year" (Edward Stanley de Groot) This England/ Evergreen C-90 n. d.

Vintage British Comedy Vol. 3. With Stanelli "All for Ten Shillings a Year" Fast Forward Music FFCD013 2004

This Song is Not to Be Broadcast: 75 Records Banned by the BBC. "We Can't Let You Broadcast That" CD 2005

Workers' Playtime 1941-46. Long delivers two monologues and sings "The Victory Song" and "Let's Have a Damned Good Grouse" in a recording dated 16 August, 1945. CD41 Recordings CD41-039 2008 (CD + DL) (Notes by James Hayward) Available from ltmrecordings@gmail.com or from CD41 Recordings, Mole End, Eastgate Street, Dereham, Norfolk, NR20 5HE

A Box of British Humour. "Ten Pahnds Dahn" / "On the Day that Chelsea Went and Won the Cup," / "My Little Austin Seven" / "We Can't Let You Broadcast That" / "Where Does Poor Pa Go in the Blackout?" JSP Records JSP 1904 (4 x CD) n. d.

Music for a Traditional Christmas. "To Wish You a Happy Christmas" AMSC 647 CD

78Man Records Vol. 1. "The Bushes at the Bottom of the Garden" CDr 78 Man Records 78M1 2017

Jolly Old Christmas. (Various Artists) "To Wish You a Happy Christmas" Windyridge VAR51

OTHER MUSIC, SONGS AND MONOLOGUES

"Norwegian Dances" (Grieg) c1912
"Henry VIII Dances" (German) c1912
"Samson & Delilah" (Saint-Saens) 1913, at the Town Hall, Luton
"Humoresque" (Dvorak) 1913
"Salut d'Amor" (Elgar) 1913
"A Fool's Paradise" 1913

"When Mr. Killjoy Comes to Town" (R. P. Weston, H. E. Darewski) Francis, Day & Hunter, 1914
"A Hundred Years Ago" (B. Hood, L. Monckton) Chappell & Co., 1915
"We Shall Sigh for the Days of the War" (N. Long) at the Rusholme Pavilion, Manchester, 1919
"Melody Interpolations" 1919
"I Never Meant to Be a Naughty Girl" ('Bay', R. Tabbush) Francis, Day & Hunter, Duet with Joy Popham, 1919
"1914 Overture" (Arr. N. Long) 1920
"I'm Forever Blowing Bubbles" (John Kellette, Kendis, Brockman, Vincent, arr. Long) Interpolations 1921
"Walter de Walnut" (N. Long) 1921
"I Live at Hampstead" (N. Long) 1922
"If Winter Doesn't Come" (N. Long, Charles Hope) 1922
"England the Land of the Free" (D. Beresford, C. A. E. Harriss) Ascherberg, Hopwood & Crew, 1924
"Down at the Listening Inn" (N. Long) 1924
"Nursery Rhymes Up to Date" (N. Long) 1924
"C-o-n-s-t-a-n-t-i-n-o-p-l-e" (H. Carlton) 1925
"Side by Side" (H. Wood, arr. N. Long) 1925
"Homes" (R. P. Weston, Bert Lee, N. Long) Francis, Day & Hunter, 1926
"Felix the Cat" (D. Archer; arr. Long) Syncopations 1926
"The Magic Waltz of Love" (N. Long) 1927
"The Glorious Month of May" (N. Long, L. Pounds) Reynolds & Co., 1927
"I'm Looking for the Window with the Pink Plant Pot" (M. Herbert, N. Long) The Lawrence Wright Music Co., 1928
"What I Know About Women" (N. Long) 1928
"The Commercial Traveller—Samples in the Bag" (N. Long) 1928
"On the Beach at Bangaloo" (N. Macbean, N. Long) 1928
"Single Versus Married Men" (N. Long) Dec. 1929
"That's Why I Love Her" (K. & G. Western) Francis, Day & Hunter, Ltd., 1929
"You Mustn't Do It After Eight o' Clock"—From *On With the Show* Blackpool (Alec McGill) 1929
"Prelude in Asia Minor" (N. Long) Mar 1929
"In the Days When Victoria Was Queen" (N. Long) 1929
"My Little Austin Seven" (C. Rose) Reynolds & Co., 1929
"Dora" (N. Long) at the Victoria Palace, April, 1929[1]
"Psychology" (H. M. Burnaby, N. Long) Reynolds & Co., 1931

"The Willows" (D. Shepherd) Reynolds & Co., 1931
"Seasons" (H. M. Burnaby, N. Long) Reynolds & Co., 1931
"For You" (N. Long) May 1933
"But" (N. Long, after Kipling) 1935
"Holidays" (N. Long) 1935
"Firty Fahsand Quid" (H. M. Burnaby, N. Long) Reynolds & Co., 1935
"It's a Marvel"—Character Song (N. Long) circa 1935
"That's How it Was" (H M. Burnaby, N. Long) Reynolds & Co., 1935
"In the Days of Good King Arthur" (H. M. Burnaby, N. Long) Reynolds & Co., 1935
"Terrible Shy Wi' the Maids" (H. M. Burnaby, N. Long) Reynolds & Co., 1935
"When Father Was a Lad" (H. M. Burnaby, N. Long) Reynolds & Co., 1935
"Resuscitated Rhymes" (H. M. Burnaby, N. Long) Reynolds & Co., 1935
"Stiff Collars" (H. M. Burnaby, N. Long) Reynolds & Co., 1935
"Tar" (N. Long) Reynolds & Co., 1936
"A Tale of Other Times" (N. Long) Reynolds & Co., 1937
"Them Days 'As Gorn" Cockney Monologue (H. M. Burnaby, N. Long) Reynolds & Co., 1938
"One Must Keep Abreast of the Times"—Humorous Curate Song (N. Long) circa 1938
"Wot For" (H. M. Burnaby, N. Long) Reynolds & Co., 1939
"Schicklgruber" (Monologue) (N. Long) 1940
"When We Win the War" (N. Long) 1941
"I'm a 1914 Soldier in 1941" (H. M. Burnaby, N. Long) Francis, Day & Hunter, 1941
"The Twirp"—Musical Monologue (R. Rutherford, N. Long) Reynolds & Co, 1942
"Norman Long's Album of Songs & Monologues" (L. Pounds, N. Long) Reynolds & Co., 1942

Filmography

Pathe Magazine No. 4. (1929) Pathe.
The Stars at Home. (1930) Pathetone. The antics of Norman Long and Charles Austin "at home."
The New Hotel. (1932). Dir.: Daniel Mainwaring. Stoll Picture Productions. Cast: Norman Long, Dan Young, Hal Gordon, Mickey Brantford, Adele Blanche, Alfred Wellesley.

Pathetone 109. (1932) Norman sings "The Barrers in the Walworth Road"
Pathetone. (1932) "Under the Bazunka Tree"
Pathetone. (1933) "I Certainly Don't Need You"
London's Famous Clubs and Cabarets—The Ace of Spades Club (1933) Norman tells jokes at the piano. Pathe
Pathetone (1934) "The Day That Chelsea Went and Won the Cup"
Pathetone 238. (1934) "Firty Fahsand Quid"
Pathe Pictorial 900 (1935) "Oles"
Royal Cavalcade aka ***Regal Cavalcade.*** (1935). Dir.: Herbert Brenon, W. P. Kellino, Norman Lee, Walter Summers, Thomas Bentley, Marcel Varnel. British International Pictures. Cast: Marie Lohr, Hermione Baddeley, Esme Percy, George Robey, Florrie Forde, Norman Long, John Mills, Ellaline Terriss et al. Long sings "Down in Our Village in Zummerset"
Pathetone 331. (1936) "Nothing Else to Do All Day"
Pathetone Parade of 1936. (1936) Pathe. Dir.: Fred Watts. Compere: Leonard Henry; with Charlie Kunz, Arthur Prince & Jim, Norman Long, et al. *Pathetone Weekly* compilation.
Starlight Parade. (1936) Viking Films. Dir.: Eric Humphriss. Cast: Norman Long, Teddy Brown, Veronica, Metaxa Girls, Julian Best & His Orchestra. Revue.
Sudbury. (1936) Pathetone short. Long with Billy Bennett, Clapham & Dwyer and other members of the Vaudeville Golfing Society larking about.
Pathetone Pictorial No. 76. (1937) Norman sings "When Your Television Set Comes Home"
Pathetone Parade of 1938 (1938) Pathe. Dir.: Fred Watts. Compere: Ronald Frankau; with Charlie Kuz, Norman Long, Stanelli, et al. Revue.
Pathetone: Out and About. (1939) Norman sings "Working for the Mayor and Corporation"
Pathetone Parade of 1940 (1939) Pathe. Dir.: Fred Watts. Cast: Robb Wilton, Nosmo King, Norman Long, The Two Leslies, Patricia Rossborough et al. Revue.

Bibliography

ONE OF THE BEST INTRODUCTIONS to the topic is the *Illustrated History of British Music Hall* by the late and much-missed Richard Anthony Baker. I well remember his obituary series, *Brief Lives*, on Radio Five many years ago. He always wrote with insight, humour and warmth, which came across in his broadcasts. The same author wrote an excellent biography of Marie Lloyd, and a book about Variety. Another good general history is Roy Busby's *British Music Hall* published in 1976. The beginnings of the halls are well documented in *The Early Doors* (Scott) and the atmosphere of a night out in gaslit days is well-evoked in Macqueen-Pope's *The Melody Lingers On*. All Macqueen-Pope's works are worth seeking out. I would also recommend Roger Wilmut's informal history of Variety, *Kindly Leave the Stage*. John Fisher's *Funny Way to Be a Hero* in any version is arguably the best single volume written about the popular comedians or indeed popular entertainment of the twentieth century. I especially like the cover of the original 1970s issue with the Peter Blake artwork a la Sergeant Pepper. Of the biographies, I highly recommend *The King's Jester* (Anthony), *Marie Lloyd* (Baker) and especially *Little Tich—Giant of the Music Hall* (Tich/Findlater). There have been many excellent books about the theatres themselves, including *Empires, Hippodromes & Palaces* (Read) which deals with those designed by the great Frank Matcham.

A WORD ON WEBSITES

Among some of the most useful websites I would strongly recommend Arthur Lloyd which is especially good on the history of theatres and has links to many other resources: http://www.arthurlloyd.co.uk/index.html

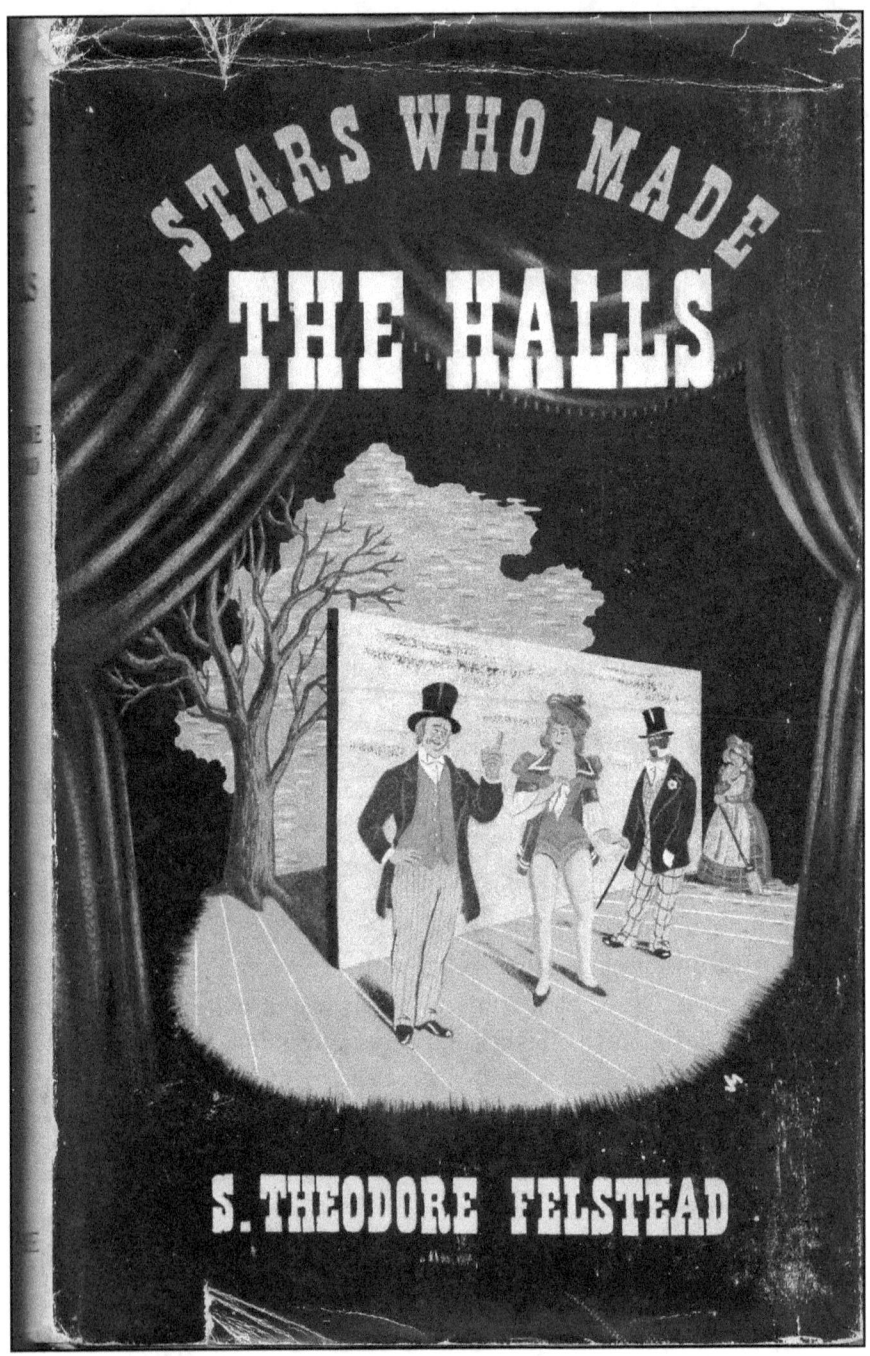

Stars Who Made the Halls (1952), one of several useful general histories of music hall written in the 1950s when there was a resurgence of interest in an era that was then passing from living memory.

Adeler, Edwin & West, Con *Remember Fred Karno?* (London, 1939)
Agate, James *First Nights* (Strand, London: Ivor Nicholson & Watson, 1934)
Agate, James *My Theatre Talks* (Arthur Barker, Ltd., London, 1933)
Alltree, George W. *Footlight Memories: Recollections of Music-Hall and Stage Life* (S. Low, Marston, London, 1932)
Amherst, Jeffrey *Wandering About: The Autobiography* (London, 1976)
Andrews, Cyrus (Compiler & Ed.) *Radio Who's Who* (London: Pendulum Publications, 1947)
Anthony, Barry *The King's Jester: The Life of Dan Leno, Victorian Comic Genius* (I. B. Tauris & Co., Ltd., London, 2010)
Aubert, Charles *The Art of Pantomime* (George Allen & Unwin, 1927)
Baddeley. Hermione *The Unsinkable Hermione Baddeley: An Autobiography* (Collins, London, 1984)
Bailey, Peter (Ed.) *Popular Music in Britain: Music Hall: The Business of Pleasure* (Milton Keynes; Open University Press, 1986)
Baker, Richard Anthony *British Music Hall: An Illustrated History* (Stroud, Gloucestershire: Sutton Publishing, 1986)
Baker, Richard Anthony *Marie Lloyd: Queen of the Music Halls* (London: Robert Hale Ltd., 1990)
Baker, Roger, Burton, Peter & Smith, Richard *Drag. A History of Female Impersonation in the Performing Arts* (New York: New York University Press, 1994)
Barker, Kathleen *Early Music Hall in Bristol* (Bristol Branch of the Historical Association of Local History Pamphlets, 1979)
Barr, Charles *All Our Yesterdays: 90 Years of British Cinema* (London: British Film Institute Publishing, 1986)
Batten, Joe *Joe Batten's Book: The Story of Sound Recording* (Rockliff, London, 1956)
Bevan, Ian *Top of the Bill: The Story of the London Palladium* (London: Frederick Mueller, 1952)
Blow, Sydney *The Ghost Walks on Friday: In & Out of the Stage Door* (Heath-Cranton, London, 1935)
Bonygne, Richard *Theatre Postcards* (Pavilion Books, London, 1987)
Booth, J. B. *The World We Knew* (T. Werner Laurie. Ltd., London, 1943)
Booth, Michael *English Melodrama* (Herbert Jenkins, London, 1965)
Bratton, J. S. *The Victorian Music Hall Ballad* (London: The Macmillan Press Ltd., 1975)

Bratton, J. S. (Ed.) *Popular Music in Britain: Music Hall Performance & Style* (Milton Keynes: Open University Press, 1986)

Broadbent, R. J., Howell, E. *Annals of the Liverpool Stage* (E. Howell, 1908)

Broadbent, R. J. *A History of Pantomime* (Simpkin Marshall, London, 1931)

Buchanan-Taylor, W. *Shake it Again* (Heath Cranton, London, 1943)

Bulliet, C. J. *Venus Castina: Famous Female Impersonators Celestial and Human* (Covici Friede, New York, 1933)

Busby, Roy *British Music Hall: An Illustrated Who's Who from 1850 to the Present Day* (Elek, London, 1976)

Byng, Douglas *As You Were: Reminiscences* (Duckworth, London, 1970)

Byng, Douglas *Byng Ballads* (The Bodley Head, London, c1933)

Calthrop, Dion Clayton *Music Hall Nights* (John Lane, The Bodley Head, London, 1925)

"Carlton" *Twenty Years of Spoof and Bluff* (Herbert Jenkins, Ltd., London, ca 1931)

Clayton, D. *Empire Palace of Varieties 1898-1921* (DBC, 1990)

Clinton-Baddeley, V. C. *The Burlesque Tradition in the English Theatre After 1660* (Methuen & Co., Ltd., London, 1952)

Clinton-Baddeley, V. C. *Some Pantomime Pedigrees* (The Society for Theatre Research, London, 1963)

Cooper, Margaret *Myself and My Piano* (John Ouseley, London, 1909)

Cotes, Peter *George Robey: The Darling of the Halls* (Cassell, London, 1972)

Croxton, Arthur *Crowded Nights—and Days: An Unconventional Pageant* (S. Low, Marston, London, 1934)

Cullen, Frank, Hackman, Florence & McNeilly, Donald *Vaudeville Old and New: An Encyclopaedia of Variety Performers in America Vol. 1* (Psychology Press, New York, 2007)

Dale, Anthony *The Theatre Royal, Brighton* (Oriel Press, London, 1980)

Davison, Peter *Songs of the British Music Hall* (New York: Oak Publications, 1971)

Dibbs, Martin *Radio Fun and the BBC Variety Department 1922-67* (Palgrave Macmillan, 2019)

Disher, H. Willson *Fairs, Circuses and Music Halls* (William Collins, London, 1942)

Disher, H. Willson *Music Hall Parade* (Charles Scribners, Sons, New York, 1938)

Disher, H. Willson *Winkles and Champagne: Comedies and Tragedies of the Music Hall* (Batsford, London, 1938)
Disher, H. Willson *Clowns and Pantomimes* (Constable, London, 1925)
Dollin, Anton *Ballet Go Round* (Michael Joseph Ltd., London, 1938)
Douglas, Stuart Charles, Park, A. J. *The Variety Stage* (A. Fisher Unwin, London, 1895)
East, John M. *Max Miller: The Cheeky Chappie* (W. H. Allen, London, 1977)
English Columbia FB 1000 Series Disc Research England, April, 1969
Fairbrother, Sydney *Through an Old Stage Door* (Frederick Mueller, Ltd., London, 1939)
Fairlie, Gerard *The Fred Emney Story* (Hutchinson, London, 1960)
Farson, Daniel *Marie Lloyd and Music Hall* (Tom Stacey, Ltd., London, 1972)
Felstead, Sidney Theodore *Stars Who Made the Halls: A Hundred Years of English Humour, Harmony and Hilarity* (T. W. Laurie, Ltd., London, 1946)
Fergusson, Jean *She Knows You Know: The Remarkable Story of Hylda Baker* (The Breedon Books Publishing Co., Derby, 1997)
Fields, Gracie *Sing as We Go! Her Autobiography* (Frederick Muller & Co., London, 1960)
Fisher, John *Funny Way to be a Hero* (Frederick Muller, Ltd., London, 1973)
Fletcher, Cyril *Nice One Cyril* (Barrie & Jenkins, London, 1978)
Foster, Andy & Furst, Steve *Radio Comedy 1938-68* (Virgin, London, 1996)
Foulkes, Richard (Ed.) *British Theatre in the 1890s: Essays on the Stage* (Cambridge University Press, Cambridge, 1992)
Frow, Gerald *"Oh Yes It Is!" The History of Pantomime* (BBC Books, London, 1985)
Gallaher, J. P. *Fred Karno: Master of Mirth and Tears* (Hale, London, 1971)
Gammond, Peter (Compiler) *Your Own, Your Very Own! A Music Hall Scrapbook* (London, Ian Allan, 1973)
Gardner, Fitzroy *Pure Folly: The Story of Those Remarkable People The Follies* (Mills & Boon, Ltd., London, 1910)
Gifford, Dennis *The Golden Age of Radio: An Illustrated Companion* (Batsford, London, 1985)
Gifford, Dennis *Entertainers in British Film: A Century of Showbiz in the Cinema* (Flicks Books, London, 1998)

Grain, Corney *Corney Grain By Himself* (John Murray, London, 1888)

Graves, Charles *The Cochran Story: The Life and Times of the Century's Greatest Showman* (W. H. Allen, London, 1952)

Green, Benny (Ed.) *The Last Empires: A Music Hall Companion* (London: Michael Joseph, 1986)

Grock *Grock King of Clowns* (Methuen, London, 1957)

Haddon, Archibald *The Story of the Music Hall: From Cave of Harmony to Cabaret* (London: Fleetway Press, Ltd., 1935)

Hall, Henry *Here's to the Next Time: The Autobiography of Henry Hall* (Odham's Press, London, 1955)

Harding, James *George Robey & the Music-Hall* (London: Hodder & Stoughton, 1990)

Hibbert, Henry George *Fifty Years of a Londoner's Life* (Dodd, Mead & Co., 1916)

Hindle, David J. *From a Gin Palace to a King's Palace: Provincial Music Hall in Preston* (The History Press, Stroud, 2007)

Holloway, Stanley with Richards, Dick *Wiv a Little Bit o' Luck* (London: Leslie Frewin, 1967)

Howard, Diana *London Theatres and Music Halls 1850-1950* (London: The Library Association, 1970)

Howard & Wyndham Pantomimes 1888-1948, Summer Seasons 1933-48 (Howard & Wyndham, Ltd., London, 1948)

Hyman. Alan *The Gaiety Years* (Cassell, London, 1975)

Iliffe, Richard, Baguley, Winifred *Victorian Nottingham, A Story in Pictures: Volume Seven Theatre Royal, St. Mary's Gate Theatre 1837-1901* (A Nottingham Historical Film Unit Publication, c1975)

Irving, Gordon *Great Scot: The Life Story of Sir Harry Lauder, Legendary Laird of the Music Hall* (Leslie Frewin, London, 1968)

Irving, Gordon *The Good Auld Days The Story of Scotland's Entertainers from Music Hall to Television* (Jupiter, London, 1977)

Jacob, Naomi *Me—Looking Back* (Hutchinson, London, 1950)

Jacob, Naomi *Me—Yesterday and Today* (Hutchinson, London, 1957)

Jacob, Naomi *Me—Likes and Dislikes* (Hutchinson, London, 1954)

Jacob, Naomi *Me- A Chronicle About Other People* (Portway, London, 1972)

Kilgarriff, Michael *Sing Us One of the Old Songs A guide to Popular Song 1860-1920* (OUP, Oxford, 1998)

Kilgarriff, Michael *Grace Beauty and Banjos* (Oberon, London, 1998)

Laird, Ross *Moanin' Low: A Discography of Female Popular Vocal Recordings 1920-1933* (Westport, Connecticut: Greenwood Press, 1996)
La Rue, Danny *From Drags to Riches* (Viking Books, London, 1987)
Le Roy, George *Music Hall Stars of the Nineties* (British Technical & General Press, London, 1952)
Laven, James *Costume in the Theatre* (George Harrap, London, 1964)
Lee, Edward *Folksong and Music Hall* (London: Routledge & Kegan Paul, 1982)
Leslie, Peter *Hard Act to Follow: Music Hall Review* (London: Paddington Press, 1978)
Littlejohn, J. H. *The Scottish Music Hall 1880-1990* (G. C. Book Publishers, 1990)
Macqueen-Pope, W. *Gaiety: Theatre of Enchantment* (W. H. Allen, London, 1949)
Macqueen-Pope, W. *The Melodies Linger On: The Story of Music Hall* (London: W. H. Allen, 1950)
Macqueen-Pope, W. *Marie Lloyd: Queen of the Music Hall* (W. H. Allen, 1954)
Macqueen-Pope, W. *Shirtfronts and Sables: A Story of the Days When Money Could Be Spent* (London: Robert Hale, Ltd., 1953)
Macqueen-Pope, W. *Theatre Royal, Drury Lane* (London: W. H. Allen, 1945)
Maitland, Sara *Vesta Tilley* (Virago Pioneers, London, 1985)
Maloney, Paul *Scotland and the Music Hall 1850-1914: Studies in Popular Culture* (Manchester University Press, Manchester, 2003)
Mander, Raymond, Mitchenson, Joe, Shaw, Bernard *Pantomime: A Story in Pictures* (Taplinger Publishing Company, 1973)
Marshall, Michael *The Book of Comic & Dramatic Monologues* (Elm Tree Books/EMI Publishing, London, 1981)
McDowell, Jim *Beyond the Footlights: A History of Belfast Music Halls and Early Theatre* (Nonsuch, Dublin, 2007)
McKechnie, Samuel *Popular Entertainments Through the Ages* (Sampson, Low, Marston & Co., Ltd., London, 1931)
Mellor, G. J. *The Northern Music Hall: A Centenary of Popular Entertainment* (F. Graham, Newcastle-Upon-Tyne, 1970)
Merson, Billy *Fixing the Stoof Oop* (Hutchinson, London, 1925)
Midwinter, Eric *Make 'Em Laugh: Famous Comedians and Their Worlds* (Allen & Unwin, London, 1979)

Milton, Billy *Milton's Paradise Mislaid* (Jupiter Books, London, 1976)

Morton, W. H. & Newton, H. Chance *Sixty Years Stage Service: Being a Record of the Life of Charles Morton the Father of the Halls* (London: Gale & Polden Ltd., 1903)

Mullen, John *The Show Must Go On! Popular Song in Britain During the First World War* (Routledge, Abingdon, Oxon., London & New York, 2016)

Nerman, [Einar] *Darlings of the Gods in Music Hall, Revue and Musical Comedy* (Alston Rivers Ltd., Adelphi, London, 1929)

Newton, H. Chance *Idols of the "Halls" Being My Music Hall Memories* (Heath Cranton, London, 1928)

Norris, Peter *A Cockney at Work: The Story of Gus Elen and His Songs* (Grosvenor House Publishing, 2014)

Nuttall, Jeff *King Twist: A Portrait of Frank Randle* (Routledge & Kegan Paul, London, 1978)

Owen, Maureen *The Crazy Gang* (Weidenfeld, London, 1986)

Parker, Dennis & Julia *The Story and the Song: A History of English Musical Plays 1916-78* (London: Chappell in association with Elm Tree Books, 1979)

Parker, John *Who's Who in the Theatre* (Sir Isaac Pitman & Sons, Ltd., London, 1916) (Also Tenth Edition, 1947)

Powell, G. Rennie *The Bristol Stage: It's Story* (Bristol: The Bristol Printing & Publishing Co., Ltd., 1919)

Powell, Sandy *Can You Hear Me Mother? Sandy Powell's Lifetime in Music Hall* (Jupiter, London, 1975)

Pulling, Christopher *They Were Singing: And What They Were Singing About* (London: G. G. Harrap, 1952)

Racster, Olga *Curtain Up! The Story of Cape Theatre* (Suta & Co., Ltd., Cape Town, 1951)

Read, Jack *Empires, Hippodromes & Palaces* (The Alderman Press, London, 1985)

Reeve, Ada *Take It for a Fact: A Record of My Seventy-Five Years on the Stage* (William Heinemann, London, 1954)

Reynolds Music *The Old Time Stars' Book of Monologues* (Wolfe Publishing, Ltd., London, 1971)

Rinaldi, Graham *Will Hay* (Tomahawk, Sheffield, 2009)

Rose, Clarkson *Beside the Seaside* (Museum Press, Ltd., 1960)

Rose, Clarkson *Red Plush and Greasepaint: A Memory of the Music Hall from the Nineties to the Sixties* (London: Museum Press, 1964)

Rose, Clarkson *With a Twinkle in My Eye* (London: Museum Press, 1951)
Rowell, George *The Victorian Theatre: A Survey* (Oxford University Press, Oxford, 1956)
Russell, Dave *Popular Music in England 1840-1914* (Manchester University Press, Manchester, 1997)
St. Pierre, Paul Matthew *Music Hall Mimesis in British Film: 1895-1960: On the Halls on the Screen* (Madison, Wisconsin, USA: Farleigh Dickinson University Press, 2009)
Scott, Harold *The Early Doors: Origins of the Music Hall* (London: Nicholson & Watson, 1946)
Seaton, Ray & Martin, Roy *Good Morning Boys: Will Hay Master of Comedy* (Barrie & Jenkins, London, 1978)
Seeley, Robert; Bunnett, Rex & Rust, Brian A. L. *London Musical Shows on Record, 1889-1989, A Hundred Years of London's Musical Theatre* (London: General Gramophone Publications, 1989)
Shaw, Chris & Oates, Arthur *A Pictorial History of the Art of Female Impersonation* (King Shaw Productions Co., Ltd., London, 1966)
Short, Ernest Henry & Compton-Rickett, Arthur *Ring Up the Curtain: Being a Pageant of English Entertainment Covering Half a Century* (London: Books for Library Press, 1938)
Short, Ernest Henry *Fifty Years of Vaudeville* (Greenwood Press, London, 1946)
Stern, G. B. *Pantomime* (Hutchinson's Colonial Library, London, 1916)
Strong, Leonard A. G. *Sea Wall* (Methuen, New York, 1946)
Sudworth, G *The Great Little Tilley* (Courtney Publications, Luton, 1984)
The Theatre Royal Nottingham 1865-1978 A Theatrical and Architectural History (Nottingham City Council, 1978)
Theatre Royal, King Street, Bristol, Founded 1766 (Theatre Trustees and Preservation Fund Committee, Bristol, 1945)
Tich, Mary & Findlater, Richard *Little Tich: Giant of the Music Hall* (London: Elm Tree Books, 1979)
Titterton, W. R. *From Theatre to Music Hall* (Stephen Swift & Co., Ltd., London, 1912)
Tyrwhitt-Drake, Sir Garrard *The English Circus and Fairground* (Methuen, London, 1946)
Underwood, Peter *Life's A Drag: Danny La Rue & the Drag Scene* (Leslie Frewin, London, 1974)
Walding, Roy *An Arm of Iron: The Life and Times of the Entertainer Stanley Holloway, C. B. E.* (Theatrical Heritage Entertains, London, 1996)

Waller, Charles *Magical Nights at the Theatre* (Gerald Taylor Productions, Ltd., Melbourne, 1980)

Wearing, J. P. *The London Stage: 1940-49: A Calendar of Productions, Performers and Personnel* (Rowman & Littlefield, Lanham, Maryland, 2014)

Jack Read's *Empires, Hippodromes and Palaces* (1985) covers the work of the great theatre architect Frank Matcham.

White, James Dillon *Born to Star: The Lupino Lane Story* (Heinemann, London, 1957)

Williams, Gordon *British Theatre in the Great War: A Revaluation* (Bloomsbury, London, 2015)

Wilmot, Roger *Kindly Leave the Stage: The Story of Variety 1919-1960* (Methuen Publishing, London, 1989)

Wilson, A. E. *Prime Minister of Mirth: The Biography of Sir George Robey, C. B. E.* (London: Odhams Press, Ltd., 1956)

Wilson, A. E. *Christmas Pantomime: The Story of an English Institution* (London: George Allen & Unwin, 1934)

Wilson, A. E. *Pantomime Pageant* (Stanley Paul, London, 1946)

Winslow, D. Forbes *Daly's the Biography of a Theatre* (W. H. Allen, London, 1944)

Young, Desmond *The Best Years* (Harper, London, 1961)

Notes

NELLIE WALLACE

(I)
1. Rainey, Lawrence *Revisiting the Wasteland* (Yale University Press, New York, 2007), p51.
2. Marriage & Baptism records, St. Giles, Colgate, Norfolk, 1855-6. With many thanks to John Lovell for genealogical information.
3. "The Jilted Lady" *Penny Illustrated Paper,* 17 June, 1911
4. "Low Comedy in Petticoats" *Birmingham Daily Gazette,* 6 June, 1906.
5. "Larks at the Athenaeum" *The Lancaster Gazette & General Advertiser for Lancashire, Westmorland & Yorkshire,* 11 April, 1888.
6. Daisy had a happy marriage but more than her share of tragedies. Seven of her ten children died before her. Three boys died in infancy, and a daughter died when her dress caught fire as she was trying to warm herself. Nellie appeared to have no contact with Daisy. Some years later the family tried to make contact with her, but she told them bluntly "If it's money you're after you can piss off!" After Nellie died, she sent a small box of mementoes and photographs to Daisy. Daisy died in 1951 aged 65. With thanks to John Lovell for the family information.
7. "The Standard" *The Era,* 25 July, 1891

8. "Theatre Royal Hartlepool" *Northern Daily Mail*, 1892
9. "The Royal" *Croydon Chronicle & East Sussex Advertiser*, 23 September, 1899
10. Reeve, Ada *Take it for a Fact*
11. "The Jilted Lady" *Penny Illustrated Paper*, 17 June, 1911
12. "Women make poor clowns; too serious" *Ballston Spa Journal, New York*, 9 March, 1933

(II)
1. "Keith and Proctor's 23rd Street" *The New York Dramatic Mirror*, 2 March, 1907
2. "De Gracia's Elephants and Nellie Wallace Next Week" *Walsall Advertiser*, 9 January 1909
3. Saunders, Walter *Reminiscences of a Rand Pioneer* (Ravan Press, South Africa, 1977)
4. "In the Theaters: The Temple" *The Detroit Times*, 18 February, 1908, p3.
5. George M. Young "Philadelphia: Keith's" *Variety*, February, 1908
6. Alec Guinness *Blessings in Disguise* (Knopf, New York, 1986), p9.
7. Nellie Wallace "Should a Woman Tell Her Age?" *The Era*, 15 June, 1921.

(III)
The opening quote: Nellie Wallace "Should a Woman Tell Her Age?" *The Era*, 15 June, 1921.
1. "Why Men Leave Home" *Variety*, 13 October, 1922, p43.
2. "The Laughter Maker" *Table Talk*, 2 December, 1926
3. "Nervous Nellie; New Turn at the Tivoli" *The Sun*, 10 October, 1926
4. "Melbourne" *The Triad*, Vol. 13, No. 1, 8 January, 1927, p46.
5. "Nellie Wallace" *The Era*, 27 April, 1927, p13.
6. With many thanks to John Lovell.
7. *The Nation & Athenaeum* Vol. 46, 673.
8. *The Play Pictorial* (Greening & Co., Ltd., 1934)
9. *Kinematograph Year Book*, 1939, p226
10. "New Cross Empire" *Woolwich Gazette*, 25 September, 1908, p8.
11. Uglow, Jennifer (Compiler & Editor) *Macmillan Dictionary of Women's Biography* (Macmillan, London, 1986), p566.
12. "Nellie Wallace Died of a Broken Heart" *Dundee Courier*, 25 November, 1948, p3.

13. "Nellie Wallace Left All to Charity" *Gloucester Citizen,* 21 February, 1949, p1.
14. Greene, Richard *Edith Sitwell: Avant Garde Poet, English Genius* (Hachette, 2011)
15. *British Vogue,* December, 1947, p54.
16. From old newspaper cutting, courtesy of John Lovell

Other Songs
1. *Dundee Evening Telegraph,* 14 April, 1893
2. "Nellie Wallace: Character Songs" *Variety,* November, 1907
3. *The New York Clipper,* 11 December, 1908
4. "De Gracia's Elephants and Nellie Wallace Next Week" *Walsall Advertiser,* 9 January, 1909, p9.
5. "Nellie Wallace" *The New York Dramatic Mirror,* 27 November, 1909
6. Saunders, Walter *Reminiscences of a Rand Pioneer* (Ravan Press, South Africa, 1977)
7. *The Scotsman,* 12 January, 1918

LILY MORRIS

(I)
1. "Shepherd's Bush Empire" *West London Observer,* 12 July, 1929, 4
2. *The Referee,* 24 June, 1894, 3.
3. "The Middlesex" *The Era,* 10 August, 1895, 14.
4. "The Canterbury" *The Era,* 24 August, 1895, 14.
5. Joe Batten was a well-known pianist/accompanist and sound recordist who was born at Hoxton. *Joe Batten's Book,* 1956 p126.
6. "Pantomime In Leeds" 28 December, 1896, 3.
7. "Local Amusements" *Nottingham Journal,* 15 February, 1898, 6.
8. "Lily Morris" *Music Hall & Theatre Review,* 1 September, 1899, 11.

(II) 'Our Lil'
1. "Lily Morris" *Exeter & Plymouth Gazette,* 25 January, 1925
2. "Princess of Wales's Kennington" *Lloyd's Weekly News,* 1 January, 1899
3. According to relatives, Lily had a son Leonard Morris (b. 31 May, 1908, died 2005) The father was Benjamin Morris. It seems curious that this son was born only a year after her marriage to Archie

McDougall. I have not been able to contact any living descendants to establish the details of this relationship.
4. *Clifton Society*, 23 January, 1908
5. "Near Tragedy in Humpty Dumpty Fifty Years Ago" *The Stage*, 24 December, 1958
6. "Mother Goose at Glasgow" *The Era*, 11 December, 1909, p12.
7. Gallaher Fred Karno: Master of Mirth & Tears (Hale, London, 1971), p87.
8. "A Popular Pantomime 'Boy'" *Newcastle Journal*, 15 January, 1917, 3.
9. "The Tyne Pantomime" *The Stage*, 2 January, 1917 "The Tank That Broke the Ranks Out in Picardy" by Harry Castling and Harry Carlton. See Russell, Dave *Popular Music in England 1840-1914* (Manchester University Press, Manchester, 1997), p157.
10. "Mrs. George Formby's Own Story" *The Sunday Post*, 13 February, 1921

(III)
1. *The Era*, 10 July, 1929
2. "Always Merry and Bright: Lily Morris, Comedian" *Table Talk*, 18 February, 1926
3. "Arrowtown Pictures" *Lake Wakatup Mail*, 8 November, 1945, p3.
4. Lily Morris "About My Next Tour" *The Era*, 16 July, 1926

(IV)
1. "The Alhambra" *Manchester Guardian*, 20 February, 1923
2. Newton, H. Chance *Idols of the Halls* (1928), p220
3. "Hippodrome" *Variety*, 25 February, 1925. The famous Hippodrome in New York was built in 1905 and was the venue for many spectacular shows in its early years when elephants were a regular feature. Houdini famously made an elephant disappear. The theatre was given over to Vaudeville shows in the 1920s by the time Lily visited and eventually closed in 1939 after which the building was demolished. The Hippodrome Centre has occupied the site since 1952. The Riverside opened in 1911 for vaudeville and movie shorts and closed in about 1974 after which it was demolished.
4. "The Feminine Side" *Variety*, 29 July, 1925
5. Robert Speare "Hippodrome Has Novelty Hits: Lily Morris Scores a Hit" *The Era*, 21 January, 1925

6. "The Variety World" *The Era*, 28 April, 1926
7. "Lily Morris Returns" *The Vaudeville News*, 24 July, 1927
8. "Poor Kiddies: Lily Morris Matinee" *The Sun* 27 January, 1926
9. "Lily Morris" *Everyone's* 17 March, 1926.
10. "The Variety World: Welcomed Everywhere" *The Era*, 28 April, 1926
11. "Lily Morris" *The Billboard*, 2 April, 1927. Keith's Fordham Theatre was built as a combined movie and vaudeville house in 1921. It was designed by William McElfatrick and seated 2,446. In 1929 it became the RKO Fordham and was demolished in 1987. Few of the theatres in which Lily played are still extant, but the State Theatre was built in 1921 with a seating capacity of 1,850 and is still a flourishing theatre.
12. "Always Merry and Bright: Lily Morris, Comedian" *Table Talk*, (Melbourne, Victoria), 18 February, 1926
13. "This Week at the Theatres" *The Buffalo Morning Express*, 18 August, 1925
14. M. Willson Disher "Joining in the Chorus at the Royal Variety Performance" *The Era*, 2 March, 1927
15. Maitland Davidson "Personality in the Theatre: A Great Variety Artist" *Britannia*, 1928

(V)
1. "The Palladium" *The Era*, 16 April, 1930
2. Raymond Bennett "The Other Immortal Bard" *The Era*, 3 October, 1934
3. Tynesider "Film World" *Shields Daily News*, 13 May, 1933
4. "Golders Green: Deaths of Elderly People" *Hendon & Finchley Times*, 29 September, 1933
5. Clarkson Rose "Peradventure" *The Stage*, 16 December, 1937
6. A. C. Astor "Just Jottings" *The Stage*, 8 August, 1929
7. "Collapsed On Stage" *Dundee Evening Telegraph*, 13 March, 1934
8. "A Popular Pantomime Boy" *Newcastle Journal*, 15 January, 1917
9. Roderick Mann "Show News" *Birmingham Daily Gazette*, 10 June, 1949
10. "Old-time Star Ill" *Birmingham Daily Gazette*, 17 March, 1950
11. "Lily Morris, Variety Star, Leaves £22,508" *Liverpool Echo*, 9 January, 1953. Probate Calendars.
12. "Lily Morris' Will" *The Stage*, 15 January, 1953
13. *The Stage*, 18 December, 1952

Discography
1. British Library listing (Ernie Bayley Bequest)

Other Songs and Sheet Music
1. "The Royal" *The Era*, 24 September, 1898
2. "The London Music Halls: Grand, Clapham" *The Era*, 15 October, 1898
3. "The Newcastle Theatre Aladdin" *Yorkshire Post & Leeds Intelligencer*, 24 December, 1906
4. "The Tyne Pantomime" *The Stage*, 2 January, 1917 "The Tank That Broke the Ranks Out in Picardy" by Harry Castling and Harry Carlton. See Russell, Dave *Popular Music in England 1840-1914* (Manchester University Press, Manchester, 1997), p157.
5. "Palace Theatre, Plymouth" *Western Morning News*, 16 November, 1920, p7.
6. "Finsbury Park Empire" *The Era*, 6 April, 1921, p16.
7. "Pantomime Songs" *Leeds Mercury*, 15 November, 1921, p6.
7. "Pantomime Songs" *Leeds Mercury*, 15 November, 1921, p6.
8. "Footlight Flashes" *The Stage*, p3.
9. "Finsbury Park Empire" *The Era*, 8 October, 1924, p16.
10. "Lawrence Wright Holiday Songs" *The Era*, 6 August, 1924, p4.
11. "Worton David" *The Era*, 9 July, 1924, p15.
12. "Palace *Variety*, 29 July, 1925
13. "Just My Way of Loving You" *The Stage*, 26 October, 1926, p18.
14. "Since Father's Joined the Mustard Club" *The Era*, 21 November, 1926
15. "Songs and Singers" *The Era*, 10 March, 1926, p14.
16. "Rexborough Music Publishing Co." *The Era*, 23 November, 1927, p19.
17. "Leo Jackson and Co" *The Stage*, 1 December, 1927
18. "That Ideal Husband" *Liverpool Echo*, 18 January, 1929, p11.
19. "The Metropolitan" *The Era*, 21 May, 1929, p11.
20. "Hackney Empire" 13 November, 1929, p4.
21. H. Willson Disher "Holborn Empire" *The Era*, 2 April, 1930, p11.
22. "Holborn Empire" *The Era*, 29 October, 1930, p11.
23. "London Music Halls" *The Era*, 11 March, 1931, p14.
24. "Song Hits are Made by Bands Now, Not By Singers" *Gloucestershire Echo*, 29 December, 1933, p4.
25. A Popular Opera" *Popular Wireless* 19 October 1935, p153.

Billy Bennett

(I)

1. "Gossip of the Day: The "Command" Performance" *Yorkshire Evening Post,* 28 May, 1926, 8.
2. "Billy Bennett's Memories of His Father" *Leeds Mercury,* 29 May, 1937
3. "The Empire" *South Wales Daily Post,* 10 November, 1897, p1.
4. "Hippodrome" *The Era,* 6 July, 1921, p3.
5. "Mr. Billy Bennett in Chester" *Cheshire Observer,* 30 October, 1937, 10.
6. "Billy Bennett for Torquay" *Torbay Express & South Devon Echo,* 12 August, 1939, 5.
7. "Proceedings of Court of Inquiry 16th (The Queens) Lancers 21 November, 1910, Cavalry Barracks, Weedon, No. 5273 Pte Bennett, C Sqdn, 16th Lancers" British Army Service Records
8. "Show World Brevities: Tom E. Hood" *Everyone's,* 18 January, 1933, p34.
9. Letter from John Bennett to Comm. Officer of Regt. 1911. British Army Service record.
10. Edward Eve "The Origin of a Make-Up" *The Era,* 19 March, 1924.
11. J. C. Canell "28 Years 'Almost a Gentleman'" *Newcastle Evening Chronicle,* 7 July, 1939, 18. The famous old Barnard's Theatre, Chatham, was built around the 1860s. The original theatre burned down in 1885 and was rebuilt the following year. Sadly, that building burned to the ground in May, 1934.
12. "Billy Bennett for Torquay" *Torbay Express & South Devon Echo,* 12 August, 1939, 5.
13. "Queen's Favourite Comedian" *Hull Daily Mail,* 8 November, 1935, 8.
14. Frederick Blanchard "Billy Bennett: An Appreciation" p7
15. "Comedian Out-Joked" *Coventry Evening Telegraph,* 4 February, 1930, 3.
16. "Billy Bennett" *The Stage,* 17 September, 1914, 8.
17. "Grand Dramatic and Musical Entertainment at Newbridge" *Kildare Observer and Eastern Counties Advertiser,* 10 April, 1915, 8.
18. "Office Report (Field Service Only) 3rd Machine Gun Regt. W Bennett" British Army Service Records
19. "Queen's Favourite Comedian" *Hull Daily Mail,* 8 November, 1935, 8.
20. "The Origin of a Make-Up" *The Era,* 19 March, 1924, p9.

21. Anthony Farrar-Hockley *Goughie: The Life of General Sir Hubert Gough* (Hart-David MacGibbon, London, 1975) p362

(II)
1. "A Soldier's Soliloquy" *Billy Bennett's Third Budget* p13. Jippo was a kind of gravy juice, dixie a large iron pot; Buckshee meant something free, and Bobajee was slang for a cook
2. "Taffy in Hunland by Arthur West, Esq." *The Stage*, 6 November, 1919
3. "The Wimbledon" *The Stage*, 6 November, 1919, 18.
4. "Wimbledon Theatre" *The Era*, 5 November, 1919, 10.
5. "The Kilburn Empire" *The Stage*, 10 June, 1920
6. A. C. Astor "Just Jottings" *The Stage*, 6 November, 1930.
7. "Swansea Empire" *The Era*, 30 November, 1921, p17.
8. *Liverpool Echo*, 15 January, 1924
9. Holt, Major & Mrs. *The Biography of Bruce Bairnsfather: In Search of the Better Ole* (1995), 124, 272.
10. "Prince of Wales" *Birmingham Daily Gazette*, 7 April, 1925.
11. "This World of Ours" *Yorkshire Post & Leeds Intelligencer*, 2 July, 1942, 2. A tanner or sixpence was a fortieth of a pound. In old money there were 12 pennies in a shilling and 20 shillings in a pound.
12. "Billy Bennett" *Everyone's*, 4 July, 1926, p52.
13. "The Shows" *Evening Post*, 13 October, 1928, 25.
14. "Billy Bennett's Sudden Return from U. S. Explained" *Dundee Evening Telegraph*, 27 August, 1928, 4.
15. "Billy Bennett Didn't Stick" *Variety*, 22 August, 1928, 3.
16. "Comedian's Return from New York" *Dundee Evening Telegraph*, 28 August, 1928, 8.
17. "The Holborn Empire" *The Stage*, 30 August, 1928, 11.
18. "Billy Bennett Didn't Stick" *Variety*, 22 August, 1928, 3.
19. J. C. Canell "28 Years 'Almost a Gentleman'" *Newcastle Evening Chronicle*, 7 July, 1939, 18.

(III)
1. Harry Taft "The Show World" *Everyone's*, 29 May, 1929, 41. "Coo-ee!" *The Era*, 1 May, 1929, 4.
2. II. Willson Disher "Melodies and Memories, Alhambra 29 October, 1929" *The Era* 30 October, 1929

4. "An Injunction Application" *The Stage*, 23 August, 1923, p11. "A Settlement" *The Stage*, 3 July, 1924, p13.
5. J. C. Canell "28 Years 'Almost a Gentleman'" *Newcastle Evening Chronicle*, 7 July, 1939, 18.

(IV)
1. H. Willson Disher "The King and the Music Hall" *The Era*, 2 June, 1926
2. "Comedian Who Made the Queen Laugh" *The People*, 30 May, 1928
3. "Billy Bennett" *Nottingham Journal*, 22 August, 1933, 1.
4. "Royal Command Show Big Success in London" 28 June, 1933, 34.
5. "Amused the Queen" *Nottingham Evening Post*, 24 May, 1933, p6.
6. "Made Queen Laugh" *Birmingham Daily Gazette*, 25 April, 1934, 7.
7. *Billy Bennett's Budget of Burlesques*, p8.
8. "Poverty Point" *The Bulletin*, 19 February, 1930, 11.
9. "Making Em Laugh" *Evening Star*, 17 December, 1935
10. Henry Hall *Here's to the Next Time* (Odham's Press, London, 1955), p127.
11. A. C. Astor "Just Jottings" 19 March, 1931
12. "The Alexander & Mose Concert Party Piccadilly Theatre" *The Times* 24 December 1931, p10
13. "King Folly" *The Era*, 2 January, 1935, 39. *The Stage*, 5 July, 1934, 11.
14. Dollin, Anton *Ballet Go Round* (1938), p124.
15. *Cornishman* 29 June, 1939, p2.
16. "Young Man's Fancy" *Motion Picture Herald*, 2 September, 1939, p48.
17. "Variety Showboat" (Programme) Palace Theatre, Manchester, 23 May, 1938
18. "Comedian Out-Joked" *Coventry Evening Telegraph*, 4 February, 1930, 3.
19. "Cabaret Corner: Billy Bennett at the Paradise" *The Stage*, 22 December, 1938, 10.
20. J. C. Canell "28 Years 'Almost a Gentleman'" *Newcastle Evening Chronicle*, 7 July, 1939, 18.

(V)
1. "Recorded Music: Really Amusing" *Northern Advocate*, 5 November, 1927, p5. The somewhat superior tone of the *Gramophone* editorial approach was maintained, and years later when the Topic LP was released, they gave it a predictably lukewarm response.

2. Tony Barker *Music Hall Records Vol 1-2*, (Tony Barker), pp60, 62.
3. John Goslin "Off the Record" *The Talking Machine Review*, p1627. Note: Despite the success of the record, Topic only produced a few other contributions to the Music Hall discography, notably a collection of Gus Elen's songs the following year.
4. Billy Bennett "Advice to Beginners" *Billy Bennett's First Budget* p5
5. "Recorded Music" *Waikato Independent*, 14 August, 1930, p2.

(VI)
1. "Death of Billy Bennett" *The Stage*, 2 July, 1942, 4.
2. "V. G. S Annual Dinner" *The Stage*, 25 November, 1937, 5.
3. Fred Russell "An Appreciation" *Billy Bennett's Budget of Burlesque Monologues Fourth Souvenir* p3
4. Holloway, Stanley *Wiv a Little Bit o Luck*
5. "The Lighter Side" *Nottingham Evening Post*, 12 September, 1942, 3.
6. "What to See at Southsea" *Hampshire Telegraph*, 9 June, 1939, 12.
7. "In the Radio World: Comedian Refuses £1 a Minute to Broadcast" *Nottingham Evening Post*, 2 June, 1926, 7.
8. "Billy Bennett Broadcasting from Luxembourg" *The Era*, 18 November, 1936, 3.
9. "Billy Bennett Comedian Who Made Royalty Laugh" *Birmingham Mail*, 1 July, 1942, 3.
10. "Billy Bennett's Loss" *The Stage*, 20 February, 1936.
11. "A Son of Liverpool" *Liverpool Echo*, 2 July, 1942, 2.
12. "Billy Bennett" *The Stage*, 21 July 1932, 5.
13. "Billy Bennett" *The Stage*, 3 July, 1930, p5.
14. "Billy Bennett" *The Stage*, 19 October, 1933, 6.
15. Clarkson Rose "Peradventure" *The Stage*, 12 August, 1937, 2.
16. Clarkson Rose "Peradventure" *The Stage*, 1 July, 1937, p2.
17. "Billy Bennett's Loss" *The Stage*, 8 June, 1939, p3.
18. "One Pantomime Running" *Birmingham Mail*, 2 April, 1940, p5.
19. "Theatres of Wartime London" *The Sketch*, 19 June, 1940, 14.
20. "Prince of Wales" *The Times*, Present Arms 14 May 1940, p4.
21. "Hit Stars at Factory" *Evening Dispatch*, 21 November, 1941, 4.
22. Fletcher, Cyril *Nice one Cyril* (1978) p47
23. "Tim Arnold Presents Boys and Girls of the BBC" *Birmingham Daily Post*, 18 November, 1941
24. "Billy Bennett" *The Era*, 20 October, 1920, 14. "Billy Bennett" *The Stage*, 16 September, 1926, 14.

25. "Billy Bennett Ill" *Daily Record,* 3 July, 1940, 4.
26. "Stoll, Kingsway" *The Stage,* 30 April, 1942. The Stoll, Kingsway was an impressive theatre originally built by Oscar Hammerstein as the London Opera House in 1911, with beautiful interiors. It was later renamed the Stoll and was at one time a cinema. The building was demolished in 1958 and the Peacock Theatre was built on the site in 1960.
27. Batten Joe *Joe Batten's Book* (1955) p71. The original Opera House, Blackpool was built by Frank Matcham in 1889. It was rebuilt and extended in 1910, and rebuilt a second time in 1939.
28. Agate, James *Ego 5 Again: More of the Autobiography of James Agate* (George G. Harrap & Co, London, 1945), 242.

Songs, Recitations & Sheet Music
1. "Grand Dramatic and Musical Entertainment at Rowbridge" *Kildare Observer & Eastern Counties Advertiser,* 10 April, 1915, 8.
2. "Brighton Royal" *The Stage,* 29 June, 1920, p3.
3. "Victoria Palace" *The Stage,* 11 July, 1923, p15.
4. "The Palladium" *The Era,* 19 December, 1923, p13.
5. "Victoria Palace" 1924 *The Era,* 7 February, 1924, p10.
6. "Ilford Hippodrome" *The Era,* 24 March, 1924, p4.
7. "The Islington Empire" *The Stage,* 23 October, 1924, p13.
8. Listed among record releases for October, 1926 "Mr. Fryer's Concert" *Burnley Express,* 9 October, 1926, p7.
9. "Victoria Palace" *The Era,* 30 March, 1927, p13.
10. "The Alhambra" *The Era,* 26 October, 1927, p13.
11. "Will o' the Whispers" The Era, 11 April, 1928
12. "Holborn Empire" *The Era,* 9 January, 1929, 11.
13. "The Pedagogue at the Palladium" *The Era,* 9 September, 1931, p12.

CHARLIE HIGGINS

(I) Double-Act
1. R. B. Marriott, *The Era* "Sherkot Burlesques at Streatham Hill" 1 August, 1934, p13.
2. Baptism Register, Ancoats St. Andrew, Manchester, 1892. "Cynical Man of World with a Moustache" *Derby Daily Telegraph,* 10 October, 1928, 8.

3. "Next Week at the Royal Hippodrome" *Belfast News-Letter*, 20 September 1918, p5. Robert Charles St. Juste was born on 19 March, 1890 in Liverpool and had a difficult childhood; he hardly knew his father and was brought up by his mother Mary Elizabeth *nee* Walton (c1855-1932). She was the daughter of a mariner and was married thrice to sailors: firstly, to William Smith (m. 15 July, 1872, St. Simon, Liverpool): (2) Charles Abram Brevnick (m. 27 January, 1874, Liverpool): Thirdly to Charles Robert St. Juste m. 1 June, 1882, St. Mary Magdalene, Liverpool. She had seven children in total but only two survived to adulthood. As a child, Charles junior spent time in the workhouse, but managed to escape a life of poverty and from at least 1910 was on the music hall stage, as was his mother. He first appeared in double acts with a Miss May in 1911 and later that year with a partner called Brennan (they appeared at the Dewsbury Empire as Brennan and St. Juste). From 1913 to about 1916 St. Juste was in partnership with Hal L. Miller as Miller and St. Juste. They were occasionally described as Americans or Canadians. Miller joined the Royal Navy Air Service in 1917 by which time St. Juste had joined the King's Liverpool Regt., (1915-19) where he rose to the rank of Lance Corporal and met Higginson. The two were part of the King's Jesters concert party troupe, but not as a double act, in 1918. By May, 1919 they were performing on the halls together, and continued until the partnership broke up in 1925. After going their separate ways, St. Juste joined up with others including George Faber as St. Juste and Faber. St. Juste was married June 1914 (W. Derby) to Annie Daley and they had a daughter Bernardine (b. Liverpool, Dec. 1915). Charles divorced Annie in 1931 and she died in 1933 aged 43. St. Juste composed a number of songs including "Rhubarb and Custard" (1928). He toured overseas in the 1930s and lived for a time in Scotland. He last appeared on variety bills around 1948, but I have been unable to discover when he died.
4. "The King's Jesters" *The Stage*, 3 April, 1919. 6 "Sheffield Courts: Hippodrome Artists Arrested" *Sheffield Daily Telegraph*, 16 May, 1919, p2.
5. "Sheffield Courts: Hippodrome Artists Arrested" *Sheffield Daily Telegraph*, 16 May, 1919, p2. "Pte. C. R. Higginson, 30 July, 1919: L/Cpl. C. R. St. Juste, 7 August, 1919" Judge Advocate General's Office. District Courts Martial, Home & Abroad SO 86; Piece No. 88.

6. "This Week in the Dublin Theatres" *Dublin Evening Telegraph*, 14 October, 1924, 6.
7. "Grand" *The Stage*, 2 April, 1925, p10.

(II)
1. *The Observer*, 2 June, 1929, p15.
2. "Magnets" *The Stage*, 15 October, 1925, p14.
3. "Coventry Entertainments" *Coventry Evening Telegraph*, 22 December, 1925, 5.
4. "Hammersmith Palace" *West London Observer*, 24 December, 1926, 4.
5. "Hippodrome" *Birmingham Daily Gazette*, 2 March, 1926, 9.
6. "The Hippodrome" *Coventry Evening Telegraph*, 20 July, 1926, p4.
7. "Out of Work" *West London Observer*, 26 August, 1927, 4.
8. "The Show World at the Hammersmith Palace" *West London Observer*, 1 June, 1928, 4.
9. The Show World" *The Era*, 18 April, 1928, 13.
10. *The Stage*, 7 June, 1928, 11.
11. "Brixton Empire" *The Stage*, 20 April, 1933, 3.
12. "The Hippodrome" *Manchester Guardian*, 15 November, 1932.
13. "The Prince's" *The Stage*, 29 December, 1933, p18.
14. "Empress, Brixton" *The Stage*, 28 December, 1939, 17.
15. R. B. Marriott "Charlie Higgins: Faithful to Buttercups and Waxworks" *The Era*, 8 August, 1934, p5.
16. "Halifax: Red Riding Hood" *The Stage*, 2 January, 1947. P13.
17. "Sunday Concert" *The Stage*, 15 October, 1953, 3.
18. "Whoopee for Charlie!" *Daily Mail*, 13 August, 2010
19. England & Wales National Probate Calendars: "Higginson, Charles Robert" 1978

Other Songs and Sheet Music
1. "St. Juste and Higgins" *The Stage*, 1 April, 1920, p14
2. "This Week's Amusements" *Belfast News-Letter*, 14 November, 1922, p8
3. "The Palladium" *The Era*, 22 August, 1923, p13.
4. "Stratford Empire" *The Era*, 9 July, 1924, p10.
5. "Charlie Higgins" *The Stage*, 1 September, 1927, p3.
6. "The Show World" *The Era*, 18 April, 1928, p13.
7. "Song Notes: Feldman" *The Stage*, 26 April, 1928
8. "The Metropolitan" *The Era*, 10 April, 1929, p4.
9. "The Palladium" *The Stage*, 23 January, 1930, p8.

10. "Live Letters: Old Timer" *Daily Mirror*, 9 August, 1967
11. "Shepherd's Bush Empire" *The Stage*, 29 December, 1950, p7.

ALFRED LESTER

Opening quote from *The Spectator*, Vol. 132, p874, 31 May, 1924.

1. Lester once told the music hall correspondent of a Nottingham paper that he was born on Mansfield Road, Nottingham in October, 1874. The family were certainly living in Nottingham at that time but it was in the following year that the five-year-old Alfred made his stage debut. Most usual online sources repeat 1874 but he could not have been on stage at the age of one, and his age was given as 10 in 1881. His parents Edgar Alfred Leslie and Annie Ross married 20 August, 1866 at Stepney. Edgar was the son of Alfred William Leslie and Annie's father was William Ross.
2. "Alfred Lester Dead" *The Leeds Mercury*, 7 May, 1925, p3.
3. "New Ealing Theatre" *The Era*, 1 September, 1900
4. "The Theatres" *The Times*, 1 October, 1906, 12.
5. "Lester's Forte" *Evening Herald*, 5 August, 1925
6. "The Tivoli" *The Times*, 25 July, 1911, 10.
7. "The Life of a Comedian" *The Times*, 16 May, 1914, p4.
8. "The Pearl Girl" *The Times*, December 22, 1913, 6.
9. "Stage Gossip" *Derby Daily Telegraph*, 9 July, 1925, 5.
10. "Musical Comedy Under a New Name" *The Times*, 13 November, 1919, 10.
11. "The Shop Girls Again" *The Times*, London, 26 March, 1920, 12.
12. "Pins and Needles!" *The Times*, May 14, 1921, 8.
13. "Alfred Lester in Dispute" *Variety*, 22 August, 1922
14. "The Coliseum" *The Times*, 26 February, 1923, 12.
15. Alltree, George *Footlight Memories: Recollections of Music-Hall and Stage Life* (S. Low, Marston, London, 1932), p133.
16. Baddeley. Hermione *The Unsinkable Hermione Baddeley: An Autobiography* (Collins, London, 1984), p39.
17. "Alfred Lester" *Nottingham Journal*, 7 May, 1925, 6.
18. "Alfred Lester" *Variety*, 30 May, 1925
19. Blow, Sydney *The Ghost Walks on Fridays* (1935), p204

Tom Foy

1. "Sudden Death of a Popular Yorkshire Comedian" *Yorkshire Evening Post,* 10 August, 1917
2. See Slout, William L. *Olympians of the Sawdust Circle* (Wildside Press, 1998), p201.
3. Pan "Between the Turns" *Penny Illustrated Paper,* 17 June, 1911, p802.
4. "Tom Foy Dead" *Nottingham Evening Post,* 10 August, 1917.
5. "Grand Opera House" *Belfast News-Letter,* 29 December, 1914.
6. "Entertainments at Birch Hill" *Rochdale Observer,* 8 November, 1916.

Songs & Sheet Music
1. *Music Hall & Theatre Review,* 5 August, 1904, p9.

Vivian Foster

1. *The Hull & Eastern Counties Herald,* 25 February, 1864
3. Tacchella, B. (Ed.) *Derby School Register 1570-1901* (Bemrose & Sons, Ltd., Snow Hill & Derby, 1902) p103.
5. "Shirland: Sudden Death of Rector" *The Derby Mercury,* 3 May, 1882
6. "Shirland: The Parish Church" *The Derby Mercury,* 28 November, 1883
7. *Canterbury Journal, Kentish Times & Farmer's Gazette,* 1 August, 1903, p5.
8. *Brighton Gazette,* 27 October, 1904, p6.
9. "The Vicar in the Troupe" *Yorkshire Evening Post,* 1 February, 1916, p3.
11. "Mystery Censorship at Broadcasting House" *Birmingham Daily Gazette,* 24 August, 1937, p8.
12. "Correspondence" *Exeter & Plymouth Gazette,* 27 July, 1916
13. Clarkson Rose "Peradventure" *The Stage,* 24 February, 1937
14. "From London Town" *The Billboard,* 4 April, 1925, p53.
15. "Injured by Falling Batten" *The Billboard,* 13 February, 1926, p13.
16. "Yes, I Think So!" *Derby Evening Telegraph,* 29 December, 1934, p4.
17. John Williams "On 'Vicar of Mirth' Vivian Foster Music Hall Eloquence and Wit" *The Stage,* 15 February, 1979, p8.

18. Frank Milne, whose real name was Frank Lionel French, was the son of a haberdasher from Leicester who played with various concert parties from the 1900s up until his death in 1937.

Songs & Monologues
1. "Shop Assistants' Concert" *Brighton Gazette*, 7 November, 1903
2. "Burgess Hill" *Mid-Sussex Times*, 29 November, 1903
3. *Brighton Gazette*, 5 December, 1903
4. "Hayward's Heath" *Mid-Sussex Times*, 28 February, 1905, p4.
5. "Rayleigh" *Southend Standard & Essex Weekly Advertiser*, 18 April, 1907, p3.
6. *Derbyshire Advertiser & Journal*, 30 August, 1907

Bert Errol

1. "Bert Errol, Princess Theatre" *Montreal Star*, 16 March, 1920
2. Isaac Whitehouse & family, 1881 Census, Aston Road, Aston, Birmingham. Also census for 1861, 1871, 1891, 1901 & 1911.
3. "Mr. Isaac Whitehouse, of the Chase, Oval Road, Gravelly Hill, Aston, Brass-founder, died on April 30, left estate valued at £5, 345." *Birmingham Daily Post*, 25 July, 1918.
4. "Bert Errol Destined for Chemistry" *The Brooklyn Standard Union*, 26 December, 1921
5. "The Transformation of a Man: Behind the Scenes with Bert and Ray Errol" *Table Talk*, 11 September, 1924, p45: "Bert Errol" *Acton Gazette*, 27 August, 1926, p7.
6. "Gossip" *The Herald, (Melbourne, Vic.)* 6 September, 1924
7. "New Acts This Week" *Variety*, November, 1914, p18.
8. Reynolds, Harry *Minstrel Memories: The Story of Burnt Cork Minstrelsy in Great Britain from 1836 to 1927* (A. Rivers, London, 1928), p238.
9. "Julian Eltinge, Attention!" *The Billboard*, 30 September, 1922, p11.
10. "Bert Errol, Princess Theatre" *Montreal Star*, 16 March, 1920
11. "The Vaudeville Mirror: Pencilled Patter" *The New York Dramatic Mirror*, 11 June, 1910, p22
12. "Ten More Weeks for Bert Erroll" *The New York Dramatic Mirror*, 14 January, 1914, p45.
13. "The Orpheum" *Brooklyn Life*, 10 April, 1920, p22.

14. "French Writer Describes the Pretty American" *Buffalo Evening News,* 26 April, 1915, p3. It is likely that the writer was confusing him with Julian Eltinge.
15. "Famous Impersonator: Bert Errol Coming to Hoyts" *The Daily News, Perth, W. A.* 29 June, 1928, p8. "Green Room Gossip: Bert Errol for Perth" *Truth,* 24 June, 1928, p10.
16. "Bert Errol in Berlin" *The Era,* 28 December, 1927, p4.
17. "English Artists in New Zealand" *The Era,* 28 January, 1925, p12.
18. "The Transformation of a Man: Behind the Scenes with Bert and Ray Errol" *Table Talk,* 11 September, 1924, p44.
19. Walter D. Hickman "Bert Errol Does Some Good Talking" *The Indianapolis Times,* 28 October, 1925, p6.
20. "The Transformation of a Man: Behind the Scenes with Bert and Ray Errol" *Table Talk,* 11 September 1924, p45
21. "Professional Apartments: Errol Hotel, 63 Gower St., London" *The Era,* 27 August, 1930, p3. Damon Runyon "The Brighter Side of the News" *Times-Union, Albany, N. Y.,* 28 July 1939. p21.
22. "Jenny Howard" *The Era,* 4 November 1931, p14.
23. "Will Rogers Stuff Rouses His Majesty's Subjects" *The Billboard,* 27 January 1927, p13.
24. "Wedding of Bert Errol's Daughter" *Birmingham Daily Gazette,* 27 June 1938, p5.
25. "Aston Hippodrome" *Birmingham Daily Post,* 7 November 1944, p4.
26. "Bert Errol" *The Stage,* 8 December, 1949, p3.
27. "The Transformation of a Man: Behind the Scenes with Bert and Ray Errol" *Table Talk,* 11 September, 1924, p45

Films
1. Denis Gifford *Entertainers in British Films: A Century of Showbiz in the Cinema* (Greenwood Press, 1998) p28

Songs & Sheet Music
1. *Rugby Advertiser,* 13 November, 1906
2. *The Era,* 30 July, 1910
3. "Vaudeville Club" *The Era,* 26 November, 1910
4. *The Era,* 16 July, 1913
5. "Song Notes" *The Stage,* 15 October, 1914
7. Introduced at the Holborn Empire, February, 1919 "Holborn Empire" *The Era,* 26 February, 1919

8. "Lawrence Wright" *The Era*, 12 November 1919
9. *The Stage*, 2 October 1919
10. "B. F. Keith's Palace Theater" *The Billboard*, 8 May 1920, p17.
11. *The Music Trade Directory: Musical Opinion & Trade Review*, Vol. 32, p28, 1921
12. *The Era*, 30 November 1922, p23.
13. "Footlight Flashes" *The Era*, 4 July 1923, p15
14. "Song Notes" *The Stage*, 23 July 1925, p4.
15. "Songs & Singers" 8 August 1925, p5.
16. William Sterling Battis "Palace, Chicago" *The Billboard*, 10 October 1925, p14.
17. "Song Notes" *The Stage*, 26 September 1926, p4.
18. *The Era*, 14 September 1927, p11.
19. "Publishers' Song Notes" *The Stage*, 8 May 1930, p18.
20. "The Metropolitan" *The Era*, 10 September 1930, p13.
21. "Lew Grade" *The Era*, 24 September 1930, p13.
22. "Jenny Howard" *The Era*, 4 November 1931, p14.
23. "West Pier Theatre, Brighton" *Sussex Agricultural Express*, 28 December 1934, p3.
24. "Provincial Pantomimes" *The Stage*, 2 January 1936

MARGARET COOPER

(I)
1. "Margaret Cooper: An Interview" *The Mail, Adelaide, SA*, 4 May, 1912, 3.
2. "Star Turns: Miss Margaret Cooper" *The Sketch*, Vol. 74, p176, 1911. The song was "Far, Far Away" Francis & Day, London, the lyrics of which were reproduced in *Jim Crow's Vagaries*.
3. "Making the Public Laugh and Cry" *Port Pirie Recorder & North Western Mail, South Australia*, 25 May, 1912, 6.
4. Kanner, Barbara *Women in Context: Two Hundred Years of British Women Autobiographers, a Reference Guide and Reader* (G. K. Hall, 1997), 236.
5. "Margaret Cooper" *The Sydney Morning Herald*, 8 June, 1912, 8.
6. Newspaper cutting from unnamed magazine. Margaret Cooper *Myself & My Piano*
7. "Drawing-Room Ballads" Letter to *The Times*, 21 April, 1961, p22.

8. *Star*, 3 March, 1919.
9. "Leicester Palace" *Leicester Chronicle*, 11 November, 1911, p7.
10. "Margaret Cooper" *Newcastle Morning Herald & Miner's Advocate*, 1 October, 1926.
11. "Margaret Cooper" *The Sydney Morning Herald*, 8 June, 1912, 8.
12. *The Berkshire Chronicle*, 18 May, 1901, 4.

(II)
1. "Miss Margaret Cooper" Theatre Programme 1912
2. W. Macqueen Pope *The Melodies Linger On* (W. H. Allen, London, 1950), pp213-14.
3. Margaret Cooper interviewed by Gwen Serjeant White "Making the Public Laugh and Cry" *Port Pirie Recorder & North Western Mail*, 25 May, 1912, p6.
4. "Palace Pier Sunday Concerts" *Brighton Gazette*, 28 March, 1908, 8.
5. B. C. Hilliam *The Times*, 29 March, 1962, p22.
6. "New Music by Ampersand: Chappell & Co." *Musical Opinion & Music Trade Review*, July, 1912, p743.
7. "Margaret Cooper" *Daily Herald, Adelaide*, 1 May, 1912, 8.
8. Gardner, Fitzroy *Pure Folly: The Story of Those Remarkable People The Follies* (Mills & Boon, Ltd., London, 1910), 17.
9. "Woman's World" *Aberdeen Press & Journal*, 4 February, 1911, 3.
10. Schafer, R. Murray (Ed.) *Ezra Pound and Music: The Complete Criticism* (New Directions, New York, 2008), p101.
11. "Stage Romance" *The Sun, Sydney (NSW)*, 10 August, 1910, 14.

(III)
1. "A. M. Humble-Crofts, Eastbourne College Roll of Honour"
2. "Stage Romance" *The Sun, Sydney, NSW*, 10 August, 1910, 14.
3. "Making the Public Laugh and Cry" *Port Pirrie Recorder & North Western Mail, SA*, 25 May, 1912, 6.
4. Miller, Geoffrey *The Bournemouth Symphony Orchestra* (Dorset Publishing Co., Bournemouth, 1970), p48.
5. Godfrey, Sir Dan *Memories & Music: Thirty-Five Years of Conducting* (Hutchinson & Co., 1924), p82.
6. Taylor, Thomas Griffith *With Scott: The Silver Lining* (Dodd, Mead & Co., Ltd., London, 1916), p265.
7. "London Notes" *Variety*, 16 June, 1910, 10.

8. "Margaret Cooper: An Interview" *The Mail, Adelaide, SA*, 4 May, 1912, 3.
9. "Talented English Entertainer" *The Daily Telegraph, Sydney, NSW*, 8 June, 1912, 22.
10. "Margaret Cooper: An Interview" *The Mail, Adelaide, SA*, 4 May, 1912, 3.
11. "A Recent Visitor" *Leader (Melbourne, Victoria)*, 1 November, 1913, 53.
12. "Miss Margaret Cooper" *The Daily Telegraph*, 29 June, 1912, 10.
13. "Margaret Cooper" *Observer*, 27 July, 1912
14. *The Bulletin*, 20 June, 1912, 24.
15. "Melbourne Chatter" *The Bulletin*, 25 April, 1912, 22.
16. "Miss M. Cooper's Relapse" *Evening Star*, 1 August, 1912, 4. "Miss Margaret Cooper" *Ashburton Guardian*, 5 August, 1912.
17. "Poverty Point" *The Bulletin*, 4 January, 1923, 36.
19. "Miss Margaret Cooper: Impressions of Australia" *The Sun*, 5 October, 1913, p21.

(IV)
1. Croxton, Arthur *Crowded Nights and Days: An Unconventional Pageant* (S. Low & Marston, London, 1934), p266.
2. "Theatrical Gossip" *Brighton Gazette, Hove Post, Sussex and Surrey Telegraph*, 10 October, 1907, p5.
3. "Margaret Cooper" *The Bendigo Independent*, 26 April, 1912, p5.
4. "A Nervous Stage Favourite" *The Sun*, 30 June, 1912, p15.
5. "Miss Margaret Cooper in Camp" Newspaper cutting from *Daily Mirror*, c1916
6. "At Mons" *Daily Mirror*, 8 June, 1916, p10.
7. "In the War News" *Daily Mirror*, 31 March, 1917.
8. "Capt. Arthur Maughan Humble-Crofts, R.A.F" *Flight*, November 28, 1918, p1363.
9. Renshaw, Andrew *Wisden on the Great War: The Lives of Cricket's Fallen 1914-1918* (A. & C. Black, London, 2014), p239.
10. Francis St. John Brougham (1890-1958) was a schoolmaster who wrote a handful of songs that achieved some fame around 1919/20. In 1923 he entered a Benedictine monastery in Yorkshire, but later returned to teaching and was a master at the Gate House School, Kingston upon-Thames in the 1930s. *The Oratorian*, 2017, pp28-29.
11. "Camp Concert Fund" *Cambridge Daily News*, 25 April, 1918, p4.

12. Coward, Noel *The Letters of Noel Coward* (Bloomsbury Publishing, London, 2014)
13. "Local Intelligence: Boxing Day at the Pump Room" *Bath Chronicle & Weekly Gazette*. 23 December, 1922, 11.
14. "Miss Margaret Cooper" *Thanet Advertiser*, 6 January, 1923, 7.
15. "Miss Margaret Cooper" *Daily Herald*, 3 January, 1923, 2.
16. National Probate Calendars: Humble-Crofts Margaret Gernon of 103 Dartmouth-road, Cricklewood Middlesex widow died 27 December 1922 Administration London 27 January to Alexander David Cooper dealer Effects £5032 8s. 9d.
17. Harry Welchman (1886-1966) married his second wife Sybil Forde in the spring of 1925. He had a long stage career and appeared in several films including *The Life and Death of Colonel Blimp* (1943).
18. Haddon, Archibald *The Story of Music Hall* 1935, p107.

Sheet Music & Additional Songs
1. "Organ Recital" *Cambridge Chronicle & Journal*, 13 November, 1896, 4.
2. "Guy d'Hardelot" *Daily Telegraph & Courier*, 15 December, 1898
3. *Musical News*, 1909, 208
4. *Catalog of Copyright Entries: Musical Compositions Part 3* 1939, p1794
5. G. A. Collard "Margaret Cooper" January, 1923
6. Collard Moutrie, 1912 *Musical Opinion & Music Trade Review, Vol. 36*, 69.
7. Coward, Noel *The Letters of Noel Coward* (Bloomsbury Publishing, London, 2014)
8. Birch, S. *The Education Outlook*, Vol 72, 1920, p434.

Norman Long

1. Norman Taylor "Meet Norman Long"
2. Historical Records: Census of 1871-1911.
3. "Miss Gladys Groom Gives a Bright and Sparkling Show" *Norwood News*, 8 May, 1914, p8.
4. "Urbanities" *Skegness Standard*, 12 April, 1944, p4. Andrews, Cyrus (Compiler & Ed.) *Radio Who's Who* (London: Pendulum Publications, 1947), p209.

5. "The Impromptus" *The Stage*, 28 May, 1914, p28. Note: Charles Heslop appeared to make at least one recording with a group: Charles Heslop and Company *The Audition*: Part 1 "The Crooner" / Part 2 "Introducing a Drinking Song" Sterno Serial 1407 This could date from c1931, but that was long after the Brownies were around. Heslop started the Brownies in 1908 and ran them until 1916 when he joined the R. F. C. After demobilisation he picked up with the group again until 1921.
6. "Pavilion Gardens" *Derbyshire Advertiser & Journal*, 18 April, 1914, p8.
7. "Pavilion Gardens, Kingstown" *Dublin Evening Telegraph*, 14 September, 1915, p2.
8. "Heard but Not Seen: Popular Broadcasters: Norman Long" (Magazine cutting, 1936)
9. Read *Empires, Palaces & Hippodromes* The Lewisham Hippodrome was built at 153/159 Rushey Green, Catford in 1911. It later became a cinema and closed in 1959. It was demolished the following year. Read pp145-50.
10. "Concert Artists and Broadcasting" *The Era*, 11 February, 1931, p20.
11. "The Zeniths" *The Stage*, 12 June, 1919, p18.
12. "Cycling Club Concert Success" *Thanet Advertiser*, 12 November, 1921, p3.

(II) All for Ten Shillings a Year: The BBC: Recording Career & Royal Variety Shows

1. Some sources place his debut as 28 November, 1922.
2. "Twinkling Radio Stars" *Nottingham Evening Post*, 24 November, 1933, p7. *Popular Wireless* 1 March 1930, p1234.
3. Norman Long "20 Years On Air" *Newcastle Evening Chronicle*, 21 November, 1942, p2.
4. "Chalet Theatre" *Skegness Standard*, 19 September, 1923, p5.
5. Terese Rose Nagel "Vaudeville Hour on the BBC" *Broadcasting*, September 15, 1932, 13.
6. "Grand Opening of Whiteley's New Restaurant" *The Times*, 19 November, 1923, p9. "Entertainments" 18 August, 1924, p8.
7. "Harrods Announce a Magnificent Gramophone Exhibition" *The Times*, 15 October, 1926, p9. "Round the Shops" *The Times*, 18 October, 1926, p11

8. Rose, Clarkson *With a Twinkle in My Eye* (1951), p223.
9. "A Good Joke" *Derby Daily Telegraph*, 25 February, 1927, p 5.
10. "Merriment" *Woking Herald*, 28 October, 1926, p5.
11. "The C. A. A. and Broadcasting" *The Stage*, 10 May, 1923, 19.
12. "Theatre Edict Defied" *The Scotsman*, 29 December, 1932, p8.
13. "Variety Gossip" *The Stage*, 30 December, 1932, p 29.

(III) "We Can't Let You Broadcast That!" His Songs of Satire and Social Comment
1. "Stanelli's Bachelor Party" *Coventry Herald*, 19 June, 1938, p3.
2. "Week-End Radio" *Sussex Agricultural Express*, 13 April, 1934, p14.
3. "Mr. Norman Long" *Portsmouth Evening News*, 13 December, 1935, p3.

(IV) His Later Career: The War Years and Retirement
1. Norman Taylor "Meet Norman Long"
2. "Norman Long Stops the Bill" *The Era*, 18 May, 1932, p23.
3. J. Manning "Norman Long's New Role" *Lincolnshire Standard & Boston Guardian*, 5 May, 1945, p8.
4. "Norman Long's Happiest Days" *Daily Herald*, 23 May, 1938, p9.
5. "Norman Long" *The Stage*, 25 March, 1937, p6.
6. "Holiday Enjoyed" *Coventry Evening Telegraph*, 29 June, 1939, p7.
7. "Stage Gossip: Geniality of Dames" 28 December, 1940, p2.
8. Huggins, Arthur A. *The Last Evacuee: Dagenham to Salcombe* p56.
9. "Masonic Rolls: Thornton Heath Lodge: 19/1/1921"
10. "Concert and Entertainment Notices" *The Stage*, 18 January, 1951, pp6, 7.
11. "Concerts and Entertainment Notes: Death of Norman Long" *The Stage*, 11 January, 1951, p6.
12. "Norman Long Memorial Service" *The Stage*, 8 February, 1951
13. "The Variety Stage" *The Stage*, 18 January, 1951, p3.
14. "The Bolt Head Hotel" *The Yorkshire Post & Leeds Intelligencer*, 24 September, 1951, p6.
15. J. Manning "Norman Long's New Role" *Lincolnshire Standard & Boston Guardian*, 5 May, 1945, p8.
16. Johnston, Brian *A Further Slice of Johnners* (Random House, 2011) Interview with George Shearing at Lord's 23 June, 1990.

Discography
1. "A Gramophone Selection" *Daily Herald,* 29 June, 1932, p13.

Other Music, Songs & Monologues
1. "Victoria Palace" *The Era,* 17 April, 1929, p11

Index

A Canterbury Tale 195
Ack-Ack, Beer-Beer 92
Adeler & Sutton 149, 150
The Adventures of Robin Hood 122
Agate, James 52, 83, 91, 93
"Agatha Green" 180
"Ain't it Grand to be Blooming Well Dead" 105
A Labour Candidate 117
Aladdin 7, 9, 17 (Theatre Royal, Newcastle, 1906-07) 33 (Empire, Wood Green, 1923-24) 36, (Liverpool, 1899-1900)
Alfonso XIII, King of Spain 64, 173
Alice in Wonderland (1941) 23
Allandale, Ethel 177
Allen, T. H. 90
All Fit 19
"All for Ten Shillings a Year" 209-10
All Poshed Up 104, *109*
Alltree, George 122
Almost a Gentleman (1928) 78, (1938) 81-82
Almost a Gentleman (Topic LP) 84
Almost an Academy 89
The Amateur Hairdresser 117
American Music Hall, Chicago *12*
Andrews, Julie 24
"And Yet I Don't Know" 164
"A N'egg and Some N'ham and an N'onion" 100
"Another Little Drink Wouldn't Do Us Any Harm" 119

The Arcadians 115, *116*, 118, 121
Arabian Nights 113
"Aren't We All?" 208
"Are We Downhearted? No!" 137
Are You Being Served? 204-05
Arnold, Tom 91
Arthurs, Robert 32
Arundale, Sybil 65
Ashcroft, Peggy 19, 20
Askey, Arthur 53, 54, 91, 214
"A Soldier's Farewell to His Horse" 78
Aston Villa F. C. 148
Astor, A. C. 54
"At the Church Door I've Been Waiting" 38
At the Drop of a Hat 166
Aubrey, Stan 60
Auden, W. H. 133, 141
Austin, Charles 67
A Woman Adrift 113
Alywin, Jean *114*

Babes in the Wood (Leeds, 1895-96) 60
Baddeley, Hermione 122-23
Bailey, Bill 216
Bairnsfather, Bruce 68
Baker, Hylda 82
The Bank of England 113
Bard, Wilkie 33
Barnum, P. T. 128
Barnard's Theatre, Chatham 62, 287n
"Barracky Bert" 74

"The Barrers in the Walworth Road" 204
Barry, Katie 11
Batten, Joe 31, 93, 283n
BBC (British Broadcasting Corporation) 16, 21, 51, 52-53, 54, 78, 89-90, 91, 92, 133, 138, 192, 197-98, 202, 208, 209, 211
"Because He Loves Me" 38-39
Beaton, Cecil 17, 25
Bennet, Harry 139
Bennett, Billy 2, 59-93, 101, 200, 204, 232-37
Bennett, Catherine 59, 65-66, 79, 90, 91
Bennett, John R. 59-60, 61-62, 90
Bennett, Kate 59, 62, 89
Bennett, Maggie 59, 62
Bennett & Martell 59-62
Bent, Buena 117
Bernhardt, Sarah 152
Berlin, Irving 35, 154
"Bertha from Balham" 190
Betsy 113
Big City 91
The Bing Boys are Here 119, *120*
"Birds in the High Hall Garden" 175
Black and Blue 91
Black-Eyed Susan 113
Black, George 60, 93
Blake, Peter 269
Blanchard, Frederick 62, 101
Blanche, Ada 28
Blow, Sydney 124
Boots at the Swan 113
Borge, Victor 216
Boys and Girls of the BBC 91
"A Boy's Best Friend is His Mother" 24
Boys Will Be Girls 21
Bray, Bert 103
Bright, John 135
The Broker's Man 117
Brougham, St. John 189, 300n
Brown, Teddy 82
Browne, Bothwell 151
Bruce, Harry 8
Bryan, Dora 39

Buchanan, Jack 119, 124
"Buck-Shee" 66
The Bulletin 184
"Burlington Bertie from Bow" 105
Burnaby, Dave 121
Burney, Herbert 196
Burra, Edward 25
Burrows, George 197
Business as Usual 136
Butcher, Ernest 211
Butt, Alfred 114, 173
Byng, Douglas 145

Cabaret (1936) 53, (1938) 107
Calling All Stars 81
"The Camel and the Butterfly" 171
Campbell, Herbert 28
Cannot, Jack 183
Can You Beat It? 214
Caractacus 171
Carbette, Rayna 47
Carew, James 80, 81
Carlyle, Thomas 135
Carter, Alexandra 216
Castling, Harry 36, 43-44
"Catch Me" 180
The Catch of the Season 172
"Champagne Charlie" 168
Champion, Harry 212
Chappell & Co. *170*, 171, 190
Chaplin, Charlie 2, 12, 48, 65, 117, 125, 218
"The Charge of the Tight Brigade" 74
"Charlie in Spain" 106
"Charlie Makes Whoopee" 103, 107
Charlot, Andre 21, 121, 124
"The Cheese it Stands Alone" 84
Chevalier, Albert 163
Child's Garden of Verses 175
The Chinese Honeymoon 171
"The Chocolate Major" 34
"Church Bells as We Hear Them" 164
Cinderella (Nottingham, 1897-98) 31, (Kennington, 1898-99) 32, (Theatre Royal, Edinburgh,

1914-15) 35, (Manchester, 1903-04) 130, (Royal Opera House, 1916-17) 130
Clapham & Dwyer 107
Clare, Tom 164, 196, 203 208
Clifton, Herbert 151
Cobden, Richard 135
Cochran, Charles B. 65, 121
Cocktails, Kippers and Capers 92
Coleridge-Taylor, Samuel 171
The Colleen Bawn 113
Collins, Charles 44
Columbia Records 43, 83, 119, 138, 139, 200, 218
Comedy Cabaret 107
"The Commissionaire" 164
Connor, T. W. 69, 78
"The Conscientious Objector's Lament" 120, 124
Coo-ee 72
Cooper, Alexander 180, 188-89, 191, 301n
Cooper, Enid 192
Cooper, Isabella C. 168
Cooper, James 168, 179
Cooper, John 168
Cooper, Margaret 168
Cooper, Margaret 166, 167-92, 208, 248-59
"The Co-Optimists" 197
Cortesi, Francisco 150
"The Council Schools are Good Enough for Me" 204
Courtneidge, Cicely 119
Courtneidge, Robert 115-16
Cowan, Maurice 18, 53
Coward, Noel 164, 190
Cranston, Sidney 113
Crawford, Percy 70
The Critic 117
Crosby, Katie 31
Crosby, Mary Ann 27, 36, 53
Crosby, Maurice 27
Cummings, Richard 169
Curran, Fred 62

Dancing Through 53
The Dandy Duke 171
Danvers, Johnny 68
Dare, Phyllis *116*, 136
David Copperfield 122
David, Worton 99, 100
Davidson, Maitland 51
Dawes, Billy 93
Dawson, Les 125
Day, Frances 91
Day, Harry 35
de Casalis, Jeanne 23
Decca 200
de Courville, Albert 67, 101, 137
del Riego, Teresa 175
Dempsey, Jack 91
Denne, David 193
de Reszke, Jean 150
de Valois, Ninette 19
d'Harelot, Guy 175
Dickson, Dorothy 72, 73
Dick Whittington 17, 28, (Theatre Royal 1896-97) 31, (Glasgow, 1910-11) 34, (Shepherd's Bush & Hackney Empire, 1947-48) 108, (Kennington, 1905-06), 114, (Hanley, 1907-08) *126*, (Belfast, 1914-15) 130
Disher, H. Willson 73
Dixon, Reginald 93
Dodd, Ken 93, 217
Dollin, Anthony 81
"Dolly Gray" 33
Donkey and Me 129, 131
"Don't Have Any More, Mrs Moore" 37, *43*, 52, 54, 55
Dora 39
"Down by the Rivah-Side" 9
"Down in Our Village in Zummersett" 197
"Down in the Fields Where the Buttercups Grow" 106
"The Drage Way" 200
Dressler, Marie 17, 173
Drover, Constance 154
The Dryad 195

Dumont, Margaret 167-68

East Lynne 111
Eaton, Frank 91
The Eclipse 121
Edgar, Marriott 137, 138
Edward VII 4, 173
Egbert Brothers 130
"Elderly Man River" 210
"The Elements" 166
"The Elephant and the Portmanteau" 171
Elgar, Sir Edward 171, 181
Elijah 171
Eliot, T. S. 25, 75, 217
Elliott, G. H. 22, 23, 55
Eltinge, Julian 145-46, 151, 154
Emery, Jim 209
Emney, Fred 130
Empire, Liverpool 85, 91
Empires, Hippodromes & Palaces 269, 278
Enough to Make a Cat Laugh 91
Elstree Calling 52
"Eric the Egg" 189
Errol, Bert 143, 144, 145, 146, 147-59, 246-48
Errol, Betty 151, 155, 158
Evans, Will 118
Evening News 122
"Every Time I Kissed Her, She Would Start to Sing" 100

Fairburn, T. C. 102
"Fairyland" 175
"Fall in and Follow Me" 34
Famous Music-Halls 52
Fields, Gracie 140, 202
Fields, W. C. 82
"Finesse" 18
The Fireman 117
"The First of April" 128
Firth, Colin 84
"Firty Fahsand Quid" 205
"Fish Sauce Shop" 189
"Five Little Flies" 163

Flanagan & Allen 87
Flanders & Swann 165-66, 216
Fletcher, Cyril 91
Flora 121
Flotsam & Jetsam 164, *165*
"The Fool of the Family" 130
Ford, Clinton 122
Forde, Florrie 180
"The Foreign Legion" 85
Formby, George, Sr. 35
Formby, George, Jr. 103, 104
Foster, John 134
Foster, Vivian 133-41, 244-45
Fowler, Reg 158
Fox, Olive 192
Foy, Catherine 127
Foy, Father Frank 131
Foy, John 127
Foy, Tom 1, 126-32, 243-44
Fragson, Harry 162, *163*, 164
Frankau, Ronald 204
Freear, Louise 9
Freberg, Stan 210
Friday: First House 92
Fromow, Stephen 5
Fryer, Bertram 198
The Fun of the Fayre 121

"The Gaieties" 153, 158
Gammon, Barclay 162, 173, 208
"The Gas Man Cometh" 166
Gay, Noel 22, 91
General Theatre Corporation (G. T. C.) 202
"Genevieve" 95
George V 50, 78, 79, 173, 200-01, 203
George VI 201
George, Muriel 211
Gerard, Teddy 121
German, Edward 171, 181
"Germs" 121-22
Gernon, Andrew 168
Gernon, Catherine 168
Gershwin, George 72
Gert and Daisy Remember 21
The Ghost Walks on Fridays 213

Gideon, Melville 73, 197
Gilday & Fox 62
Gilbert W. S. 161, 166, 171
Gish, Lillian 85
Gitana, Gertie 23, 53
"Give My Regards to Leicester Square" 105
Godfrey, Dan 181
"The Glorious Month of May" 207
The Golden Pippin Girl 17
The Golden Toy *19*, 20-21
Gomez, Alice 170
The Gondoliers 171
Good Boy 70
The Good Old Days 4, 217
"The Good Old Summer Time" 33
Good Old Timers 55
"Good Queen Bess" 158
Goosey Gander 33
Glorie Aston 8
"Goodbye-ee" 124
Gough, General 64
"The Gnu" 166
Grain, Corney 161, 162
The Grass Widow 119
"The Green Eye of the Yellow God" 73
"The Green Fly on the Little Yellow Dog" 73
"The Green Tie of the Little Yellow Dog" 73
Grenfell, Joyce 192
Grock 10
Groom, Gladys 195
Grossmith, George 161, 162, 163, 169, 180
Grossmith, Weedon 162
The Grotesques 177
Guilbert, Yvette 173
Guinness, Alec 12-13,
Gulliver, Charles 60
Gutterb, Pierre 152
Gwenn, Edmund 121

Haddon, Archibald 192
"Had the Old Noah's Ark Got Wrecked" 162

Hail, Variety! 52
Hales, Binny 52
Hale, Robert 123
Hale, Sonny 23
Hall, Ethel 135
Hall, Harry 196
Hall, Henry 80
Hall, Rev. Joseph 133-35
Hall, Leslie 136
Hall, Lillian 135
Hall, Sarah Ann 133-35
Hancock's Half Hour 93
Handley, Tommy 107
The Happidrome 54, 92, 213
Happiness Boys 47
Hardie, Keir 10
Hargreaves, William 105
Harker, Gordon 52
Harlow, Jean 91
Harmer, Dolly 55
Harris, Sir Augustus 28, 30
Harris, Leslie 162-63
Harris, Phil 122
Harrison, Kathleen 81
Hartley, Betty 154
Hartley, Ray 150-51, 155, 158
Harvey, Al 212
Harvey, Bob 212
Hastings, Ernest 164
Havana 114, 115
Hay, Will 65
Hayes, Charles 211
Hayes, J. Milton 73-74
"Heaps o' Lickens" 175
"Hello, Hello, Who's Your Lady Friend?" 163
Henderson, Dickie 127
Henson, Leslie 153
Heslop, Charles 195, 302n
"He Was a Careful Man" 169
Hiawatha 171
Hibbert, Stuart 214
Hicks, Seymour 118, 121, 172
"Hidden Heroes" 205
Higgins, Charlie 2, 68-69, 95-110, 237-41

Higginson, Alitia 109
Higginson, Robert 95
Higginson, Sarah 95
Hill, Benny 108
Hill, Hamilton 162
Hill, Jenny 9
"The Hinglishman" 163
Hippodrome, New York 46, 47, 284n
"The Hippopotamus" 166
His Master's Voice 192, 200
Hitchcock, Alfred 52
Hobbs, Jack 78
Hoffnung, Gerard 216
Holloway, Stanley 72, 79, 89, 137, 138, 164, 212
"Hollywood, Hollywood, City of Sin" 84-85
Holmes, Leslie 209
"Hometown" 87-88
"Honolulu Eyes" 153
Hood, Tom E. 60, 61-62
Houdini, Harry 46, 47
The House That Jack Built 34
"How Does a Fly Keep Its Weight Down?" 43
"How I Wish My Mother-in-Law Were Far, Far Away" 168, 298n
How I Won the War 84
Hulbert, Claude 72
Hulbert, Jack 119
"Hullo Tu Tu" 175, 180,
Humble-Crofts, Arthur M. 179-80, 184, 187, 188, 189
Humble-Crofts, Cyril M. 189
Humour from Pulpit and Pew 140
Humoresque 195
Humpty Dumpty (Royal Court, Liverpool, 1908-09) 33, *34*
"Hunting Trouble" 129, 131
Hutchinson, Leslie "Hutch" 82, 91, 212
Hylton, Jack 199

Ici on Parle Francais 113
"Ideal Homes" 204
"I Do Like to Sing in the Bath" 121
Idols of the Halls 45

"I Don't Want to Get Old" 43
"If Winter Comes" 86-87
"If You Were the Only Girl in the World" 119
"I Know Where the Flies Go" 105
"I'll Be Thinking of You" 75
"I'll Build You a Gunyah" 183
"I Love Me" 122
"I'm A Daddy at 63" 105
"I'm As Old as I Look and as Young as I Feel" 43
"I'm Better Off in My Little Dug Out" 35
"I'm Coming Home to You Love" 33
"I'm Forever Blowing Bubbles" 197
"I'm Going to Be an Old Man's Darling" 38
"I'm Looking Now for Any Kind of Sweetheart" 207
"I'm Not One as Wants to Say Owt" 130
"I'm Not What I Used ter Be" 21, 52
"The Impromptus" 195
"I'm Waiting Now for Any Kind of Sweetheart"
Ingomar 113
"In Our Village ARP" 212
"In the Dingle Dongle Dell" *191*
"In the Waxworks Late at Night" 107-08
"In Trouble Again" 129
Isaacs, Lewis 150
"Is it British?" 205
"Isn't it a Cruel World?" 15
"Is Variety Dead?" 72
"It's All Too Terribly Thrilling" 204
"It's the Usual Thing to Say" 163
"It Wouldn't Have Done for the Duke, Sir" 204
"I've Been to America" 129
"I've Gotta Motter" 115, 116
Ivel, Grace 149
"I Want Somebody to Love Me" 176-77
"I Was Born on a Friday" 14
"I Wasn't Born with a Silver Spoon" 31
"I Wonder if You Miss Me Sometimes" 39

"I Wonder What Made Her Go" 204

Jack and Jill 9 (Bristol, 1907-08) 33, (Theatre Royal, Birmingham, 1911-12) 34, (Coliseum, Glasgow, 1919-20, Empire, Newcastle, 1920-21) 35, (Prince of Wales, Birmingham, 1939-40), 91
Jack Horner 34
Jack and the Beanstalk 21 (King's, Edinburgh 1915-16, 1917-18) 35, (Empire, Sheffield, 1922-23) 36, (Drury Lane, 1910-11), 62
Jackson, Nelson 162, 208
Janotha, Natalia 179
"The Jewel Song" 149, 154, 172
Johnston, Brian 93, 216
"Jolly Old Uncle Joe" 105
"Just as the Sun Goes Down" 63
"Just Like a Rainbow" *148*

Karno, Fred 34, 65
Kaye, Danny 24
Keaton, Buster 111
"Keep A Little Bit of Something in the Larder" 40
"Keep Off the Grass" 128
"Keep the Home Fires Burning" 35
Keith's Fordham Theatre 285n
Kellogg, Susan 68
Keys, Nelson 120
King Folly 81
King, Hetty 144
King Pins of Comedy 92, 212-13
Kipling, Rudyard 73, 75
"K-K-K-Katy" 98
Kunz, Charlie 91

The Ladies of the Halls 21
Lady Land 171
A Lady's First Lesson on a Bicycle 9
Lait, Jack 46
Lamb, Harry 121
Lambert, Frank 171
Lane, Jack 130

Langley, Percival 78
"Lardy-Doody-Day" 29, 30
La Revue Artistique 102
Larks 7
La Rue, Danny 159
Lauder, Harry 11
Laughter Zone 20
Laurel & Hardy 12
Laurel, Stan 65
"La Veeda" *153*
Lawrence, Charles 182
Lawrence, Gertrude 124
Laye, Evelyn 121
Layton & Johnstone 202
"The League of Nations" 85
Leamore, Matt 103
Lee, Anna 82
Lehmann, Lisa 175
Lehrer, Tom 166
Leigh, Fred 44
Lennon, John 84
Leno, Dan 1, 4, 28, 59, 269
Lenton, Wilbur 103
Leslie, Annie 111-12
Leslie, Edgar A. 111-12, 294n
Leslie, H. S. 182
Leslie, Kate 111, 112
Lester, Alfred 111-25, 241-43, 294n
"Let's Have a Damned Good Grouse" 212
"Let's Have a Tiddley at the Milk Bar" 22
Levis, Carol 108
Lewisham Hippodrome *196*, 301n
Leybourne, George 4
Liddy, William H. 8, 17
Liddy, Nora 8, 23, 25
Life and Honour 113
The Lights o' London 113
Lillie, Beatrice 124
Lind, John 144
"The Lion and Albert" 138
"Little Betty Bouncer" 165
Little Jack Horner 130
Little Tich 1, 269
Lloyd, Alice 203

Lloyd George, David 203
Lloyd, Marie 1, 4, 10, 27, 31, 40, 52, 217, 269
"Lo, Hear the Gentle Lark" 21, 149
Lohr, Herman 190
"London and Daventry Calling" 209
Long, George H. 193-94, 195
Long, Maud 193-94, 195, 215
Long, Maud 212, 213,
Long, Norman 2, 89, 138, 166, 193-216, 260-68
Loraine, Violet 119, 120, 137
Love and Money 18
"Love is Meant to Make Us Glad" 182
Lucas, E. V. 137
Lupino family 7
Lupino, Mark 63
Lupino, Stanley 125
"Luxembourg Calling" 209
Lynn, Vera 92

Macpherson, Sandy 89
Magnets 100
"The Maiden with the Dreamy Eyes" 175
Maison, Trixie 108
"Major General's Song" 166
Makeham, Eliot 195
Manchester Guardian 45
Manzone, Oreste 182
Marconi, Ernest 209
"Marrers" 204
Marriott, R. B. 95
Martell, Charles 59, 60, 61
Marx Bros. 167
Queen Mary 50, 59, 78-79, 200-01
Masterpieces 67
Matcham, Frank 4
Matthews, Ernestine 128, 131
Matthews Family 128
Matthews, Rev. C. H. S. 190
The May Queen 171
McCormack, John 172
McDougal, Archie 33, 46, 47, 53-54, 55
McGhee, Thomas 44
McGiveny, Owen 67, 82

McLaughlin, Gibb 82
Macqueen-Pope, W. 88, 167, 173, 218, 269
"Me and a Spade" 88
The Merry Widow 173
Merson, Billy 18, 202
"Middle Class Society Tea" 163
Milland, Ray 93
Miller, Hal L. 96
Miller, Max 65, 104, 217
Milne, Frank 141, 296n
"Miss Annabelle Lee" 72
Mix, Tom 48
Moncrieff, Catherine 55
Monday Night at Eight 214
Monkhouse, Harry 7
Morecambe & Wise 52, 59, 85, 93, 218
Morning Star 212
Morris, Lily 2, 21, *22*, 27-57, 73, 200, 223-232
Morris, William 11
Morton, Charles 3
Moss & Thornton 30
"Mother Always Sends the Very Thing" 164
Mother Goose (Grand, Glasgow, 1909-10), 28, (Palace, Newcastle, 1949-50), 108
Mother Hubbard (Prince's Theatre, Glasgow, 1903-04), 33 (Prince's Theatre, Bristol, 1905-06) 33
"Mother's Walking Round in Father's Trousers" 105
Motion Picture Herald 82
"Mrs. McGrath and Mrs. O'Rafferty" 105
"Mr. Waterhouse's House" 101
"Much Obliged to Me" 130
Mundin, Herbert 122
Music-Hall 52, 89, 92, 107, 208, 214
"My Angel Jim (Of the Flying Corps)" 189
"My Bungalow in Bond Street" 190
"My Hero" 154
"My House is Haunted" 99
My Little Austin Seven 215
"My Little Friend" 175-76

"My Moon" 176
"My Mother Doesn't Know I'm On the Stage" 84
"My Old Man" 52
Myself and My Piano 178, 179
"My Soldier Boy" 30
"My Soldier Laddie" 35
"My Mother's Piecrust" 14
"My Word, You Do Look Queer" 164

Naafi Presents the Ensa Half Hour 212
"Navvies Jazz" 101
Nell Gwynn 113
The New Aladdin 112, 113, 114
The New Barmaid 8
The New Hotel 203
Newman, Sir Robert 140
Newton, H. Chance 45
Nicholson, Ben 25
The Night Porter 122
"Nobody Loves a Fairy When She's Forty" 56
No, No, Nanette 139
"No Power on Earth" 204
Norton, Frederic 171
"Nothing Else to Do All Day" 204
"Nothing Over Sixpence in the Store" 164

The Officer's Mess 113
"Oh, Dry Those Tears" 175
"The Old Apple Tree" 42, 52
Old Mother Riley's Christmas Party 92
"The Old School Tie" 164
Old Time Music Hall 218
Oliver Twist 67
Once in a Blue Moon 139
"Only A Few of Us Left" 165
"Only A Working Man" 48-49, 50, 52
"The Only Girl I Ever Loved" 76-77
"On the Banks of the Serpentine" 185
On the Halls 2
On the Dot 92
On with the Show 107, 201
Opera House, Blackpool 93, 291n
O'Shea, Tessie 56

Osborne, John 93
"The Other Department Please" 163
"Otherwise She's Mother's Kind of Girl" 206
Our Boys 113
"Ours is a Nice 'ouse, Ours Is" 121
Ouseley, John 179
Out of Work 68-69, 101
The Owl 60

Paget, Henry 151
Palace of Varieties 21
"The Paper Fan" 171
"The Paramount Pierrots" 211
Parnell, Archie 67, 68, 80
Parry, Sir Hubert 181
Parry, Orlando 161
"The Parson and the Sewing Party" 137
"Passionetta" 40
Pathe Magazine No. 35 78
Pathe Records 43
Patience 171
Paxton, W. & Co. 90
The Pearl Girl 119
Peel, John 2, 84, 92, 209
Pelissier, J. G. 162, 176, 177
"Perverted Placards" 164
Peter Wilkins 130
Phi Phi 122
Pickles, Wilfred 92, 213
Pins and Needles! 121
Play Pictorial 20
"Play the Game, You Cads" 164
"Poisoning Pigeons in the Park" 166
Poor Old Parker 67
"A Poor Soldier's Daughter in England" 31
"The Porter's Blues" 102
Potter, Gillie 138
Pound, Ezra 75, 177-78
Powell, Sandy 127
"Prelude in Asia Minor" 204
Present Arms 91
The Punch Bowl 122-23, 124
Puss in Boots (Grand, Woolwich, 1901-02) 33

"Put Me Amongst the Girls" 33

"Queenie the Carnival Queen" 14
The Queen of Clubs 20

Radiolympia 52
Radio Parade of 1935 21, *22*, 52, 81
Radio Revels 107
"Rag-time Cowboy Joe" 62
"Rahnd the Houses" *199*, 205
The Rainbow 67
Rainer, Louise 91
Randle, Frank 105
Rats! 122
Ray, Ted 24, 214
Red Hot 65-66
Red Riding Hood (Empress, Brixton, 1939-40) 107, (Tour, 1946-47) 108
Reed, Thomas German 161
The Referee 28
Reeve, Ada 9, 121
Regal Records 43, 83, 200
Reminiscences of Piano Humour 208
Restaurant Episode 117
Retford, Ella 108, 130
Revolving Stage 54
Reynolds, Harry 150
"Rhapsody in Blue" 72
Rice, Gitz 121
The Rich and Poor of London 113
Rickaby, J. W. 63
Ringing the Changes 155
Ring Out the Old 212
Rinso Music Hall 89
Road to Mandalay 75
Roberts, Arthur 31, 33
Robertson, Forbes 169
Robertson, Ian 169
Robey, George 1, 18, 21, 55, 73, 119, 123-24, 141, 173, 203
Robinson Crusoe 32
Roche, Dorothy 97
Rock, Joe 21-22
Rogers, Arthur 108
Rogers, Florence 108-09

Rogers, Will 173
Rogez, Marcell 82
"Romanca" 170
The Romany Rye 113
Rose, Clarkson 54, 82, 91, 100, 107, 140, 192, 200, 203, 211
Ross, Don 23, 54-55
Round the Map 120
Royal Cavalcade 203
Rubens, Paul 190
Rule, Herbert 44, 121
"Running Up and Down Our Street" 105
Russell, Fred 89
Russell, Harry 62
Russell Lillian 153
Russell, Tommy 209

Sadler, Iris 108
St. Juste & Higgins 68,
St. Juste, Robert C. 96-100, 292n
Samson and Delilah 195
Sarah's Young Man 136
Saratoga 91
Sarony, Leslie 105, 209
Savoy, Bert 146
"The Scene-Shifter's Lament" 112, 113
Schumann, Robert 20
Scott, Maidie 22, 34
Scott, Malcolm 2, 9, 130, 144, 145, 158, 173
Scott, Capt. Robert F. 182, 203
Scott-Barrie, K. 144-45
Secombe, Harry 108
"Seven Veils" 206-07
Sewell, Gladdy 73
Shanghai 121
The Shaughraun 113
Shearing, George 216
"She's A Lassie from Lancashire" 33
"She's Mine" 85
"She's No Lady Some Might Say" 31
"Shikelgruber" 212
Shields, Ella 23, 47, 55, 105
"Ship Ahoy" 33
"The Shooting of Dan McGrew" 73

The Shop Girl 121
"Show Me the Way to Go Home" 78
The Show World 101
Siddons, Sarah 31
Simpson Stores 119
Sinbad the Sailor 7, (Hippodrome, 1941-42) 107
Sing Me a Song of Social Significance 208
Sing Song 54
Sitwell, Edith 25
Sitwell, Sacheverell 25
"Six What-Nots" 189
Sky High 18
Sleeping Beauty 21
Slingsby, Harry 62, 63
"Slow Train" 166
Smith, Vere 136, 171, 177
Smith, "Whispering" Jack 72
Smithers, Selwyn 18-19
Soft Lights and Sweet Music 81
"Soldier's Reminiscences" 164
"Some Little Bug" 122
"Some Madeira M' Dear?" 166
"The Song of the Ford Motor Car" 164
Speare, Robert 46
"The Spooning of the Knife and Fork" 165
Spurr, Mel B. 162, 163
The Stage 17, 63, 81, 99, 195, 214
Stanelli's Stag Party 208, 212
Stanelli, Edward 209
Stanford, Sir Charles 181
Starlight 53
Stanley, Burton 146
Stars Who Made the Halls 270
State Theatre (NY) 285n
"Stay Out of the North" 84
Sterndale Bennett, T. C. 189
Stevens, Guy 195
Stevenson, R. L. 175
Stewart, Gordon 158
"Stiff Collars" 207
Stoll, Oswald 35, 62, 187, 190
Stoll, Lady 190
Stoll Theatre, Kingsway 92, 291n

Stone, Reg 145
Stratton, Eugene 130
"Street of a Thousand Lanterns" 85
Sullivan, Arthur 161, 166, 171
The Sundowner 117
Sutton, Randolph 23

Tabrar, Joseph 29, 30, 32
Taffy in Hunland 65
Tait, E. J. 18
"Take Me Back to Dear Old Blighty" 35, 73
"The Tanks That Broke the Ranks Out in Picardy" 35
A Taste of Honey 39
Tate, Harry 137
Tayler, Eleanor (nee Fromow) 5, 7
Tayler, Francis 5
Tayler, Francis G. 5, 7
Taylor, Jack 81
Taylor, Thomas G. 182
Taylor, Rev. West 190
Teasdale, Richard 139
Tennyson, Alfred Lord 74, 75, 175
"Ten Pahnds Dahn" 204
Terry, Ellen 190
Test Match Special 93, 216
Thanks for the Memory 23-25, 52, 54-55, 56
"That Kentucky Home of Mine" 98
"That Little Back Garden of Mine" 204
That'll Be the Day 23
"Them Days 'as Gorn" 204
"There Ain't No Flies on Auntie" 47
"There Isn't Any Girl Like My Girl" 164
There's a Long, Long Trail 213
These Radio Times 138, 215
Thesiger, Ernest 20
"They Built Piccadilly for Me" 63
"They'll Never Know Me in Old Dahomey" 100
This is the Life 52
This Week of Grace 140
Those Were the Days 52
Thorne, George 113
The Three Musketeers 113

Through the Looking Glass 23
"Tiddley Hi" 44
Tiller Girls 19
Tiller, John 81
Tillett, Ben 10
Tilley, Vesta 114, 144, 173
"Till We Meet Again" 35
The Times 75, 80, 114
Timmins, James 7
Timmins, Agnes 7
"The Tin Gee-Gee" 173
"Tipperary" 35, 67
"Toasts" 206
To Meet the Army 212
Tom Jones 172
Top of the Bill (BBC) 20, 92
Topic Records 84, 290n
Toplis, George 112
Tracy, Spencer 91
Travers, Ben 66-67
"Tried By the Centre Court" 166
Trinder, Tommy 83
Trinder's Hall of Fame 20
Tucker, Charles L. 82
Tucker, Sophie 46
Tudor-Thomas, Sarah E. 136, 138
Turbutt, Gladwyn
"Turned Up" 38, *50*
Twinkle 82, 211
Two Hussars 8
"Two Little Girls in Blue" 30

'Ullo 68
"Under the Bazunka Tree" 206
"Under the Bed" 14
Unnatural History 78

Valentino, Rudolph 18
Vance, Alfred 4
Vanities 93
Variety 17, 70, 114
Variety (BBC) 21, 107, 208
Variety (1935) 21
Variety Revels 108
Variety Roadshow 82
Vastersavendts, August 169

Vaudeville 21, 52, 208
"Venetian Moon" 154, *157*
Queen Victoria 4, 158
Victoria, Vesta 11
The Village Fire Brigade 117, 118
Vincent, Ruth 154
The Voyage of the Mael Dune 171

Waite, Ted 102
"Waiting at the Church" 54
Wakefield, Willa H. 182
Waldon, Max 144
Wall, Max 82, 91, 125
Wallace, Ian 166
Wallace, Nellie (Tayler, Eleanor) 2,
    5-26, 27, 35, 52, 54, 55, 202, 212,
    221-23
Wallis, Alfred 25
Wallis, Daisy 7, 281n
"Waltz Me Around Again, Willie" 173,
    180, 192
Wappat, Frank 2, 110
Ward, Theo 67
Watch Your Step 35
Weatherly, Fred `175
Webb, Clifton 121
"We Can't Let You Broadcast That!"
    203, 209-10
"We Don't Want to Lose You (But We
    Think You Ought to Go)" 73
Welchman, Harry 191-92, 301n
Weldy, Max 67
Wells, Wilfred 158
"We Montmorencies" 207
"We Must All Fall In" 35
Wentworth, Fanny 162
"We're Frightfully BBC" 164
West, Arthur 65
West London Observer 101
West, Mae 146, 158
Western Brothers 164, 204, 208
"What Are You Going to Do About
    Selina?" 40-41
"What Did You Do in the Great War,
    Daddy?" 164
Whatever Next 214

"What's the Use?" 52
"What's To Be Done?" 41-42
Wheeler & Wolsey 67
Whelan, Albert 80-81
"When Cleopatra Got the Needle" 158
"When Day is Done" 72
"When Fairyland Was Young" 170
"When I'm A Little Older" 28
"When I See an Oyster Walk Upstairs" 101
"When Mr. Killjoy Came to Town" 195
"When the Jolly Good Times are Booming Later On" 105
"When We've Would Up the Watch on the Rhine" 137
"When We Win the War" 212
"When Your Television Set Comes Home" 210
"Where Does Poor Pa Go in the Blackout?" 212
"Where the Cross-Eyed Claras Grow" 97, 98-99, 100
"Where the Violets are Blue" 106
"Which of the Three?" 38
"The Whistling Blacksmith" 98
Whitehouse, Elizabeth 147
Whitehouse, Isaac 147-48, 296n
Whiting, Richard 35
"Who Does the Lady Belong To?" 49
Who's Your Lady Friend? 54
"Why Am I Always the Bridesmaid?" 37, 52, 56
"Why Did You Have Your Hair Bobbed, Mary?" 47
"Why is the Bacon So Tough?" 204
Wilde, Oscar 144
Williams, Bransby 73, 141
Williams, Charles 8
Williams, Percy 11
Williams, P. G. 182
Williamson, James 9
Will o the Whispers 72
"The Willows" 207-08
Wilton, Robb 138
The Wishbone 21

"With Me Gloves in Me 'and and Me 'at on One Side" 103
"The Wives of Commercial Travellers" 44-45
"The Woman That's Coming" 163
Wood, Henry 169, 190
Wood, Muriel 190
Wood, Wee Georgie 55
Woodhouse, Vernon 80
Workers' Playtime 212
"Working for the Mayor and Corporation" 204
Wright, Lawrence 107, 201
Wyndham, Charles 112

Yankee Doodle Comes to Town 108
Yarde, Margaret 72
"Yachting in Regent's Park" 190
"Yes! We Have No Bananas" 122
"The Yorkshire Lad in London" 128
"You Always Have to Pay a Little More" 180
"You Mustn't Do It After Eight O' Clock" *201*, 208
Young, George 11
Young Man's Fancy 82

"The Zeniths" 196
Zonophone Records 127, 129